COLONIES, CULTS AND EVOLUTION

The concept of culture, now such an important term within both the arts and the sciences, is a legacy of the nineteenth century. By closely analysing writings by evolutionary scientists such as Charles Darwin, Alfred Russel Wallace and Herbert Spencer, alongside those of literary figures including Wordsworth, Coleridge, Arnold, Butler and Gosse, David Amigoni shows how the modern concept of 'culture' developed out of the interdisciplinary interactions between literature, philosophy, anthropology, colonialism, and, in particular, Darwin's theories of evolution. He goes on to explore the relationship between literature and evolutionary science by arguing that culture was seen less as a singular idea or concept, and more as a field of debate and conflict. This timely and highly original book includes much new material on the history of evolutionary thought and its cultural impact, and will be of interest to scholars of intellectual and scientific history as well as of literature.

DAVID AMIGONI is Professor of Victorian Literature at Keele University.

CAMBRIDGE STUDIES IN NINETEENTH-CENTURY
LITERATURE AND CULTURE

General editor
Gillian Beer, *University of Cambridge*

Editorial board
Isobel Armstrong, *Birkbeck, University of London*
Kate Flint, *Rutgers University*
Catherine Gallagher, *University of California, Berkeley*
D. A. Miller, *Columbia University*
J. Hillis Miller, *University of California, Irvine*
Daniel Pick, *Birkbeck, University of London*
Mary Poovey, *New York University*
Sally Shuttleworth, *University of Oxford*
Herbert Tucker, *University of Virginia*

Nineteenth-century British literature and culture have been rich fields for inter-disciplinary studies. Since the turn of the twentieth century, scholars and critics have tracked the intersections and tensions between Victorian literature and the visual arts, polities, social organisation, economic life, technical innovations, scientific thought – in short, culture in its broadest sense. In recent years, theoretical challenges and historiographical shifts have unsettled the assumptions of previous scholarly synthesis and called into question the terms of older debates. Whereas the tendency in much past literary critical interpretation was to use the metaphor of culture as 'background', feminist, Foucauldian and other analyses have employed more dynamic models that raise questions of power and of circulation. Such developments have reanimated the field.

   This series aims to accommodate and promote the most interesting work being undertaken on the frontiers of the field of nineteenth-century literary studies: work which intersects fruitfully with other fields of study such as history, or literary theory, or the history of science. Comparative as well as interdisciplinary approaches are welcomed.

A complete list of titles published will be found at the end of the book.

COLONIES, CULTS AND EVOLUTION

Literature, Science and Culture in Nineteenth-Century Writing

DAVID AMIGONI

Keele University

CAMBRIDGE
UNIVERSITY PRESS

CAMBRIDGE UNIVERSITY PRESS
Cambridge, New York, Melbourne, Madrid, Cape Town, Singapore,
São Paulo, Delhi, Dubai, Tokyo, Mexico City

Cambridge University Press
The Edinburgh Building, Cambridge CB2 8RU, UK

Published in the United States of America by Cambridge University Press, New York

www.cambridge.org
Information on this title: www.cambridge.org/9780521174053

First published 2007
First paperback edition 2010

A catalogue record for this publication is available from the British Library

ISBN 978-0-521-88458-7 Hardback
ISBN 978-0-521-17405-3 Paperback

For Barbara, Fiona and Tom

Contents

Acknowledgements

I am grateful to the Arts and Humanities Research Council and Keele University for generously funding a period of research leave, enabling me to complete the research and what turned out to be the first phase of the writing of this project. I am grateful to the original anonymous reader for Cambridge University Press, who was encouraging, while pointing out that there were still issues that needed to be thought through. The revised book has subsequently been re-evaluated by that reader, and read for the first time by another reader, and I greatly appreciate their generous responses and wise insight. This project has, consequently, been long in the making, but I did not expect the revisions and re-thinking to take such a long time to complete. Attempts to bring it to a conclusion coincided with an unexpectedly heavy load of administrative responsibilities, and the arrival of a family in the form of twins. That said, I am grateful to Keele University for providing me with a period of leave that has enabled me finally to revise the manuscript; and I am grateful to Fiona and Tom for just being here, making life rich, and for confirming chapter 6's arguments about the unconsciously subversive nature of imitations.

A number of conferences have kindly given me the opportunity to present aspects of this work; special thanks should go to the organisers of 'Victorian Boundaries' (Exeter University, 2002, Angelique Richardson and Regenia Gagnier), and the BAVS (British Association of Victorian Studies) conference 'Victorian Idealism and Materialism' (Hull University, 2003, Valerie Sanders). I have been fortunate to have been invited to present aspects of this work at research seminars, and I am grateful to Phil Shaw and Joanne Shattock at the University of Leicester; Eleanor Byrne at Manchester Metropolitan University; Jo McDonagh for the English Faculty's Nineteenth-Century Seminar, Oxford University; Peter Widdowson, University of Gloucestershire, and John Holmes, University of Reading. I'd like to thank Helen Small, Roger Ebbatson and Simon Dentith for their valued feedback. I have been sustained throughout the writing of this project by a community of literature and science scholars: I am especially grateful to Sally Shuttleworth, Gowan Dawson and John Holmes. And very special thanks must go to Rebecca Stott; not only has she been generous with feedback, but her own work is constantly inspiring. At Keele, I am grateful to my colleagues (present and former) for providing a stimulating and collegial environment in which to share ideas; particular thanks must be expressed to Jim McLaverty, Anthea Trodd, John Bowen, Julie Sanders, Simon Bainbridge, Fred Botting, Ian F. A. Bell, Scott McCracken, Sharon Ruston and James Knowles. I am grateful to Tim Lustig for generously commenting on an early portion of the manuscript, and sharing his own work on the emergence of the culture concept in American writing. My long-standing involvement with the *Journal of Victorian Culture*, which I now have the privilege to edit, has provided me with a wonderful insight into the vibrancy and vigour of nineteenth-century studies on both sides of the Atlantic. It saddens me deeply that Charles Swann is with us no longer to contribute to that scene. Charles's characteristic generosity in the long loaning of books has left a very tangible impression on this study. His astonishing breadth of reading casts a long shadow over what I have achieved here: all the deficiencies in the book belong to me.

Some parts of this work have been published previously: a limited amount of material from chapter 4 appears in my contribution in Louise Henson *et al.* (eds.) *Culture and Science in the Nineteenth-Century Media* (Ashgate, 2004); some paragraphs from chapter 5 appear in my contribution to Jim Paradis (ed.), *Samuel Butler: Victorian Against the Grain* (Toronto, 2007); and some material from chapter 6 appears in my contribution to Roger Luckhurst and Josephine McDonagh (eds.), *Transactions and Encounters: Science and Culture in the Nineteenth Century* (Manchester, 2002). Thanks to all for their permission to reproduce.

Thanks to Simone Clarke and Julie Street at Keele for shouldering more than their fair share of administrative work during the last push to finalise the manuscript. Warm thanks too to Linda Bree and Gillian Beer at Cambridge University Press for their interest in and patient support for this project. Finally, my biggest and most emphatic expression of thanks for emotional and intellectual support, and a partnership in family life, is reserved for Barbara Kelly.

Introduction: literature, science and the hothouse of culture

I. 'LIFE, LIFE, LIFE': A READING AND WRITING RELATION

In *Culture and Anarchy* (1869), Matthew Arnold offered his gospel proclaiming sweetness and light. 'Culture' would speak through '*all* the voices of human experience . . . of art, science, poetry, philosophy, history, as well as of religion'.[1] The many-sided receptor of culture would then look and listen: 'Consider these people, then, their way of life, their habits, their manners, the very tones of their voice' (97). Arnold had listened, and his response was to satirise. One vocal tone to receive this treatment belonged to the poet Robert Buchanan, who had celebrated God's 'move to multiplicity' and 'divine philoprogenitiveness'.[2] Arnold cites Buchanan's language praising God's 'love of distribution and expansion into living forms' at length:

Every animal added seems a new ecstasy to the Maker; every life added, a new embodiment of his love. He would *swarm* the earth with beings. There are never enough. Life, life, life, — faces gleaming, hearts beating, must fill every cranny. Not a corner is suffered to remain empty. The whole earth breeds and God glories. (215)

Arnold's discourse on 'culture' here cites and confronts a discourse on 'life' and its divinely sanctioned reproductive urges. Buchanan's language celebrating divinely created and cherished swarms of living things is derived in part from Christian traditions of agape, and in part from the popular science of phrenology. 'Philoprogenitiveness' was one of George Combe's 'affective propensities', a mental faculty common to man and 'the lower animals'; situated at the back of the head, this faculty cultivated an 'affection for young and tender beings'.[3] Buchanan's language, in its concern with 'distribution' and 'expansion', also drew on another nineteenth-century fascination: the power of biological science to explain the diversity of teeming life forms, and their patterns of distribution into every available 'cranny'. *Culture and Anarchy* was published in the same year as Alfred Russel Wallace's great travel narrative about the distribution of exotic life forms in the Malay Archipelago, one of the world's foremost regions for posing questions about life's distribution, diversity and sheer inventiveness. Arnold's extensive citation of Buchanan's linguistic celebration of 'life' is strategic, for Buchanan's language becomes the object of Arnold's satire:

how inspiriting is here the whole strain of thought! and these beautiful words, too, I carry about with me in the East of London, and often read them there. They are quite in agreement with the popular language one is accustomed to hear about children and large families, which describes children as *sent*. And a line of poetry which Mr. Robert Buchanan throws in presently after the poetical prose I have quoted:–
    'Tis the old story of the fig-leaf time–
    this fine line, too, naturally connects itself, when one is in the East of London, with the idea of God's desire to *swarm* the earth with beings; because the swarming of the earth with beings does indeed, in the East of London, so seem to revive *the old story of the fig-leaf time*, such a number of the people one meets there having hardly a rag to cover them; and the more the swarming goes on, the more it promises to revive the old story. (*Culture and Anarchy*, 214–15)

Buchanan's language is countered by Arnold's satire upon the swarming population of the East End of London, a satire haunted by Thomas Malthus' principle of population. Ten years prior to the publication of *Culture and Anarchy*, Malthus was cited as an important theoretical building block in Charles Darwin's theory of transmutation or evolution by natural selection.[4] Malthus became one of Darwin's ways of explaining life's distribution, expansion – and, crucially, its contractions or extinctions. Alfred Russel Wallace's *Malay Archipelago* also offered a Malthusian account of nature; Wallace dedicated his text to Darwin and the extension of the principle of natural selection. If Arnold's culture was a 'criticism of life' then biological finitude, or death, was visible, more or less explicitly, from its critical horizon. Arnold plays with Buchanan's line about 'the old story of the fig-leaf time' to re-locate the Fall in a degenerating area of London, a colony in the East where the savage populations are bereft of culture's garments. In satirising the felicitousness of Buchanan's language and allusiveness, Arnold makes the worth of Buchanan's 'poetical-prose' and popular language a vital issue, devaluing it as cultural capital for the reader's consumption. As Jon Klancher has remarked, cultural capital is

not a stock of particular ideological positions, nor even a particular content . . . It is, rather, a framework of reading, a habitual energy, a mode of reception and comprehension. That mode must be inscribed in language as well as in social relations, in prose style as well as in publishing institutions.[5]

In describing cultural capital as a 'habitual energy', Klancher gives Pierre Bourdieu's concept a foothold in the sciences of life, and the intellectual field in which they were articulated in the nineteenth century. To be sure, cultural capital is inscribed in social relations, registers, styles and discourses, and the modes of publication that disseminate its materials. It accumulates and disseminates in the practice of reading, that new horizon of research in the history of nineteenth-century science.[6] But in being read, it is also re-invented and re-invested in new forms of expression that perhaps break up and interrogate habitual, familiar conventions. Such new forms emerge as literary responses that are located in either 'higher' or 'lower' niches of that field. In other words, the responses are located in that meticulously zoned yet reproductively promiscuous 'hothouse', as Thomas Henry Huxley would describe it, of sprouting intellectual and affective forms: the field of symbolic power that we have come to know as 'culture'.[7]

It can be defamiliarising to note Arnold's influential account of culture for its inclusion of a Malthusian anxiety about population and swarming life.[8] This book offers a new reading of 'culture' and its linguistic derivatives as immensely complex forms of mediation. It argues that 'culture' is less a concept in itself than the product of competing accounts of the different dimensions of material reality. By examining the multiple faces of 'culture' in nineteenth-century writing, especially the writing of evolutionary theory, the book argues that some of the most active interpretive devices in the cultural discourse of the present – defamiliarisation, hybridity, mimicry, cybernetics – carry a genealogy that can be linked back to 'culture' as the nineteenth-century field of symbolic power that hosted complex encounters between literary and scientific discourse, and was in turn shaped by those encounters.[9]

To illustrate this further, let me balance the example from Arnold, writing when biological evolution was emerging as an authoritative descriptive and critical discourse, with an earlier nineteenth-century example from Charles Darwin, writing when 'transmutation' was significantly different, and intellectually risky. In 1837–8, Darwin was reading the *Edinburgh New Philosophical Journal* as part of an eclectic reading programme ranging from natural history, to the philosophy of the sensorium, to the poetry of William Wordsworth. Darwin's reading embraced the speculative possibilities of the intellectual field, and it was, according to Sydney Smith, 'about the last time when such an activity was within the capacity of a single man'.[10]

Recently returned from the exploratory voyage of H.M.S. *Beagle* (1831–6), Darwin was busy making his name as a geologist and natural historian through elite scientific societies in London, and writing up his travel narrative of the voyage. Having been exposed to geological evidence of the depth and scale of the earth's history, Darwin was also occupied in making notes towards answering speculative questions concerning the origins and distribution of its various organic productions: did living organisms evolve or transmute from one species into another, and if this did occur, by what means did it happen in natural history? Darwin noted points towards a potential public answer secretly, in private notebooks, for the question conveyed dangerously materialist philosophical implications for orthodox religion and its account of life – especially human life – as a divinely ordained vital energy. In reading and making notes from this periodical in pursuit of a transmutational theory, Darwin did not always transcribe from the most obvious sources carried by the journal.[11]

Instead, he made a note from another essay published in the same number of the journal, entitled 'An Account of Mr Crawfurd's Mission to Ava'; the editors of the journal had published it in the expectation that it 'will be read with interest by the general reader and also by the natural historian'.[12] For although Darwin was selectively focused on the question of transmutation, the materials that he read and noted in the desire to answer it were wide ranging, and the possible openings that Darwin noted were varied, and to our eyes surprising. In reading Crawfurd's travel narrative about a diplomatic mission to Burma, Darwin transcribed Crawfurd's anecdote of an albino Burman that he encountered: this man had been given by his people to a Portuguese priest because he was strange, a monstrosity, and they were ashamed of him and considered him 'little better than a European' (368). Darwin wondered what effect the banishment of monstrosities might have on the propagation of a race: if, in colonising a new territory, they were split into isolated groups, would their peculiar variations be maintained and spread by the new populations that they created?[13]

Crawfurd's text contained observations with the potential to contribute to a theory of evolution, but also ethnographic observations that would contribute to the formation of what is now recognised as a conception of culture. Crawfurd trained as a military surgeon, and went on to become a scholarly Orientalist and a diplomat. He was thus one of the great, though now largely forgotten, generalists produced by the drives of nineteenth-century colonialism. His ethnographic and natural history of the Malay Archipelago would be read with approval by Samuel Taylor Coleridge, and his experience of Asia would lead him to mentor Alfred Russel Wallace. His knowledge of ethnology and race led to his election as President of the Ethnological Society in 1861. And yet, as I shall show, his reading of

Darwin's published work would, in the 1860s, trouble his view of the means by which races populated and colonised the earth.

But in the 1820s, Crawfurd had been sent by Lord Ameherst, the Governor-General of India, as envoy to the Burmese court at Ava. In 1826, the *Calcutta Gazette* first published his account of the mission, but it was the *Edinburgh New Philosophical Journal* which gave it a broader circulation. The journal's inscribed 'general reader' would have been professional and highly educated, with particular interests in natural science and philosophy. Crawfurd's narrative offered such a reader insights into a territory recently colonised by the British: its population, resources, the language, manners, customs, tastes and religious practices of its native inhabitants. In simultaneously appealing to the interests of the 'natural historian', the narrative draws attention to Crawfurd's comment on his mission's collection of eighteen thousand botanical specimens, some of which were to be lodged in the Botanical Gardens of Calcutta, for they were 'rare and curious . . . combining, in a great degree, the characters of the *Floras* of continental India and the Malayan countries' (367). In addition, Crawfurd comments on the geological formation of the territory, in particular the vestiges, or fossil evidence, of life forms that had passed from the territory; indeed, in some cases, from the face of the earth itself. Darwin was Crawfurd's ideal reader.

For the region that Darwin read about was 'abounding every where with fossil remains of one of the last great changes the world has undergone' (360). Crawfurd saw that the earth's surface had been subject to processes of evolutionary change and transformation. This was evinced by the 'petrified' remains of life forms which were either extinct (mammoths), or which, as in the case of the 'abundance of sea shells', could no longer occupy the area because of radical environmental change (369). Natural history and archaeological ethnography were linked by their interest in commemorative monuments, and one of the last details that Crawfurd mentions relates to the discovery of vestiges of an earlier braminical civilisation, its places of worship, and the epitaphic inscriptions to the dead recorded on stones which resemble the monuments 'placed at the head of graves in an English church-yard' (369–70). Burma may have been the embodiment of the Orient in all its difference and otherness – Crawfurd could not help thinking of an 'Arabian Nights Entertainment' as he viewed a festival (361) – yet, uncannily, its survivals from the past conveyed impressions of England. Crawfurd thus found that observations derived from encounters with the colonised 'primitive' could cast an estranging perspective on the familiarities of home.

As Crawfurd tries to calculate the population of the area surrounding the capital, Ava, he reports that he sees little 'evidence of culture or occupation' (360). He uses 'culture' to signify pastoral activity, past and present. This is entirely consistent with usage at the time.[14] Yet his use of 'culture' in relation to a synonym – 'culture or occupation' – throws our attention towards the word 'occupation'. In its localised context, 'occupation' means little more than simply the process of inhabiting and tilling the soil. But as it stands, the term cannot be dissociated from the context of Crawfurd's entire narrative, which records an episode in the history of Britain's colonial occupation of Asia. Crawfurd represents colonial 'culture' in a narrative form, revealed in his recording the passing of 'the spot at which the Burmese contemplated making their last effort, had the British army not been arrested in its progress by the treaty of Yandabu' (360).

The experience of colonial activity was all-pervasive, and yet immensely varied and highly mediated, in the nineteenth century, as David Cannadine's work has demonstrated.[15] Crawfurd's mission needs to be seen in the context of a very specific moment of Britain's imperial history: having lost its North American colonies in the late eighteenth century, its attention and activity became focused on consolidation in India and its surrounding territories, which also meant engaging in post-Napoleonic rivalries with other European colonial powers.[16] This very reading of British colonial history became available in the late nineteenth century when the historian J. R. Seeley published *The Expansion of England* (1883) at a time of increased, if politically controversial, imperial consciousness. While Seeley claimed that the revolution in print and the production of mass reading materials would consolidate his vision of 'Greater Britain' overseas, such productive capacity also generated political and ideological contestation.[17] Colonial governance was a different question for a 'squarson' whig liberal such as Charles Darwin, a liberal meritocrat such as T. H. Huxley (in the 1860s at least), and a socialist such as Alfred Russel Wallace.[18] Indeed, political positions would be further complicated by the deeper implications of Darwinian evolutionary discourse, as my reading of Huxley's 'Evolution and Ethics' (later in this chapter) will demonstrate. For evolutionary thought identified a proliferating range of agencies at work in the world which complicated understandings of colonialism and political affiliation themselves.[19]

Colonial ideologies were conveyed imaginatively and powerfully in relationships founded on writing and reading: when Charles Darwin published the second edition of his *Journal of Researches* (his account of the *Beagle* voyage, an expedition substantially concerned with exploiting new advantages in the context of shifting colonial relations²⁰) in 1845 with the house of John Murray, he did so in the publisher's series entitled 'Colonial and Home Library', a series which imagined serving 'the highly intelligent and educated population of our Colonies' with English literature, and domestic readers with reading about the history of travel and the occupation of far away lands.²¹ 'Occupiers' assumed many identities: they included the white settler colonists who emigrated to what would become the dominions (Canada, Australia, and New Zealand) and Darwin would write sympathetically of these agrarian cultivators in his *Journal of Researches*; indeed, this identity would also be the basis of his initial warm response to Samuel Butler, a former sheep farmer in New Zealand. But occupiers could also wield martial power: Crawfurd's narrative presents the reader with images of trading ships and gun-boats arrayed in the harbour created by 'the new settlement of Amherst . . . a curious spectacle . . . a harbour which was not known to exist ten months ago' (364). Crawfurd represents the signs of British colonial 'culture', carved into the landscape as unmistakably as the vestiges of past, natural creations.

Crawfurd's colonial mission also furnished his readers with ethnographic insights. Arriving at the court of Ava, Crawfurd's mission was 'detained for nearly three hours, to afford us the magnificence of the Burmese court, but, above all, to afford the court an opportunity of displaying it' (361). The performance of Burmese hierarchies through deferential antics is contrasted with the reserve of the British: before King Hpagyidoa 'the courtiers humbly prostrated themselves. The English gentlemen made a bow . . . touching the forehead with the right hand' (362). In Crawfurd's account, this display honours a peculiarly Burmese cult of regal authority. Later in Crawfurd's narrative, having departed Ava, the mission encounters a group of 'insurgent' ethnic Talains who had just risen against the Burmese: 'Our visitors saluted us in the manner of English sepoys, standing up. This, they said, was the positive order of his Talain majesty, who declared he would permit no one henceforth to crouch in his presence, or any other chief (363). The insurgents are ordered to imitate the posture of sepoys, native Indian soldiers trained under English discipline. Crawfurd's ethnography thus includes the practice of imitation as a category observation and an engine of diffusion.

Towards the end of his narrative, Crawfurd becomes a philologer, recording some of the details of 'the language and literature of the Burmans' that had been collected in the course of the mission: enshrined in portable, diffusable form, they record the modes of symbolic signification that had been performed in ceremonial gatherings. Burman books were donated by the King, including 'some histories of Guatama . . . highly esteemed by the Burmans', as well as 'vocabularies . . . of some of the numerous dialects spoken' (369). In the 1970s Clifford Geertz urged ethnographers to see their practice as the interpretation of webs of symbolic signification, which Geertz held to encode the fundamental meanings comprising what had come, by his time, to be known as a 'culture'. Some sense of this literary critical practice – 'sorting out the structures of significations' to use Geertz's words – underpins Crawfurd's interpretation of Burmese 'fit objects of worship' and their symbolic encodings.[22] Applying this to Crawfurd's text, one can begin to 'sort out structures of signification' that seem to blur distinctions between human and animal economies, precisely as monstrous animal and human 'specimens' enter different circuits of social exchange. Such conceptual blurrings resonated for Charles Darwin.

Crawfurd mentions a 'white elephant' of the court at Ava as a 'royal curiosity' that was shown to men of the mission. Towards the end of his narrative he returns to this specimen, remarking that 'there is but one Albino elephant':

this, a male of about twenty five years of age, was repeatedly seen and examined by the gentlemen of the mission; and his Majesty has made a present to the Governor-General of a drawing of the animal in its state of caparison, which is no bad specimen of Burman art.

As connected with this department, may be mentioned the existence at Ava of a man covered from head to foot in hair, whose history is not less remarkable than that of the celebrated porcupine man, who excited so much curiosity in England, and other parts of Europe, near a century ago . . . At Ava he married a pretty Burmese woman, by whom he has two daughters; the eldest resembles her mother, the youngest is covered with hair like her father, only that it is white or fair, whereas his is now white or black, having, however, been fair when a child, like that of the infant . . . Albinos occur, now and then, among the Burmese, as among other races of men. We saw two examples; one of these, a young man of twenty, was born of Burmese parents. They were ashamed of him, considering him little better than a European, they made him over to the Portuguese clergyman. The reverend father, in due course, made him a Christian. (368)

A representation of the twenty-five-year-old albino elephant is given to the Governor; the hairy man enters networks of marital and sexual exchange, propagating his peculiarities through heredity; the twenty-year old albino man becomes a 'gift' to a priest, and the priest 'makes' or cultivates the man into a Christian. Of course, this is the moment of Crawfurd's narrative that so fascinates Darwin that he transcribes a version of it into his notebook account of HAIRY man (**because ancestors hairy**) with one hairy child, and of *albino* DISEASE being banished, and given to Portuguese priest.– In first settling a country.– people very apt to be split up into many isolated races! Are there any instances of peculiar people banished by the rest? –

∴ most monstrous form has tendency to propagate as well as diseases.[23]

Darwin moves from speculations on monstrosity to colonisation as a source of the reproduction of peculiarities, perhaps indeed of speciation itself. But it is perhaps Crawfurd's blurring of the human/animal distinction ('as connected with this department') that initiates a response from Darwin; it prompts an evolutionary, or transformist, speculation, but one that is bound up in complex ways with notions of cultivation, colonisation, religion and practices of signification.

In focusing on this obscure but revealingly rich moment in Charles Darwin's notebooks, I am suggesting that it is misplaced to assume that evolutionary speculation led inexorably to Darwin's 'Malthusian moment' in October 1838, the most obvious source of the 'discovery' of natural selection that distinguished the argument of the *Origin of Species* from earlier, 'vulgar' theories of transformism put forward by Jean-Baptiste Lamarck and Erasmus Darwin.[24] Malthus was crucial to Darwin's theoretical mix; but Darwin's notebooks are remarkably eclectic in their coverage of late eighteenth- and early nineteenth-century arguments about 'the laws' of life and its transformational potential: the first notebook that Darwin opened began with the headnote 'Zoonomia', a reference to his grandfather Erasmus Darwin's work of that title (1794), subtitled *The Laws of Organic Life*. The older Darwin's work stimulated the grandson into notations that reflected on the mysterious relations of sameness and difference between horticultural and natural processes of generation: 'seeds of plants sown in rich soil, many kinds are produced, though individuals produced by buds are constant'.[25] On a related theme, and just prior to his notation from Crawfurd's account of the 'monstrosities', Darwin reproduced verbatim an observation from Frédéric Cuvier's 1828 essay on domesticated animals, indicating that there must be some mysterious relation between the cultivation of domesticated creatures, and the modification of 'races' in nature into 'durable form[s]', and 'accidental habits into instincts'.[26] Erasmus Darwin and Lamarck also speculated on the parallel logics of variation under, on the one hand, 'culture' and, on the other, nature. The possibility that nature was always already 'cultured' (in being shaped, modified, supplemented) became a powerful yet troubling source of analogy for Charles Darwin.

The *Origin*, far from beginning with Malthus, begins with a chapter on 'Variation under Domestication', or variation produced by culture that imitates, though by no means perfectly, what happens in nature. Little wonder that when the writer Samuel Butler went on to contest natural selection, and to 'unroll' the theory of evolution in directions that sought to remind readers of sources of evolutionary speculation that preceded the writings of Charles Darwin, Butler's techniques of reading could demonstrate theoretical affinities with predecessors that Charles Darwin was keen not to claim; beyond this, Butler read and inscribed in ways that could break existing thought conventions, and invent new possibilities. Evolutionary theory consisted of a great variety of observational orientations and inscribed accents that played uneasily and ambiguously on shifting fault lines of semantic distinction: the human and the animal, the cultivated and the natural, the colonial and the home, the living and the dead.

As Darwin attempted in the *Origin* to articulate some of the difficulties of constructing evidence of evolutionary change in the face of gaps in the geological record, he reached for an image of a text fragmented by waste and linguistic change that proves difficult to read:

I look at the natural geological record, as a history of the world imperfectly kept, and written in a changing dialect; of this history we possess the last volume alone, relating only to two or three countries. Of this volume, only here and there a short chapter has been preserved; and of each page, only here and there a few lines. Each word of the slowly-changing language, in which the history is supposed to be written, being more or less different in the interrupted succession of chapters, may represent the apparently abruptly changed forms of life, entombed in our consecutive, but widely separated formations (*Origin* 317)

Evolution's theatre of action during the nineteenth century was as much the intellectual field as the field of nature. Language was of course the medium through which the idea of evolution was conceived and refined: as the embodiment of historical change and transformation, it could also function as a source of analogy to be tapped in cases of epistemological difficulty. Darwin conceived of the problem of evidence for evolution in terms of a 'slowly-changing language'; etymological and philological approaches to language were common to the construction of knowledge in both evolutionary theory and ideas of culture. As Stephen Alter has demonstrated in detail, Darwin borrowed many of his insights into evolution from researches into philology. Philology was still present in influential accounts of 'culture' from late 1950s Britain, but I shall suggest that this is a legacy of the contact between nineteenth-century discourses of culture, literature and evolutionary science.[27]

In 1958 Raymond Williams observed that the word *culture* amounted to 'a special kind of map'. In the last decades of the eighteenth century, and in the first half of the nineteenth, the meaning of *culture* changed: 'Before this period, it had meant, primarily, the "tending of natural growth", and then, by analogy, a process of human training. But this latter use, which had usually been a culture *of* something, was changed . . . to *culture* as such, a thing in itself.'[28] This marked the beginning of Williams's long interrogation of the idea of culture. He went further in his etymological speculations in *Keywords* (1976), where he argued that culture 'is one of the two or three most complicated words in the English language':

The [immediate forerunner of culture] is *cultura*, L, from [the root word] *colere*, L *Colere* had a range of meanings: inhabit, cultivate, protect, honour with worship . . . 'inhabit' developed through *colonus*, L to *colony*. 'Honour with worship' developed through *cultus*, L to *cult*.[29]

This was an etymology that returned 'culture' to explicit contact with both colonisation and religion, and it has had an impact on reassessing nineteenth-century thought on colonialism. As Robert J. C. Young has argued, 'colonisation rests at the heart of culture, or culture always involves a form of colonisation, even in relation to its conventional meaning as to the tilling of the soil'.[30] This is borne out, as we have seen, in John Crawfurd's prosaic use of the term in the 1820s, but also in Thomas Carlyle's visionary and influential naturalisation of colonisation and cultivation in 'Chartism' (1840), imagining 'everywhere else' as 'a whole vacant Earth . . . call[ing] to us Come and till me, come and reap me.'[31] And Seeley, in 1883, would highlight another pastorally inspired convention of colonial imagery: 'colonisation . . . is like the swarming of bees', he wrote, which is precisely, as chapter 2 shows, one of the ways in which Wordsworth troped the activity in *The Excursion* (1814).[32]

Terry Eagleton observes that the root *colere* 'ends up via the Latin *cultus* as the religious term "cult"' so that culture 'inherits the imposing mantle of religious authority, but also has uneasy affinities with occupation and invasion'. Eagleton suggests that on grasping this, it is possible to see how 'cultural truths – whether high art or the traditions of a people – are sometimes sacred ones, to be protected and revered'. It can also explain how 'the idea of culture itself in the modern age came to substitute itself for a fading sense of divinity and transcendence': the very problem to which Samuel Taylor Coleridge's theologically inspired 'clerisy' was to address itself, discriminating between discourses and ways of reading and preserving them.[33] However, the function of Coleridge's 'clerisy' needs to be understood in terms of the way in which its theorist expected it to resist certain developments in the field of early nineteenth-century life science. Taking a broader view of evolutionary thought, any consideration of the place of the 'cult' in 'culture' needs to be aware of a long history of sectarian religious fragmentation, and the way in which the 'cult' came to figure as a category in ethnographic explanations of theology, denoting a particular phase in, and identity formed by, the evolution of thought.[34] Williams's map of culture bypassed both of these contexts; consequently, the nineteenth-century tradition of the culture concept that he constructed was not especially able to exploit and interrogate the connections that his later etymology promised.

A new map of the word 'culture' in the nineteenth century needs a fresh starting point. In 1893 the critic John Addington Symonds published an essay entitled 'Culture: its Meaning and Uses'. Symonds was prompted to enquire into the meaning of the term precisely because 'overuse' had passed 'culture' into 'the jargon of cliques'.[35] Certainly 'culture' had been regularly invoked in polemical debate since Arnold's *Culture and Anarchy*; indeed, as Williams noted in the late 1950s as he started to map a literary tradition of usage in *Culture and Society*, the term was used extensively both before and after Arnold by writers such as Coleridge, Carlyle, Mill, Newman, Ruskin, Morris, Pater and T. S. Eliot. Symond's text is generally overlooked in the established maps, of which Williams's is perhaps the most powerful. And yet, like Williams, Symonds looked to etymology to grasp the concept of culture, and judged that 'by the etymology of the word, culture is not a natural gift. It implies tillage of the soil, artificial improvement of qualities supplied by nature' (196), so that 'culture is self-tillage, the ploughing and the harrowing of self by use of what ages have transmitted to us from the work of gifted minds' (200).

Symonds is also an important alternative starting point because his account of culture accorded scientific knowledge an important role in what was transmitted to till and harrow the self. For Symonds the 'ends of culture' could be advanced by 'Humanism and Science' (203), for both poetry and metaphysics contributed to the formation of the evolutionary hypothesis. Without habits of strict investigation, on the other hand, we should not possess the great historical works of the nineteenth century, its discoveries in comparative philology, its ethnological theories and inquiries into primitive conditions of society . . . Humanists and scientists have been engaged together for nearly five centuries in weaving a magic robe, warp and woof combined into one fabric, which gradually through their accumulated industry, approximates to something like an organic tissue. The hope of the future is that any exact investigation of one part will imply an adequate acquaintance with the whole. (204, 206–7)

Symonds's text on culture is an illustration of how important discourses of evolutionary science had become to the discourse of culture by the late nineteenth century. His sense of 'organic wholeness' – a characteristic traced by Williams in his 'culture and society' tradition – is given a distinctive intellectual hue by the presence of evolutionary discourses. For Symonds, literature, poetry and metaphysics have contributed to the formation of the evolutionary hypothesis itself: but the evolutionary sciences of ethnology and philology also constitute major interpretive contributions to 'culture' as a great woven textual garment, an enchanted robe of some five hundred years' standing.

   The anthropologist J. G. Frazer, who started to publish *The Golden Bough* during the 1890s, also represented the history of human culture by turning to the metaphor of weaving, likening it 'to a web woven of three different threads – the black thread of magic, the red thread of religion, and the white thread of science'. Frazer goes on:

Could we then survey the web of thought from the beginning, we should probably perceive it to be at first a chequer of black and white, a patchwork of true and false notions, hardly tinged as yet by the red thread of religion. But carry your eye farther along the fabric and you will remark that, while the black and white chequer still runs through it, there rests on the middle portion of the web, where religion has entered most deeply into its texture, a dark crimson stain, which shades off insensibly into a lighter tint as the white thread of science is woven more and more into the tissue. To a web thus chequered and stained, thus shot with threads of diverse hues, but gradually changing colour the farther it is unrolled, the state of modern thought, with all its divergent aims and conflicting tendencies, may be compared.[36]

Frazer integrates religion into this metaphoric attempt to grasp the history of thought and culture: rather than being positively 'magical' and enchanted in itself, the strands comprising the huge woven web include magic as a weapon in a great war of thought, alongside, but weaving in and out of (or staining?), science and religion. Culture, for Frazer, is not a garment of common ownership to be proudly worn, but an ensnaring web of conflict extending from the ancients to modernity itself.

Symonds's emphasis on culture's inter-weaving of the humanist and scientific traditions drafts a map of the term that opens up the conflicted vistas of evolutionary discourse. It opens not only a wider range of intellectual traditions, including Frazer's ethnology, but also the principle of culture as contestation. Raymond Williams was alert, of course, to the contests that 'culture' as a conceptual space was carved out to hear and judge. In 'culture' Williams traced an idea concerned initially 'with an area of personal and apparently private experience, which was notably to affect the meaning and practice of art'. This initial meaning developed into 'a separate body of moral and intellectual activities . . . offering a court of human appeal'; witness Arnold's 'hearing' of Buchanan on 'life', and the way in which 'culture' found against it. For Williams, culture emerged finally as a means of asserting 'a whole way of life, not only as a scale of integrity, but as a mode of interpreting all our common experience, and, in this new interpretation, changing it' (*Culture and Society*, 17–18). In generating interpretive practice directed at understanding patterns of 'life', but also, crucially, effecting change, these new interpretive practices were viewed as vital to communal solidarity and resistance in the face of capitalist modernisation, a 'mitigating and rallying alternative' (17). Williams argued that 'we need a common culture . . . because we shall not *survive* without it' (304 [my emphasis]); he concluded by arguing that there 'are ideas, and ways of thinking, with the seeds of life in them, and there are others, perhaps deep in our minds, with the seeds of a general death' (323). Without the interpretive devices of culture, extinction beckons: culture as interpretation is life-sustaining. But this does raise the question of the emergence, variety and reach of those interpretive devices. In a sense, the very confidence of Williams's prose in *Culture and Society* belies the troubled intellectual waters in which arguments about culture and 'life' had circulated since the nineteenth century. Symonds's text enriches and complicates Williams's way of accounting for culture, given that the relation between literature, religion and science was virtually ignored in Williams's account. And it helpfully re-directs us to some of the other writers who were writing on culture in 1950s Britain.

F. R. Cowell's wide ranging *Culture in Private and Public Life*, published just one year later in 1959, also saw culture as a 'key-word to explain all manner of contemporary topics and problems'.[37] As a classicist, Cowell sought to re-instate Arnold's idealist, classicist account of the concept as the authoritative meaning (175). In seeking to grasp the concept, Cowell also invoked etymology, observing that the earliest use of the term 'culture' signifies an effort to assist the growth and development of natural products, while also being aware that culture was both a 'mystery' and a 'problem' to be solved, for it has 'something of the elusive, attractive quality of the rainbow' (3). Cowell acknowledged Williams's work as a detailed account of nineteenth-century writings on culture, but he also pointed to Williams's failure to address the concept from the perspective of religion, philosophy and science (237); and Cowell acknowledged that Darwin's evolutionary science had 'contributed to swell the stream of cultural tradition' (159). But part of the mysterious problem of culture resides in its workings and new directions of development, given its vast cumulative extent: for the 'stream of cultural tradition' to which Darwin had contributed is, for Cowell, in constant danger of turning into a deluge given the 'flood of knowledge [that] threatens to overwhelm anyone who would voyage upon it' (25). For Cowell, as for Williams, culture has become inseparable from complex problems of symbolic mass production and mass literacy. Indeed, Cowell invokes a version of Coleridge's 'clerisy', calling for the creation of a 'minority capable of being affected to a greater or lesser degree by written and printed material' (21), an agency for cultivating taste and selecting the good amidst the 'flood of knowledge'. Like Williams, Cowell saw culture as a court of appeal. But Cowell's writings on culture register a sense of deep anxiety about culture as a problem of knowledge accumulation and dissemination.

Anxieties were also at play in the so-called 'Two Cultures debate' between C. P. Snow and F. R. Leavis, an encounter between the discourses of science and the humanities with enduring resonance, and contemporaneous with the appearance of Williams's early work on culture. As Snow acknowledged in his later essay, 'The Two Cultures: A Second Look' (1963), he took 'culture' to mean, on the one hand, 'intellectual development, development of the mind'.[38] But he also acknowledged that 'the term "culture" in my title has two meanings'. Snow moves through a number of synonyms that equate ways of knowing the world with the ways in which anthropologists came to use the term 'culture' – 'subjects', 'disciplines', then 'cultures' in the plural, suggesting 'distinct ways of life'. In his original Rede Lecture 'The Two Cultures', Snow specifically identifies the 'anthropological sense' of culture as a way of understanding what it means to inhabit a discipline: 'common attitudes, common standards and patterns of behaviour, common approaches and assumptions' (9). Indeed, Snow goes so far as to suggest that a 'culture' in this sense can inhabit human selves, stripping those subjected to it of agency and spontaneity: 'Without thinking about it', Snow remarked of scientists' social attitudes, 'they respond alike. That is what a culture means' (10). Williams identified an 'anthropological' meaning of culture in *Culture and Society* in his reading of T. S. Eliot (229), but Snow appeared to push this meaning in a more ontologically troubling direction: 'subjects' of disciplinary cultures were mere automata or imitators who lacked spontaneity and individual agency. In fact, Snow had stumbled upon an anxiety about imitation that had been present since the late eighteenth century in anthropological and cultural discourse.

F. R. Leavis condemned Snow's dealings with the term 'culture', in particular his contention about the 'unconsciousness' that follows from subjection to a culture. But at the root of Leavis's attack on Snow was a contest to re-define the meaning of 'life' as vital force. Leavis's appeal to 'life' is almost overwhelming: 'nothing matters but life'; 'only in living individuals is life there'[39]; '"Live", of course, is a word of many possible values, as great novelists and poets make us know' (21): 'something of the livingness of the deepest vital instinct; as intelligence, a power – rooted, strong in experience and supremely human – of creative response to the new challenges of time' (27). For Leavis as a literary critic, the language of English literature was the place where minds met and conscious 'life' could be generated and experienced, communally: 'It gives us, too, the nature of the existence of English literature, a living whole that can have its life only in the living present, in the creative response of individuals, who collaboratively renew and perpetuate what they participate in – a cultural community or consciousness' (28); 'life is growth' – such growth should be fostered by the university, and centrally from 'a vital English School' (29).

Leavis's appeal for a university English school charged with 'vital' forces owed much to a romantic nineteenth-century tradition of vitalist life science, anti-materialist and championed by Coleridge, which held 'life' to be a divine, unknowable force that inhered in the living being, in opposition to the inert, material environment.[40] Leavis's defence of 'vital' literary criticism points to the way in which the discussion of culture in late 1950s Britain was linguistically suffused with previous encounters and contests between nineteenth-century scientific and literary discourses, and the complex range of significations that played around the term 'culture'. As V. N. Voloshinov was to argue in another context, 'life' was not so much an inward and innate property of the word and the literature written in its name; instead, it was a deeply active and contested sign, for it is through the 'intersecting of accents that a sign maintains its vitality and dynamism and the capacity for further development'.[41]

The same would apply to 'culture'. Michael Yudkin, in an essay that accompanied Leavis's, observed that 'there is a real danger that the problem of the "two cultures" may gradually cease to exist. There will be no building of a bridge across the gap, no appearance of modern Leonardos, no migration of scientists to literature. Instead there will be the atrophy of the traditional culture, and its gradual annexation by the scientific – annexation not of territory but of men' (*Two Cultures*, 44–5). Culture is about the tilling of minds under particular regimes of intellectual organisation, but also, in the context of conflicts between theories of life and processes of habitation, about migration and drives to 'annexation'. To return to Williams's extended etymology of the term, the sign of 'culture' reveals its complex political faces, its multiple perspectives on different dimensions of material reality, through its philological origins in *colere, colonus* and 'colonisation'.

What follows from this philological understanding of the 'sign' of culture? It provides a way of exploring textual dialogues that have been overlooked by established traditions, in effect expanding the breadth and inclusiveness of Williams's 'culture and society' corpus of texts. It also expands the range of interpretive devices that can be deployed in the interrogation of politics and morals under the banner of 'culture' and its etymological derivatives. As Voloshinov argued, the textual monuments comprising a tradition, and so revered by philological methods, are in practice 'one link in a continuous chain of speech performances. Each work carries on the work of its predecessors, polemicising with them, expecting active, responsive understanding, and anticipating such understanding in return. Each monument in actuality is an integral part of science, literature and political life.'[42]

Such a philological approach to the politics of literature and science provides the ground for a new reading of T. H. Huxley's 'Prolegomena' and 'Evolution and Ethics' as 1890s texts that were responding to and broadening, in an estranging fashion, Matthew Arnold's discourse on culture. An allegory of 'culture' that traverses the concept's philological origins in horticulture, colonisation and religion, Huxley's lecture provides a viewpoint on culture's imbrication with evolutionary discourse at a particularly high and confident point of the latter's elaboration. 'Prolegomena' and 'Evolution and Ethics' follow in the footsteps of Huxley's *Lay Sermons* by inscribing the 'man of science' in the role of authoritative critical commentator.[43] They explore principles and figures of intellectual authority, while finally promoting literature and the intellectual field as a compelling but unstable historical locus of authority. In doing this, Huxley's texts articulate discourses associated with culture that cast the received accounts of the term in an estranging light.

3. HUXLEY'S GARDEN-COLONY: HORTICULTURALISTS,
ADMINISTRATORS AND EMOTIONAL CHAMELEONS

It is well known that Thomas Henry Huxley jousted with Arnold through
public lectures and essays, speaking up, as it were, for the contribution of
'science' to culture (chapter 4 explores the encounters) – a rehearsal of the
'two cultures' joust for intellectual authority that Leavis and Snow would
engage in during the middle of the following century. It is less easy to recognise the contribution that Huxley's 'Evolution and Ethics' (the Romanes
Lecture of 1893), and its 'Prolegomena' (1894) made to the discourse of culture. Thus a highly influential essay on evolution is also a late-nineteenth-
century map of key semantic strands that went into the formation of the
discourse of culture.[44] Known as a major anti-socialist statement on the
limits of eugenics in the sphere of ethics, the essay achieves its effects by
means of an imagined journey through horticultural and, by extension, late
nineteenth-century colonial discourse marked by the conservative Unionist
position to which Huxley had drifted.[45] Yet, despite this conservatism, the
prose which guides the reader orchestrates an estranging encounter between
the discourses of colonialism, cultivation, belief, evolution, mechanisation
and, indeed, modern culture itself.[46] Huxley foregrounds the strategy of
estrangement. Huxley begins his Romanes Lecture with a reference to 'a
delightful child's story, known by the title of "Jack and the Bean-stalk"',
and the magical journey up and around a bean-stalk becomes for him an
introduction to 'cyclical evolution' and a new platform from which to see
the place of culture in cosmic struggle: 'We have climbed our bean-stalk
and have reached a wonderland in which the common and the familiar
become things new and strange.'[47]

Huxley spoke in his 'Prolegomena' against what Arnold called 'doing as
one likes', and made it clear that self-restraint was an end of cultivation:
'every child born into the world will still bring with him the instinct of
unlimited self-assertion. He will have to learn the lesson of self-restraint
and renunciation.'[48] However, for Huxley, as an expositor of Darwinian
evolutionary theory, cultivation was a process subject to reversals and complications. While Arnold focused on the 'bear garden' horrors of Hyde Park
rioting, Huxley began the 'Prolegomena' with a glance at the view from his
study window, towards land in a state of nature and its scarcely visible, yet
profound and discernible, historicity. Huxley contrasts this with a focus
upon a plot of land recently reclaimed from nature, set aside and converted
into a garden, a site of horticulture. The work of the gardener in selecting
some plants and weeding out others that might threaten those selected,

effectively removes the garden from the state of nature; horticulture is 'antithetic' to the 'cosmic process', conditioned as it is by 'the struggle for existence' (13), though removal of the watchful supervision of the gardener would see the return of the cultivated space to a state of nature.

The gardener is one of two 'artificer-authority' figures that Huxley's essay fashions, for, in a moment of footnoted etymological reflection, he guards against a narrowing in the meaning of 'Art': 'The sense of the term "Art" is becoming narrowed; "work of Art" to most people means a picture, a statue . . . by way of compensation, "artist" has included in its wide embrace cooks and ballet girls . . .' (10). Yet, the artificers that were truly interesting to Huxley were versed in the art of governance. This is apparent in the shift of imaginative ground that Huxley's 'Prolegomena' undertakes as it moves from the space of a garden to that of the colony: 'The process of colonisation presents analogies to the formation of a garden which are highly instructive' (16).[49] For in imagining this 'composite unit', peopled by 'a shipload of English colonists sent to form a settlement' and reclaiming it from a state of nature, Huxley also imagines the governor of the unit, 'some administrative authority, as far superior in power and intelligence to men, as men are to their cattle' (17). This is Huxley's version of Matthew Arnold's authoritative state and the cultured 'best selves' that would govern from it, filtered through an analogy derived from Charles Darwin's *Origin of Species*; the administrator as cattle breeder and 'artificial' domestic selector.

Of course, the whole point of Huxley's discourse is to expose the fantasy of social eugenics, which he satirises as a 'pigeon-fanciers' polity' (23), an allusion to the opening chapters from the *Origin*. In another allusion to the myth of the Fall, Huxley contends that any administrative fantasy of an artificially created 'garden of Eden' from which struggle had been eliminated by far-sighted, selective cultivation would be undone by a 'serpent, and a very subtle beast too' (20). This beast was the Malthusian law of population, which Darwin had integrated into his theory of transmutation by natural selection. The artificial elimination of struggle from the garden colony would, paradoxically, lead to its re-introduction as colonists, with time on their hands and desire in their loins, sexually reproduce, thereby intensifying again the competition for the colony's resources. For Huxley, the administrator-cultivator would always be fighting a losing battle in the drive for an ideal colony, for in reality, cultivation is always in danger of being reversed by the natural processes which cultivation mimics, but which are unconscious and randomly directed.

Huxley draws attention to that unsettling implication that Darwin's theory made explicit: that the state of nature is always already governed by a process leading to selection and amounting to random, unconsciously generated cultivation. Huxley acknowledges this when contemplating the formation and functioning of insect colonies: the beehive, for example, functions on the basis of a strict division of labour and is 'the direct product of an organic necessity, impelling every member of it to a course of action which tends to the good of the whole' (24). The resonant phrase here is 'organic necessity': Huxley dismisses the idea that 'organic necessity' might reside in 'an eternal and immutable principle, innate in each bee'. Instead, it is the intellectually authoritative biologist 'who traces out all the extant stages of gradation between solitary and hive bees, as clearly sees in the latter, simply the perfection of an automatic mechanism, hammered out by the blows of the struggle for existence upon the progeny of the former, during long ages of constant variation' (25). Huxley is alluding to Darwin's observations of bees in his chapter on instinct in the *Origin*, but he is also re-working Darwin's famously industrial 'face of Nature' image from the first edition of the same work, which held nature to be comparable to 'a yielding surface, with ten thousand sharp wedges packed close together and driven inwards by incessant blows, sometimes one wedge being struck, and then another with greater force'.[50] In the 'culture and society' tradition mapped by Williams, 'mechanisms' are presented as characteristically outside of, and other to, the organic wholeness of culture. Williams cites early Carlyle critiquing undue 'faith in mechanism', and Arnold warning against the tendency to 'follow staunchly but mechanically' stock notions and habits (*Culture and Society*, 88, 124). In one sense, this might simply confirm that Huxley, Carlyle and Arnold came to subscribe to opposed mechanistic and romantic traditions, Huxley having shifted from an early attachment to a romanticism inspired by Carlyle, which was marked by a tendency to vitalism in his theory of life.[51]

As ever, the imbrications are more complex. Williams himself glimpsed the complexity, for he included an arresting philological 'Note on "Organic"' in *Culture and Society* (a lengthy endnote to his discussion of Leavis and Thompson's *Culture and Environment*, clearly important but difficult to assimilate to the main argument), urging 'caution' in the use of the word, pointing out that, in the original Greek, 'organic' 'first meant "tool" or "instrument", and . . . was equivalent to our "mechanical"'. This meaning transferred to physical organs, in phrases such as the 'instrument of the eye'; 'organs' became living tissues in general (256–7). This is the language of organic design and function that had been important to the tradition of natural theology exemplified in William Paley's *Natural Theology* (1802). Huxley's discourse on culture is enmeshed into, rather than estranged from, the romantic tradition precisely because of its evolution-ary frame.[52] To argue this cuts against the dominant tradition mapped by Williams in suggesting that mechanism is not separate from, but rather a participant and constant presence in, the cultivation of living tissue. This had a powerful and unsettling impact on conceptions of human subjectivity and cultivation. Robert Chambers's *Vestiges of the Natural History of Creation* (1844), one of the earliest, most widely read and controversial public contri-butions to the evolutionary hypothesis in Britain, could observe that 'Man is . . . a piece of mechanism, which can never act so as to satisfy his own ideas of what he might be.'[53] Such formulations could generate, as in the case of Samuel Butler, highly inventive openings that would interrogate the workings of culture, and Darwinian evolutionary theory, simultaneously.

Huxley concludes that the composite figure of the colonial administra-tor and domestic breeder is an 'unattainable' fantasy because the severity implied by the will to select would fatally 'loosen' and erode the bonds that ultimately hold human society together (23–4). Huxley's discussion shifts its ground to the invisible but restraining bonds of cooperation and sym-pathy that hold societies of humans together, if precariously. Huxley begins with the premise that 'at its origin, human society was as much a product of organic necessity as that of the bees' (26), though it was a necessity that had to accommodate the diverse capacities of individual humans, rather than impose a strict division of function. And yet, tempered necessity had still to curb a tendency to indulge the 'free play of self assertion' (27), or 'doing as one likes'. Huxley identified mutual affection, especially of the kind generated by the infant and parent bond, as one of the means by which self-assertion would be curbed. But it was the reproduction of feelings in general, or 'the state of mind we call sympathy' (28), that was the most distinctive bond at work in human society.

'Sympathy' and 'fellow-feeling' were cornerstones of Victorian moral and artistic discourse. George Eliot's 'aesthetic of sympathy' is the best-known example, the theoretical announcement of which appeared in the *Westmin-ster Review*, the periodical that at mid-century did perhaps the most to disseminate the approach and values of the naturalistic paradigm.[54] Huxley presented 'sympathy' with an estranging twist: for 'man is the most consum-mate of all mimics in the animal world . . . there is no such another emotional chameleon. By a purely reflex operation of the mind, we take the hue and passion of those who are about us, or, it may be, the complementary colour' (28). Human sympathy thus becomes an effect of mimicry and imitation, aptitudes which paradoxically bring humans closer to the animal world, as Huxley suggests in his image of the 'emotional chameleon'. Moreover, the act of mind that brings about sympathetic identification, putting oneself in the 'place' of the other, is a 'reflex' action, which poses a question about the reflective involvement of the subject in acts of identification.

In linking imitation with sympathy, Huxley invoked a conceptual connection that had been activated by the philosophy, anthropology and zoology of the Enlightenment, and problematically so because of the uncertain place of mind in the material process of bodily action to which mimicry bore witness. Thus, when Dugald Stewart of the Common Sense school wrote on 'Sympathetic Imitation' as one of the most central, but also ambiguous, *Elements of the Philosophy of the Human Mind* (1826), he observed that 'it depends on the mimical powers connected with our *bodily frame*; and which . . . seem to result with little intervention of our will'. In advancing this definition, Stewart was keen to distinguish sympathetic imitation from the sense established by the French naturalist and transmutational speculator Buffon, and named as 'l'imitation machinal', or that instinctual uniformity of bodily organisation and disposition in a species that was 'without intention'. Despite Stewart's insistence on a distinction between his own definition, with its exclusively human range of reference, and the zoological definition offered by Buffon, it remains the case that Stewart's sense of 'imitation' is haunted by the materialist implications of Buffon's zoology, and the spectre of machinate activity in supposedly 'vital' things.[55] Huxley's image of the 'emotional chameleon' is similarly haunted, and it is a spectre that stalks many of the encounters between literary and scientific discourses in the nineteenth-century cultural field, often with a subversively comic force. As Robert Chambers observed of 'our faculty of imitation' in the *Vestiges*, 'whole tribes of monkeys must have walked about the pre-human world, playing off those tricks in which we see the comicality and mischief-making of our character so curiously exaggerated'.[56] The subversive, literary and parodic force of imitation would continue to be explored into the early twentieth century, as my account of Edmund Gosse's *Father and Son* (1907) illustrates.

4. FIELD WORK

In one sense, Huxley's account of sympathetic imitation as a 'reflex' imagined a primitive reaction: an evolutionary account would stress, as Huxley's did, the way in which such identifications and reactions became more refined, and organised. Reaching for a philological metaphor, Huxley referred to this as acquiring 'the dialect of morals'. Huxley appeals again to the Common Sense school in his attempt to grasp the effect of this organisation, borrowing Adam Smith's notion of conscience as 'the man within', or an 'artificial personality' (30). Crucially, the artificer-cultivator function transfers from the figures of the gardener and colonial administrator to networks and institutions of sympathy building: that is to say writing, literature, and the cultural field that organises them – a field in which the sympathies, identifications and curiosities are cultivated through symbolic imitation, exploration and experimentation.

In 'Evolution and Ethics', Huxley continued to work out the implications of his horticultural metaphor while reflecting on the mixed 'blessings of culture', now imagined as a 'an intellectual field':

Two thousand five hundred years ago, the value of civilization was as apparent as it is now; then as now, it was obvious that only in the garden of an orderly polity can the finest fruits humanity is capable of bearing be produced. But it had also become evident that the blessings of culture were not unmixed. The garden was apt to turn into a hothouse. The stimulation of the senses, the pampering of the emotions, endlessly multiplied the sources of pleasure. The constant widening of the intellectual field indefinitely extended the range of that especially human faculty of looking before and after, which adds to the fleeting present those old and new worlds of the past and the future, wherein men dwell the more the higher their culture. But that very sharpening of the sense and that subtle refinement of emotion, which brought such a wealth of pleasures, were fatally attended by a proportional enlargement of the capacity for suffering; and the divine faculty of imagination, while it created new heavens and new earths, provided them with the corresponding hells of futile regret for the past, and morbid anxiety for the future. Finally, the inevitable penalty of over-stimulation, exhaustion, opened the gates of civilisation to its great enemy, ennui ... when all things are vanity and vexation ...

Even purely intellectual progress brings about its revenges ... The beneficent demon, doubt, whose name is Legion and who dwells among the tombs of the old faiths, enters into mankind and thenceforth refuses to be cast out. Sacred customs, venerable dooms of ancient wisdom, hallowed by tradition and professing to hold good for all time, are put to the question. Cultured reflection asks for their credentials; judges them by its own standards. (55–6)

For Huxley, there are two versions of culture at work. On the one hand, culture is, as Raymond Williams came to see it, a court of appeal; on the other, the 'field' of culture is also a 'hothouse' of spiritual and intellectual productivity, a cauldron of inventiveness generating sensations of pleasure, anxiety, ennui and doubt. It enables a complex symbolic life through significations of the present, future, but also the past, resurrecting the dead encased in 'tombs of the old faiths'. When Charles Darwin came to write about extinction in his *Journal of Researches*, he borrowed from Wordsworth's 'epitaphic' language. For Huxley, culture was imagined simultaneously as a garden-colony, a sepulchre and a volatile 'hothouse'.

The conception of culture as a field of symbolised bonds, restraints, but also inventive possibilities, was a feature of speculative nineteenth-century evolutionary theory. In his *Principles of Sociology* (1873), Herbert Spencer conceived culture as a meta-sphere or field comprising an ensemble of material 'super-organic products' which had their origins in primitive society: 'the recital of the chief's deeds with mimetic accompaniment gives origin to epics, dramas, lyrics, and the vast mass of poetry, fiction, biography and history'.[57] These super-organic symbolic products 'are ever modifying individuals and modifying society while being modified by both': they comprise 'a secondary environment, which eventually becomes more important than the primary environments – so much so that there arises the possibility of carrying on a high kind of social life under inorganic and organic conditions which originally would have prevented it'. Consequently, an ensemble of symbolic practices is conceived as a powerful, ghostly agency in this secondary environment, creating coherence among apparently unconnected elements of a social organism, for though 'not in contact, they nevertheless affect each other through intervening spaces, both by emotional language and by the language, oral and written, of the intellect' and 'the signs of feelings and thoughts'. In common with Huxley's sense that the field played host to discourses on doubt and death, Spencer contended that the cultural field was an 'agency for social control', the effectiveness of which was in large part owing to discourses on 'the dead'. This ensemble of powers produces a constraining 'invisible framework' in primitive societies, and, still less visibly but no less powerfully, in modern societies: 'this invisible framework has been slowly and unconsciously shaped'. For Spencer, the 'secondary environment' or 'meta-sphere' of culture was an organised inter-generic space, but there was a sense in which its diachronic and synchronic complexity rendered it a space in which individual agency was circumscribed, prompting speculations on the unconscious dimensions in representation.[58]

Huxley and Spencer were articulating a version of what Pierre Bourdieu would later theorise as an 'intellectual field', defined as a system of power lines comprising 'agents or systems of agents . . . which by their existence, opposition or combination, determine [the field's] given structure at a given moment of time', and its distributions of what Bourdieu would describe as 'symbolic power'.[59] Evolutionary discourse in the nineteenth century forced explicitly into the field of culture a debate about the origin, making, substance and value of the bonds of sympathy, and, thereby, the forms of politics and collective belonging, that could be sustained, or perhaps challenged and dismantled. The making or 'harrowing' (Symonds) of selves, and the question of the impulses, symbolic materials and values from which they are made and shaped, became a recurrent concern for contributors to the nineteenth-century field. It is significant that the otherwise very different genres discussed in the following chapters all contribute to a dialogue about the cultivation of selves, and the different kinds of symbolic capital that validate representations: from Coleridge's theological *Aids to Reflection*, to Wordsworth's long poem *The Excursion*, to the travel journals of Charles Darwin and Alfred Russel Wallace, to Samuel Butler's *Life and Habit* and *Erewhon*, and finally Edmund Gosse's story of self-making, *Father and Son* (1907). Methods for evaluating writing – measuring symbolic or 'cultural' worth – map, I argue, on to scientific and philosophical arguments about the sources of power energising life.

To conclude, I'll extend this point about varied genres of 'self-culture' in the intellectual field to outline in more detail the rationale for the chapters that follow, and the texts and authors that are discussed in them. While Matthew Arnold, 'the apostle of culture', is retained as a kind of touchstone who appears not only at the beginning of the book but at strategic points throughout, I began this introduction with Darwin's notebooks quite deliberately, for they provide both a framing perspective on, and a brilliant cross-section of, the early nineteenth-century intellectual field in all its manifestations: from Erasmus Darwin's theories of organic life, to the travel and natural history writing of John Crawfurd, to the philosophical writings of Dugald Stewart, to Coleridge's dramas, and writings about Coleridge.[60] Darwin's much later autobiography would also recall the importance of Wordsworth's *Excursion* to this intensive period of reading and note-taking in pursuit of an answer to the species question.

There is an important point about the form of the 'note', and the function it performs in my study: it is fragmentary, and generates a connection between areas of discourse that our own disciplinary separations and generic protocols have tended to keep apart. The informal, privately scribbled note finds its more formal analogue in footnoted or endnoted text in published work. Consequently, I investigate the potential of footnotes and endnotes as sources of reading. In chapter 1 I explore the way in which Coleridge's *Constitution of the Church and State*, a conscious contribution to the formation of a concept of culture, cites approvingly John Crawfurd's ethnographic study of the Indian (or Malay) Archipelago on the politics of a cultivated territory. Additionally, in chapter 2 I analyse the significance of the extensive endnotes on migrant pedlars, epitaphs and colonial education that Wordsworth appended to *The Excursion*; and in chapter 3, I address the attentive way in which Charles Darwin responded to a headnote attached to a Wordsworth poem about a 'savage' native American's intimations of immortality, which has implications both for Darwin's notes on 'culture' as a tool of evolutionary explanation, and his narration of a key episode in his *Journal of Researches*. In chapter 6, I look at the exemplary usages of the term 'imitation' noted by the *Oxford English Dictionary*, usages which contributed to a late nineteenth-century debate about the universality of Darwinian evolution.

By noting these notes, I suggest, the critic and historian gains insight into linked dialogic acts of reading and writing which cumulatively were constitutive of a field of culture, and often formative of 'culture' as a keyword. One also begins to grasp the intertextual resonances which both consolidate and diverge around those readings, and which merit close analysis and a measure of Clifford Geertz's celebrated 'thick description'. As Catherine Gallagher and Stephen Greenblatt recall, Geertz's thick description is initiated by an anecdote, or what he called 'raw data, a note in a bottle', that arouses curiosity. This is an especially appealing image for my study as the 'note in a bottle' also suggests a text that is generically framed, but transportable in a multiplicity of possible directions (rather like the ocean-borne seeds that fascinated Darwin in the *Origin*).[61] Here I should distinguish my approach to reading from J. A. Secord's approach, set forth in his exemplary and groundbreaking study of Chambers's *Vestiges*, *Victorian Sensation*. Secord has revolutionised the history of science, and its place in culture, by focusing on a wide range of unpublished records of the experience of reading and discussing Chambers's *Vestiges* (diaries, letters, press reports of gatherings), and his approach to publishing and dissemination is designed to broaden perspectives beyond the prominent canonical figures in the history of science.[62] While I have learned much from Secord's exemplary 'history of the book' approach, and an attention to issues of publication, editions and dissemination informs this study, my approach continues to focus on canonical figures (Darwin, Wordsworth, Coleridge, Matthew Arnold), but locates within their writings the marginal notes and asides that link them, intertextually and dialogically, into the wider making of a contested culture. If the ghostly, ether-like properties of readerly connectivity fascinated Victorians such as Herbert Spencer, leading to his theories of culture as a 'secondary environment', or inter-generic field that rivalled the theatre of organic evolution itself in power and influence, they hold analogous fascinations for us, which we seek to theorise through intertextuality (rather than simple 'influence'). Intertextual resonances also demonstrate that the site of reading was significant, whether it be a metropolitan centre or a colonial periphery, as my account of Samuel Butler's reception of Darwin in New Zealand suggests. Intertextuality serves, ultimately, to 'describe thickly' the earliest iterations of the present-day interpretive devices of hybridity, mimicry, defamiliarisation and the cybernetic.

The six chapters therefore conduct one long but multi-layered argument about the relations between literature, science and culture in the nineteenth century and beyond, or, as J. A. Symonds put it in 1893, about the 'magic garment' woven between poetry, metaphysics, criticism and the aspirant scientific disciplines of philology, life science and ethnography. In effect, the two distinct terms from my sub-title, 'literature' and 'science', cannot easily be thought of as distinct domains in the nineteenth century: as areas of disciplinary specialisation they were in the process of formation. 'Culture' was crucial because it figured as the intermediary field or 'hothouse' in which, at different moments in the nineteenth century, the limits of the forging power of 'matter' could be debated, and meanings exchanged between 'literature' and 'science' in the 'two-way traffic' that Gillian Beer's seminal work has done so much to theorise and demonstrate.[63] Indeed, my argument is that 'literature' became a widely embracing practice because, first, publication opportunities were constantly expanding, which prompted a continuous re-assessment of the relationship between writers as intellectual producers and their audiences; and, secondly, as the evolutionary aesthetics of Grant Allen and others would show, 'science' in the public domain was made of symbolic material, and thus always already literary. Huxley could not help but be literary when imagining science's contribution to culture's 'hothouse', or network of symbolic bonds and inventive possibilities. Moreover, the expansion of literature prompted debates about its cultural value as a tool of pedagogy, to which 'men of science' like Huxley contributed; in turn, an alternative practice of 'literature', energised by contact with the discourses of life science, inserted what Derrida has called 'a logic of supplementarity' into the field.

The chapters trace the shifting tensions and conflicts that these relations generated across nineteenth-century writing about evolution. In fact, John Crawfurd can be seen as an interesting barometer of shifting intellectual paradigms; cited by both Darwin and Coleridge in the 1830s (introduction; chapter 1), Crawfurd ended his life in the late 1860s arguing against Darwin's theories, a point that I analyse in chapter 4. In this study, 1859 is seen as an important date, but not primarily because of the publication of Darwin's *Origin*, even though the book had a massive impact on subsequent decades. Rather than celebrating a 'Darwinian revolution', chapter 4 argues that the

1860s–1890s is an important period mainly because of shifts in lecturing and publishing opportunities, and the way this fashioned new and far from straightforward relations between audiences and intellectuals in pursuit of new ways of expressing 'culture'. I take J. Baxter Langley's 'Church of the Future' of 1866 to be symptomatic of these relations, and of a discourse on 'culture' which was different from the influential contemporaneous version expressed by Matthew Arnold. Inevitably, T. H. Huxley's lectures and essays are an important focus of this chapter, but so too are the socialist-biological writings of George Henry Lewes ('Studies in Animal Life') and Alfred Russel Wallace (*The Malay Archipelago*), which also, I argue, contributed to a debate about culture. Among those literary intellectuals who diverged from Arnold was Walter Pater, who in the context of an emergent evo-lutionary aesthetic, initiated a distinctively aesthetico-relativist perspective on the science–literature–culture relation, and in articulating it under new conditions, attempted to grasp comparatively the nature of those condi-tions by looking back to the writings of Coleridge and Wordsworth, and their different conceptions of symbolic practice.

This is a book about the long nineteenth century, so it begins with chapters on Coleridge and Wordsworth, focusing on their writings from 1810 to 1832, and their struggles to fashion discriminating readers in the name of 'culture'. Chapter 1 focuses on Coleridge's later prose writings (*The Friend, Aids to Reflection* and *Constitution of Church and State*) in order to establish the way in which they strenuously resisted a tradition of sensational, materialist science (Erasmus Darwin, Lamarck) and theology (Paley and Malthus) that Coleridge dismissed as 'mechanic dogmatism'. The chapter also examines the part played by ethnographic speculations about priesthoods and observations from colonised territories in the for-mation of a regulative idea of culture, maintained by an intellectual class (the clerisy), which, nonetheless, Coleridge's own philological energy places under pressure.

Chapter 2 focuses on Wordsworth's long poem *The Excursion*, which Coleridge hoped might refute 'mechanic dogmatist' science. Wordsworth's poem became a text that was valued by a generation of Christian 'gentlemen' science dons in the Cambridge of the 1820s and 1830s, notably William Whewell and Adam Sedgwick, which accounts for the Cambridge-educated Charles Darwin's keen interest in the work. The poem contributed to a wider ambition to construct a 'cultured' subjectivity from ideas about sympathetic ethnographic observation, sympathy for the dead, and the duty to disseminate both education and excess population to the colonies. The chapter explores the way in which Wordsworth imagined that the language of his poem – indeed any symbolic practice – could be appropriated by what he called 'counter-spirit', and set against its own overt intentions and philosophical orientations. I argue that this appropriation was carried out by Charles Darwin, particularly in his account of his *Beagle* voyage.

Chapter 3 examines Charles Darwin's *Journal of Researches*, a text that explicitly reflected on travel as a source of self-culture, and which was most clearly marked by Darwin's immersion in romantic discourse. The chapter focuses on the first and second editions of the work, and the fact that the second edition was published in 1845 once Darwin had become a transmutationist with a theory to match, but which could not be expressed publicly. The chapter explores the way in which Wordsworthian 'epitaphic' language palliated Darwin's increasingly Malthusian observations on the extinction of living beings. The chapter also focuses on the fact that the second edition of the *Journal* was published in Murray's Colonial and Home Library, and that this opposition – the familiar of the home, the otherness of the colonial – can be read as a frame in which the defamiliarising relations that characterised Darwin's emerging theory, between domestic cultivation and natural processes of random growth, variation and selection, were played out. The chapter looks at the way in which Darwin's frame of 'self-culture' stimulated other naturalists such as Alfred Russel Wallace into evolutionary speculations.

My argument thus stresses contexts of reception and dissemination, and the increasing recognition of scientific discourses as symbolic practices, and chapter 4 concludes with a discussion of the theory of the symbol in post-Darwinian evolutionary discussions of culture, including the evolutionary aesthetics of Grant Allen. The focus on science as symbolic practice, and the fact of the increasing authority of Darwin's model of evolution in the 1870s and 1880s, is a context for chapter 5, which is a major reassessment of Samuel Butler's dispute with Charles Darwin, and Butler's own 'idiosyncratic' contribution to evolutionary theory. I take the colonial origins of Butler's work, in New Zealand, to be important to the emerging awareness of what we might now recognise as the impact of distinctive 'cultural' locations on the reception of concepts and theories; in fact, Butler's brilliant *Erewhon* is an extended humorous meditation on that idea. The chapter also examines the fact that the Butler–Darwin dispute was produced by and carried out through print culture, and that, simultaneously, Butler was devising a theory of symbolic action. Butler's interest in the machine within the human sought to take Darwinism in a Lamarckian direction, but is also, I argue, a way of suggesting that texts themselves might be cybernetic inventions in thought, or contrivances that take thought in new directions.

Finally, in chapter 6, I examine Edmund Gosse's *Father and Son* as an early twentieth-century text on self-culture that looks back to the moment of the publication of the *Origin*, and charts a connection between the progress of evolutionary thought and the trajectory of artistic self-fashioning. The chapter argues, however, that Gosse's intertextual allusions to Frazerian anthropology and magic undermine this trajectory, and open up alternative ways of conceiving literariness, as both transgressive invention and contagion. This represents a radically different form of literariness to the pedagogic account of 'literature' proposed by Arnold and T. H. Huxley in the 1880s. Chapters 5 and 6 become ways of re-thinking the concept of culture as a symbolic practice; they suggest that evolutionary theory, in curious and hitherto unrecognised ways, helped to prompt a re-thinking of the nature of literary practice as supplementarity.

CHAPTER I

'Symbolical of more important things': writing science, religion and colonialism in Coleridge's 'culture'

I. RE-LOCATING COLERIDGE'S 'CULTURE'

As Robert J. Richards has pointed out, Charles Darwin read John Stuart Mill's famous essay on Coleridge during the course of his reading on the species question. He used it to speculate on instincts, but consigned the notation to a bundle of notebooks that were labelled 'Old and Useless Notes'.[1] Coleridge has in fact proved to be highly usable, and his legacy has resonated widely in a variety of domains of the intellectual field. Raymond Williams's *Culture and Society* explored the legacy of Coleridge's contribution to the formation of the culture concept by focusing on John Stuart Mill's essays on Coleridge and Bentham. While Williams thought it would be a 'mistake' to suppose that Mill was presenting 'an *impartial* judgement of the ideas of Bentham and Coleridge' (65), if anything Mill was being excessively judicious, striving to occupy the place of 'culture' imaged as a court of appeal. Mill crafted a unity of purpose between Jeremy Bentham and Samuel Taylor Coleridge in two essays for the *Westminster Review*, 'Bentham' (1838) and 'Coleridge' (1840). As Adrian Desmond's work has argued, Benthamites and Coleridgeans had been at intellectual war with one another from their respective enclaves of University College and King's College, London. Medical education and the politics of transmutational speculation in the life sciences were battlegrounds in the warfare between these institutions and the intellectual formations that gathered around them; they have left their mark on Coleridge's invention of an idea of 'culture'.[2]

In literary history the same 'two systems of concentric circles' (Mill) that organised political and aesthetic argument in the 1830s are an important focus for Isobel Armstrong's account of the discourses that Matthew Arnold, in the 1850s and 1860s, would repress in composing his account of culture. Armstrong detects in Arnold's culture 'a dislike of the plebification of knowledge', a dislike that had its origins in Coleridge's project.

As Armstrong points out, the Coleridgean legacy, in particular his theory of the poetic symbol, passed to Tennyson, Hallam and the Apostles. It was precisely this inheritance that Arnold repressed from his discourse. In the process, Arnold also repressed the Coleridgean Apostles' antagonist, the dissenting Benthamite formation that grouped around W. J. Fox's South Place Unitarian chapel, and the periodical *The Monthly Repository*. Along with it was elided Fox's discourse of progress, social transformation and reform. Fox's dissenting, utilitarian politics pointed in 1832 to a disjunction between a developing 'public mind' and ossified institutions, such as the established church. A concern with authoritative 'establishments' was also at the centre of Coleridge's discourse; in turn it would be adopted by Arnold. Fox, by contrast, had called for education, particularly scientific education, as part of a general dissemination of knowledge to the people.[3]

Arnold's repression of these late romantic and radical reformist battles over culture perhaps helps to explain the absence of science from Raymond Williams's account of the 'culture and society' tradition. Mill's essays neutralised the warfare to differences between seminal figures whom he fashioned as 'the teachers of the teachers', the office of the clerisy being their common pursuit.[4] The energetic intertextual resonances of Coleridge's later prose can be re-read in the light of the intellectual conflicts that Desmond and Armstrong have highlighted. For Coleridge's texts helped to carve out a place in the field for the nineteenth-century conflict between 'science' and 'religion', shaping the conflict into re-usable symbolic capital. At the same time, Coleridge's rhetorical war with a sensationalist tradition of science, and his reflections on colonial order, helped to fashion an influential discourse on 'culture' that was at once defensive and symbolically suggestive. Its suggestiveness would condition relations between discourses of 'literature' and 'science' throughout the nineteenth century; Walter Pater would comment critically on Coleridge's legacy in the watershed decade of the 1860s.

This conception of culture was central to Mill's essay on Coleridge. Contemplating the historical means by which 'systems of restraining discipline' have emerged from anarchy, Mill identified 'the culture of the inward man as the problem of problems' because, as 'the Germano-Coleridgean school' argued,

The culture of the human being had been carried to no ordinary height, and human nature had exhibited many of its noblest manifestations, not in Christian countries only, but in the ancient world, in Athens, Sparta, Rome; nay, even barbarians, as the Germans, or still more unmitigated savages, the wild Indians, and again the Chinese, the Egyptians, the Arabs, all had their own education, their own culture; a culture which, whatever might be its tendency upon the whole, had been successful in some respect or another.[5]

Williams criticised Mill's apparent tendency to mix up 'different orders of experience' by 'arbitrarily grouping' civilised man, the Noble Savage and the industrial worker together.[6] Yet it may be more productive to see Mill's reading of Coleridge leading him to a historicism conditioned by an 'anthropological turn' which was, for Foucault, characteristic of postclassical discourse.[7] For Mill does not just arrive at culture as court of final appeal, but glimpses instead some sense of culture*s* in the plural: that is, distinctive educative and symbolic systems for sustaining life against the threat of death, which have evolved, operated, degenerated and themselves faced extinction in specific historical circumstances. Indeed, far from seeing culture as a court of final appeal in all matters of the social, Mill follows Coleridge in conceiving of 'the culture of the inward man' as 'the problem of problems', given that inwardness has never been an exclusive property of Christianity, but rather an evolving and degenerating possession of other ethnicities, cults and educative systems. Thus, as the second part of this chapter will demonstrate, when Coleridge came to write about the place of landed occupation, culture, and its overseeing clerisy in Britain in *On the Constitution of the Church and State*, he recognised the parallels between his own preoccupations and what he had derived from reading John Crawfurd's ethnographic work on the history of the Indian (or Malay) Archipelago. In other words, by acknowledging the anthropological turn taken by Coleridge and recognised by Mill, the formation of an early nineteenth-century concept of culture can be re-connected to colonialism, ethnography, and the early nineteenth-century battles that were waged between transformist life science and religious establishments. One is consequently reminded of the way in which 'culture' was split between being the solution – the court of final appeal – and 'the problem of problems'.

Coleridge's prose writings on Christian Revelation, such as *Aids to Reflection*, which will be discussed in the first part of the chapter, become resonantly charged here, in that they seek to advance a case for a distinctive human inwardness that reveals the presence of God, a case formulated by Coleridge in opposition to the perceived threats posed by materialist theories of life and self-evolving matter. Indeed, Coleridge's writings on the concept of culture, particularly *On the Constitution of the Church and State*, are permeated by a discourse of 'organic' evolution which rhetorically resists the claims advanced by 'mechanistic' sensationalist science. To begin with, the chapter will establish a context for this science, examining the complex, overlapping presence of 'materialisms' in early nineteenth-century discourses of theology and evolutionary speculations, and the way in which Coleridge's philology, and his textual practice, negotiated them to produce some very complex, supplementary effects. As Charles

Darwin would come to see, there could be no 'cure' for religious or other forms of doubt from a reading of Coleridge. Mill contended that 'the name of Coleridge . . . [would] become symbolical of more important things', and Mill was exactly right to locate the power of Coleridge's project in the domain of the intellectual field where his own contest with the languages of life science and evolution were waged.[8] The problem was that ethnography and materialist life science possessed the potential to critically undermine traditionally constituted interpretations of the bonds of human sympathy and reflective self-understanding, which seemed to source the 'inward' sustenance offered by culture. It confirms Homi Bhabha's sense that while culture is held up as 'a moment of . . . enlightenment or liberation' it can also become an 'uncomfortable, disturbing practice of supplementarity'.[9]

2. 'MECHANIC DOGMATISTS': EYES, MOUTHS AND MATERIALISMS IN THEOLOGY AND TRANSFORMIST SPECULATION

Writing to William Wordworth in May 1815, Coleridge expressed a guarded disappointment at his friend's philosophical poem *The Excursion*, published a year earlier. While the next chapter will show how Wordsworth's poem was a complex text that maintained a complex textual after-life in nineteenth-century scientific speculation, we can begin with Coleridge's dashed hope for a poem that would emphatically refute the 'sandy Sophisms of Locke and the Mechanic Dogmatists'. Because he could see clearly where such 'sandy Sophisms' of mechanistic thought might lead, he also desired that the true philosophical poem should 'have exploded the absurd notion of Pope's Essay on Man, [Erasmus] Darwin, and the countless Believers . . . of Man's having progressed from an Ouran Outang state'.[10] Coleridge was particularly driven to defend theology from the consequences of mechanistic thought: in his *Aids to Reflection* (1825), he praised William Paley for the 'incomparable grace, propriety, and persuasive facility of his writings'; but this was itself, to Coleridge's eye, a specious sophism, for 'on this very account', he believed himself 'bound in conscience to throw the whole force of my intellect in the way of this triumphal Car, on which the tutelary Genius of modern Idolatory is borne, even at the risk of being crushed under the wheels'.[11] The juggernaut-like 'triumphal Car' was William Paley's *Natural Theology* (1802); the 'argument from design' was Paley's device for crushing the atheistic contention of creation without an artificer. Coleridge feared that Paley's 'mechanic' mode of argument and its rhetorical support would be pushed in dangerously materialist directions, and opened up to the very atheist logic it sought to crush.

Beginning his argument with the discovery of a watch in a field, a manifestly designed mechanism, Paley famously asked his readers to recognise, on the grounds of analogy, the mechanistic design of all living organs, an acknowledgement that would at once concede their origin in a designer or artificer. In order to mark sexual reproduction and the generation of new life as the points at which the analogy might break down, Paley even asks his readers to conceive that within the watch, they might observe a mechanism for 'producing, in the course of its movement, another watch like itself . . . a system of parts, a mould for instance, or a complex adjustment of laths, files and tools, evidently and separately calculated for this purpose'.[12] For Paley, laths, files and tools are, first, the analogical means by which reproduction is assured; secondly, the means by which God is confirmed as first cause and designer (such contrived arrangements could not come about spontaneously, by themselves); and thirdly, evidence that the reproduction of new, young life was nurtured under his powers.

And yet, the analogy between living tissue and a mechanical contrivance was open to refutation. Conceding that some may be sceptical concerning 'the similitude between the eye and the telescope', Paley nonetheless insists that 'the fact is, they are both instruments', returning the 'organic' to its Greek origins in conceptions of the mechanical and instrumental (12). Eyes are rhetorically fashioned as instruments that interact harmoniously with the other organs comprising the perfectly designed living being. In the case of birds, as Paley points out, eyes are very close to the beak, or the means by which the creatures 'procure their food' (18). However, because birds also have to be able to see over great distances from the air, the muscles of their eyes permit rapid switches of focalisation. For Paley, disciplined, anatomical investigation into the instrument of the eye reveals the presence of the Creator, the designer, the deity, almost looking through the creature's own window on the world, ensuring the stable maintenance of its perfectly designed equilibrium. No wonder that the examination of the eye 'was a cure for atheism' (20).

But what happens when the focus shifts, and when a more excursive, speculative mind begins to plot design from a different organ – say an orifice such as the bird's beak? Whereas Paley kept the bird's beak in subservient relation to the sovereign position of the eye, for Erasmus Darwin in *Zoonomia* (1794), beaks as procurers of food told a different story and led to a different conclusion: 'some birds have acquired harder beaks to crack nuts, as the parrot. Others have acquired beaks adapted to break the harder seeds, as sparrows. Others for the softer seeds of flowers, or the buds of the trees, as the finches.' For Darwin, such differences did not reveal a creator; instead they were evidence of 'what had gradually been produced during many generations by the perpetual endeavour to supply the want of food, and to have been delivered to their posterity with constant improvement of them for the purposes required'.[13] Mouths had been shaped by the random colonisation of space, rather than grand design. And yet, the will and wants of the individual organism in that particular space modified the shape and function of the mouth, and the character could be passed down the generations once acquired. The inheritance of acquired characteristics was also being theorised by Erasmus Darwin's French contemporary, Jean-Baptiste Lamarck.

Darwin's materialist sense of an organ's shape and powers of development was differently premised, as he illustrated in his poem *The Temple of Nature* (1803):

> Nurs'd by warm sun-beams in primeval caves
> Organic life began beneath the waves . . .[14]

> Hence without parent by spontaneous birth
> Rise the first specks of animated earth;
> From Nature's womb the plant or insect swims,
> And buds or breathes with microscopic limbs . . .
> (I, ll. 247–50)

> From embryon births her changeful forms improve,
> Grow, as they live, and strengthen as they move . . .
> (I, ll. 225–6)

Darwin presents a materialist account of the origins of life in chemical and heat-based processes of 'parentless' spontaneous generation. There is no evident system of contrivances pointing to the existence of an artificer; instead there is self-directed progress, whereby nature's 'changeful forms improve'. Darwin's concern with mouths generates other, disturbingly materialist implications. In the fourth and final Canto, he presents the reader with an image of life decimated in 'one great Slaughter-house the warring world' (IV, l. 66). In a world of struggle vast numbers of living things can never be, unconditionally, ends in themselves, for they also exist as potential food for other organisms; mouths become, paradoxically, living graves: 'With monstrous gape sepulchral whales devour / Shoals at a gulp, a million in an hour' (IV, 61–2). In the case of the whale, the mouth becomes a consumption mechanism on an industrial scale.

Erasmus Darwin's vision of 'one great Slaughter-house the warring world' bore a strong resemblance to Thomas Malthus' 1798 thesis in *An Essay on the Principle of Population*, which was written precisely to contest the philosophical basis of radical 'optimism' advocated by Condorcet and Godwin.[15] Coleridge and Wordsworth read and responded to Malthus; in Joseph Johnson they shared the same liberal London publisher as Malthus (and Erasmus Darwin). Johnson presented Coleridge with a copy of Malthus' newly published book when he and Wordsworth visited the publisher in 1798.[16] Paley had to assimilate Malthus' insistence upon strict limits to the otherwise 'delighted existence' he celebrated in *Natural Theology*.[17] Malthus' theology of struggle wove together discourses of deity, matter and mind. In doing so it produced some striking linguistic congruencies with naturalistic speculations about transmutation that linked colonisation with notions of cultivation.

In Malthus' *Essay*, the occupation of overseas territory is viewed as a kind of controlling experiment measuring the validity of his theory in the pressured, over-populated old world. As population in the old world increases, cultivation necessarily intensifies, but never at a rate to meet the expansion: parsimony and death constantly threaten. By contrast, happiness and plenty depend on a small population and a surplus of uncultivated but fertile land, as experienced in the American colonies and other territories that European nations were subjecting to 'culture'.[18] Malthusian theory epitomises Foucault's sense of an anthropological turn in western thought, or the discovery of that 'perilous region where life is in confrontation with death'.[19]

In articulating a version of this anthropological turn, Malthus claims that 'some of the noblest exertions of the human mind have been set in motion by the necessity of satisfying the wants of the body'. Malthus' theory of need implied that the colonial enterprise could enable European civilisation to re-encounter the founding drives which gave birth to social and mental progress. For Malthus, mind is an entity which is stimulated and given shape by the body's desire to satisfy its physical needs, leading to the labour expended on inhabiting and cultivating space – in short, the practice of primitive colonisation:

The first great awakeners of the mind seem to be the wants of the body . . . The savage would slumber for ever under his tree unless he were roused from his torpor by the cravings of hunger or the pinchings of cold, and the exertions that he makes to avoid these evils, by procuring food, and building himself a covering, are the exercises which form and keep in motion his faculties, which otherwise would sink into listless inactivity.[20]

Malthus' theory of need also constructs a God who oversees a still more elemental process governing the evolution of matter. Malthus' Deity can, accordingly, be read in 'the book of nature', which reveals the way in which life is created and then selectively cultivated. Reaching for a materialist, promethean metaphor, Malthus holds that 'many vessels will come out of this mighty creative furnace in wrong shapes' because the overall profusion of existence is always in excess of the resources to sustain, free from pain, the matter that develops into sentient being.[21] A new way of seeing is required, taking readers beyond 'the crude and puerile conceptions which we sometimes form of . . . the Deity', for

we might imagine that God could call into being myriads and myriads of existences, all free from pain and imperfection, all eminent in goodness and wisdom, all capable of the highest enjoyments, and unnumbered as the points throughout infinite space. But when from these vain and extravagant dreams of fancy, we turn our eyes to the book of nature, where alone we can read God as he is, we see a constant succession of sentient beings, rising apparently from so many specks of matter, going through a long and sometimes painful process in this world, but many of them attaining, ere the termination of it, such high qualities and powers as seem to indicate their fitness for some superior state . . .

. . . I should be inclined, therefore . . . to consider the world and this life as the mighty process of God, not for the trial, but for the creation and formation of mind, a process necessary to awaken inert, chaotic matter into spirit, to sublimate the dust of the earth into soul, to elicit an ethereal spark from the clod of clay. And in this view of the subject, the various impressions and excitements which man receives through life may be considered as the forming hand of his Creator, acting by general laws, and awakening his sluggish existence, by the animating touches of the Divinity, into a capacity of superior enjoyment. The original sin of man is the torpor and corruption of the chaotic matter in which he may be said to be born.[22]

Malthus' materialist theology describes an idea of bounteous God calling teeming life forms into existence by separate acts of creation as 'puerile'. Reading God in 'the book of nature' involves a focus on the process by which 'specks of matter' are developed into 'sentient beings'. Yet Malthus' theology side-steps materialist and transmutational heterodoxy by distinguishing between matter on the one hand, and spirit and soul on the other. Moreover, a more subtle, yet crucial, shift which Malthus registers resides in his distinction between, on the one hand, a religion envisioning life on earth as God's trial of preordained mind, and on the other, one which recognises the Deity's overseeing of the evolutionary process of mind 'creation and *formation*' (my emphasis). It is this strain which will re-appear in influential strands of the nineteenth-century conception of culture as *Bildung* or 'self-culture'. For if 'original sin' for Malthus is no longer the story of the Fall, but rather the morass of proliferating 'chaotic matter' into and out of which the subject is born, then salvation, in earthly terms at least, is the acquisition and cultivation of those 'high qualities and powers' which lead the subject out of this morass towards an elevated process of formation, and 'fitness for some superior state'.

In constructing a discourse of nature that is predicated upon a vast productive and reproductive capacity for generating more and more 'chaotic matter', which yet contained within it the possibility of mind-driven moral and intellectual selectiveness and order, Malthus posited a nature that distinguished between chaos and cultivation, or anarchy and culture. A nineteenth-century discourse on culture can be traced from Malthus' injunction to read these actions of God in the book of nature. As we have seen, Matthew Arnold drew on it when he satirised Robert Buchanan. Coleridge, as we shall see, resisted its materialist implications when writing his own texts on self-culture.

He resisted them because materialist discourse also played an important role in the formation of evolutionary speculation. For there are parallels between Malthus' sense of sentient being emerging from the 'dust of the earth' and Erasmus Darwin's celebration of life being re-cycled from 'specks of animated earth':

> HENCE when a Monarch or a mushroom dies,
> Awhile extinct the organic matter lies;
> But, as few short hours or years revolve,
> Alchemic powers the changing mass dissolve;
> Born to new life unnumber'd insects pant,
> New buds surround the microscopic plant;
> Whose embryon senses, and unwearied frames,
> Feel finer goads, and blush with purer flames; . . .
>
> (IV, ll. 383–90)

For Darwin self-organising, self-directed matter is at once the means by which seemingly 'extinct' and inert organic monads are re-cycled into new life forms, and also the means for dismantling the hierarchical barrier separating high-caste humans (monarchs) from fungus (mushrooms).

But this was not the most sensitive barrier that Darwin was to breach. Consisting of four cantos of rhyming couplets framed by the mythic and allusive machinery of Augustan convention, Darwin's *The Temple of Nature* also employs the characteristic 'apparatus' of the Enlightenment philosophical poem, exemplified in Pope's *Essay on Man* (1733), in the form of footnotes which give the poem a powerful and generative intertextual resonance in the intellectual field. In these, Darwin's sources are cited as speculative possibilities, as in this footnote to Canto II of the poem, in which Darwin's materialist and transmutationist views of the origins of life are explictly pushed to their final, and controversial, conclusion:

Philosophers, with Buffon and Helvetius, seem to imagine, that mankind arose from one family of monkeys on the banks of the Mediterranean; who accidentally had learned to use the adductor pollicis, or the strong muscle which constitutes the ball of the thumb, and draw the point of it to meet the point of the fingers, which common monkeys do not; and that this muscle gradually increased in size, strength and activity, in successive generations; and by this improved use of the sense of touch, that monkeys acquired clear ideas, and gradually became men. (II, 54)

Darwin's footnote on the transition from ape to man draws on a number of sources of philosophical and scientific speculation (Buffon and Helvetius). The note also draws implicitly on the science of comparative anatomy, which made visible the structural similarities between man and beast at the level of organ, muscle and bone. The very science that inspired Paley's confidence in the presence of a designer is also a ground for Darwin's speculation on self-evolving matter. Finally the speculation rests on Lockean empiricism, the idea that knowledge is derived mechanically from the senses, for it is a heightened degree of tactile capacity that leads to the formation of ideas and the gradual emergence of men. The speculation subscribes to a contingent, random and 'mindless' view of evolution: it is by 'accident' that the structural advantage derived from the configuration of muscle and bone peculiar to a particular species of monkey is put to the use that results in the production of ideas and, thereafter, men. This neatly sums up Coleridge's fear of the 'mechanic dogmatists': there was a route from Locke, through Paley and Malthus, and it could lead to Erasmus Darwin's claim about the simian origin of humans.

3. ADDRESSING THE FEW: PERIODICALS AND THE INTELLECTUAL FIELD

Mill observed that Bentham and Coleridge 'have never been read by the multitude . . . their readers have been few'.[23] But it was resistance to the consequences of multitudinous reading, the plebification of knowledge concerning science and materialist transformism that drove Coleridge. He conceived his periodical *The Friend* as a select, minority publication. The publication was financed by an elaborate system of subscription and had a circulation of around six hundred. Writing to the chemist Humphrey

Davy, Coleridge distinguished his periodical from competitors such as the *Edinburgh Review, Examiner* and *Weekly Register*. 'I do not write in the Work for the *Multitude*; but for those who by Rank, or Fortune, or official Situation, or Talents or Habits of Reflection, are to *influence* the Multitude.'[24] Thus, Coleridge was beginning, with *The Friend*, to put into practice his theory of intellectual instruction and reading which was to achieve mature expression in *On the Constitution of the Church and State*.

The *Friend* projected itself as an organ for establishing 'true PRINCIPLES, to oppose false PRINCIPLES'.[25] It was a forum for establishing the philosophic grounds for the distinctiveness of living things, and in particular the unique value attached to human life. The first number opened with a statement of the way in which the self-contradicting tendency in human nature which distinguishes 'man from . . . all other animals' (1 June, 1809, 7). Coleridge's strategy depended in part on vitalist theories of life, and his essay on metaphysics (14 September 1809) alludes to the counter-materialism of vitalist thought elaborated by the English surgeons John Hunter and John Abernathy. A good example of a piece which sought to uphold truth against the falsehoods of materialist science was William Wordsworth's 'Essay Upon Epitaphs', which appeared in the periodical in 1810: a prose meditation on the uniquely human capacity for glimpsing intimations of immortality, it invoked anthropological and antiquarian research to furnish the material evidence (epitaphs) for these intimations, and it drew distinctions between human and animal impulses and sympathies. (The next chapter will situate Wordsworth's essay in context, given its attachment as an endnote to his poem *The Excursion*.) Coleridge's essay defending metaphysics in the fifth number of *The Friend* (14 September 1809) invoked ethnographic strategies for identifying primitivism to assert those true, life-defining principles:

To connect with the objects of our senses the obscure notions and consequent vivid feelings, which are due only to Ideas of immortal and permanent Things, is profanation relatively to the heart, and superstition in the understanding. It is in this sense, that the philosophic Apostle calls Covetousness Idolatory. Could we emancipate ourselves from the bedimming influences of Custom, and the transforming witchcraft of early associations, we should see as numerous Tribes of *Fetish-Worshippers* in the streets of London or Paris, as we hear of on the Coasts of Africa.[26]

In common with the argument of Wordsworth's 'Essay Upon Epitaphs', Coleridge holds that immortality and 'Ideas' of 'permanent Things' cannot be accessed through 'the objects of our senses'. However, whereas Wordsworth glimpsed intimations of immortality in the anthropological and archaeological evidences of burial site monuments, Coleridge uses the ethnographic imagination to unsettle the reader by highlighting impact of the 'bedimming influence of Custom' upon the everyday. It is not merely that the sensationalism of materialist science is a 'superstition'; it is also that the powerful persistence of 'early associations' prevents civilisation from apprehending the extent to which 'fetish worship' is practised in London and Paris at the same time as it is in Africa. Coleridge's anthropological turn is thus also a strategy of defamiliarisation: it brings a supposedly 'primitive' condition into the heart of the present, and to an unexpected location.

In all respects *The Friend* was an avant-garde intervention into the intellectual field, re-moulding the discourses of criticism, legislation, philosophy and morals. In his letter to Davy Coleridge claimed that *The Friend* comprised more than a set of 'Labourers pocket knifes' for cutting bread and cheese, and was instead a 'Case of Lancets' for dissecting the anatomy of a national condition.[27] Coleridge thus styled his project through a metaphor that distinguishes between classes and professions, and which draws attention to the power of the medical profession for the business of dissecting the ills of the nation. In formulating his theory of the clerisy in *On the Constitution of the Church and State*, Coleridge pitched his sense of a surgical mission against radical members of the medical profession who professed an adherence to materialist science and transmutationism, or 'revolutionary Amputators' as he styled them in *The Friend*. Coleridge's complex engagement with the professional and intellectual authority of medicine and science was intimately embedded in his project to fashion an adjudicative idea of culture out of distinctive reading experiences that revealed the divine, vitalised inwardness of the human. In inventing 'culture', Coleridge was also devising a counter-medicine, and counter-science through complex symbolisations.

4. REFLECTIONS ON CATERPILLARS, SELF-CULTURE AND
COPULAS: WORDS, EMBRYOS AND UNCONSCIOUS SELECTIONS

Coleridge's work of self-improving practical theology, *Aids to Reflection* (1825), started life as a collection of aphorisms selected from the writings of the seventeenth-century divine Archbishop Leighton. These aphorisms were supported by Coleridge's own burgeoning commentary which had grown out of positions negotiated in the writing of *The Friend* fifteen years earlier. Trevor H. Levere's study of Coleridge and science argues that the *Aids* were beyond the scope of his study, even though they were richly endowed with scientific observations and speculations.[28] But when the text's science is considered in relation to self-culture and philological reflection, it deserves fresh consideration in an assessment of the place of science in Coleridge's invention of 'culture'. The *Aids* were a phase in Coleridge's longer-term project of making an audience, given Jon Klancher's interpretation of Coleridge's determination that '[t]he mind of the middle-class audience would . . . have to be *formed* to know the Truth, shaped in those deliberate ways he would begin to essay in *The Friend* and not complete until *On the Constitution of the Church and State*'.[29] *Aids to Reflection* was a text designed to make an audience in the image of culture, in so far as its reading was conceived as a source of reflection and inward improvement. Coleridge's text aimed, in the words of its sub-title, to complete the 'Formation of a Manly Character on the Several Grounds of Prudence, Morality and Religion', the religion in question being Protestant Christianity, which Coleridge took to be the embodied perfection of reflective human intelligence.[30]

Aids to Reflection is reflective precisely about language and symbolic practice, styling itself a study of 'the Science of Words and their Use and Abuse' (6–7). Coleridge was acknowledging a particular inflection of the philological science of language that was exerting an ever larger impact on the understanding of religion.[31] The structure of religions in general was supposed to have originated in forms of symbolic signification that could be analysed comparatively. Primitive rituals surrounding death – the disposal of the corpse and symbolic imaginings of an after-life – were thought to draw on the natural world and record the common origins of religious customs and thought practices, as Erasmus Darwin had noted in his observation that 'a butterfly was the ancient emblem of the soul after death as rising from the tomb of its former state' (*Temple of Nature*, II, 60). This was linked to the propensity to imitate, 'imitation' being defined as 'repetition . . . the easiest kind of animal action' (III, p. 109). Imitation is also the origin of language – 'Thus the first LANGUAGE, when we frown'd or smiled / Rose from the cradle, Imitation's child' (III, ll. 363–4). The force of imitation is poeticised by Darwin as the gift of 'the Muse of MIMICRY' (III, l. 319). Imitation underpinned a theory of language as the naming of things, which found one expression in Horne Tooke's theory of etymological development: that the aim of language was to communicate thoughts and do it 'with dispatch' (*Aids to Reflection*, 93). In contributing to the 'Science of Words', Coleridge countered these materialist constructions of philology and imitation as forms of useful knowledge, given that 'more value may be conveyed by the history of a *word* than by the history of a Campaign' (*Aids to Reflection*, 17). Coleridge insists that words, as incarnate history, are '*LIVING POWERS*', a position he derives from Horne Tooke's radically materialist etymologies, supplemented by the visionary authority of the Book of Ezekiel (10).[32] Coleridge sought very different links between the science of life and language.

Indeed, while Coleridge began by filtering the thought of a seventeenth-century divine through a counter-science of words, the science of living things came to play an increasingly prominent role in his commentary. The importance of living things to Coleridge's argument is evinced in his observations on the stomach of a caterpillar and the creature's eating habits:

> I ask my self, under what words can I generalise the action of this Organ; and I see that it selects and adapts the appropriate means (ie. the assimilable part of the vegetable *congesta*) to the proximate end, ie. the growth and reproduction of the Insect's Body . . . Well! from the Power of the Stomach I pass to the Power exerted by the whole animal. I trace it wandering from spot to spot, and plant to plant, till it finds the appropriate vegetable; and again on this chosen vegetable I mark it seeking out and fixing on a plant, bark, leaf or petal, suited to its nourishment . . . Here I see a power of selecting and adapting means to proximate ends *according to circumstances*; and this higher species of Adaptive Power we call INSTINCT. (246–7)

In prose recording the excursive movements of eyes and mind, Coleridge self-consciously poses the question of the 'words' that he should use to describe what he observes: first, the actions of the caterpillar's stomach, and, secondly, the whole creature as it simultaneously occupies space and finds a food source to nourish and reproduce itself. Coleridge identifies the second as 'instinct' through the language of 'selection' and 'adaptation': adaptation was already a resonant word in Paley's natural theology, and selection would, of course, be conceptually revolutionised by Charles Darwin later in the century.[33] However, Coleridge goes on to note differences between these words and words from a higher status register: 'there is selection, but not *choice*: volition rather than Will' (247). Coleridge encounters the boundary which also preoccupies Wordsworth in the 'Essay Upon Epitaphs' when he asserts that 'fore-thought without Reflection is but a metaphorical phrase for the *instinct* of a beast' (13). Reflection, the key word of Coleridge's title, is the activity which distinguishes man from the beast. Accordingly, reflection is inherent in 'the words you use, hear or read . . . by which the things of most importance to mankind are actuated, combined and humanised' (10). Thus, to use words at all is to distinguish between human choice and bestial selection, human will and animal volition.

Aids to Reflection maps the symbolic capital associated with word choice about living things, given the 'primary, derivative and metaphorical senses' of words (7). In promoting the importance of precision in word choice,

Coleridge acknowledges that customary word usage does not always con-
form to this standard results in a kind of deviousness – and that, consequently, 'to expose a sophism and to detect the equivocal or double meaning of a word is, in the majority of cases, one and the same thing' (7).
Coleridge notes that increasing scientific specialisation and intellectual differentiation observe the same drive for precision in that the 'botanist, the
chemist, the anatomist & c., feel and submit to this necessity at all costs,
even at the cost of exposing their several pursuits to the ridicule of the
many, by technical terms . . . alike quarrelsome to the ear and the tongue'.
Coleridge distinguishes the development of field-specific vocabularies from
his own commitment to 'rescue' words which denote 'clear and distinct conceptions of our duties', an act of rescue that constitutes resistance to the
'chipping and debasing misusage of the market' (46–7). And yet, Coleridge
encountered difficulties in transcending a linguistic marketplace and the
consequences of the division of intellectual labour that it imposes, a difficulty that is practically manifest in the hybrid generic make-up of *Aids to
Reflection.*

 In the 'Advertisement' to the first edition of *Aids to Reflection* (it was
removed from the second edition of 1831), Coleridge acknowledged that his
intended book, ostensibly devoted to the writings of Archbishop Leighton,
had evolved during the process of writing:

The various Reflections, however, that pressed on me while I was considering the
motives for selecting this or that passage; the desire of enforcing, and as it were
integrating, the truths contained in the Original Author, by adding theses which
the words suggested or recalled to my own mind; the conversations with men of
eminence in Literary and Religious Circles, occasioned by the Objects which I had
in view; and lastly, the increasing disproportion of the Commentary to the Text,
and the two marked differences in the frame, character and colours of the styles;
soon induced me to adopt a revolution in my plan and object, which had in fact
actually taken place without my intention, and almost unawares.[34] (534)

Coleridge reflects on the 'revolution' that has transformed his attempt at
'rescuing' Leighton's thoughts and words, given that these words from the
seventeenth century have been subsequently accented by multiple inter-
textualities and dialogics. Coleridge's own thoughts clearly intrude upon
his reading and selection of Leighton's words, as have his conversations
'with men of eminence in Literary and Religious Circles', a form of intellectual and spiritual association which strives to lift Coleridge's project
above 'the debasing misusage of the market'. Nonetheless, supplements have
accrued to Leighton's religious thought, and the greatest supplement of all
is Coleridge's prose commentary, which he acknowledges has become dis-
proportionate to the text of his 'Original Author'. What is more, Coleridge

acknowledges that he has not intended this development, it has taken him 'almost unawares.' Thus Coleridge is placed in the paradoxical position of reflecting upon the 'selections' he has made from Leighton and discovering that, not unlike the caterpillar's instinctual settlement upon the leaf from which it feeds, rather than having exercised 'choice', he has 'selected' without being wholly aware of what he has done.

But Coleridge begins the 'Advertisement' to the first edition of *Aids to Reflection* by casting these reflections into striking metaphorical terms which attempt to rescue him from this paradox. He constructs an analogy between reading the text on which the reader is about to embark and practices derived from the sciences of life, specifically comparative anatomy and embryology:

In the bodies of several species of Animals are to be found certain Parts, of which neither the office, the functions, nor the relations could be ascertained by the Comparative Anatomist, till he had become acquainted with the state of the Animal before birth. Something sufficiently like this (for the purpose of an illustration, at least) applies to the work here offered to the Public . . . and the Changes it has undergone during its immature and embryonic state.[35] (533)

Coleridge's initial explanation of his changing intentions presents his writing as a 'living' thing, analogously amenable to analysis by the practices of comparative anatomy and embryology: what the reader as comparative anatomist might not be able to discern from a dissection of the formed work of living literature, the reader as embryologist could discover from exploring the early stages of growth manifest in embryonic intentions. Crucially, Coleridge's analogy imagines that the works which will consolidate 'culture' are evolving life forms in which continuities underlie apparent changes. As Scott F. Gilbert and Marion Faber have argued, the symmetrical structure of embryos has consistently, from the late eighteenth century, licensed a heightened, aestheticised way of appreciating their form. Coleridge appears to be drawing upon Goethe's observation that similarities between structures which might be distorted or hidden in adult organisms are revealed more clearly in embryos.[36] Embryology thus had an impact on Coleridge's romantic-aesthetic conceptions of organic form, and the role they would play in his historical, social and political thought.

Coleridge's organic sense of the relationship between science, politics and history underpinned the purpose of *On the Constitution of the Church and State* (1830), his late treatise, written in response to the Catholic Emancipation debate, addressing the historic and philosophic foundations of the English church, state, and caste of moral teachers or 'clerisy'.

The practices of comparative anatomy and embryology are invoked in Coleridge's observation that

A naturalist, (in the infancy of physiology, we will suppose, and before the first attempts at comparative anatomy) whose knowledge had been confined exclusively to the human frame, or that of animals similarly organised; and who, by this experience, had been led inductively to the idea of respiration, as the copula and mediator of the vascular and nervous systems,– might, very possibly, have regarded the lungs, with their appurtenants, as the only form in which this idea, or ultimate aim, was realizable. Ignorant of the functions of the spiracula in the insects, and of the gills of the fish, he would, perhaps, with great confidence, degrade both to the class of non-respirants. . . . [A]like in the work of nature and the institutions of man.[37]

Again, comparative anatomy will reveal structural similarities and relations that would not be apparent to the eye in a less advanced state of knowledge. Comparative anatomy will demonstrate how a gill and a spiraculum perform the same function as a lung. They are, in effect, embryonic versions of a highly evolved manifestation of a particular idea, or the ultimate aim: to breathe. Coleridge proposes that this teleological way of looking at evolving ideas in the works of nature can be applied to evolving ideas in the institutions of man, from primitive modes of social organisation to advanced, class-stratified civilisations. The discovery of the functional 'copula' in a comparison between ostensibly different material, bodily organisations has important symbolic consequences for the copula as moral metaphor; as Coleridge was to put it in his *Table Talk*, 'I wish, in short, to connect by a moral *copula* natural history with political history; or in other words, to make history scientific and science historical; to take from history its accidentality, and from science its fatalism.'[38]

But there were other impulses pushing scientific fatalism in more populist directions. Embryology also was to emerge as an important science in the debate about transmutation. As James A. Secord has noted, in the decade following 1825 embryology became important scientific currency in popular medical textbooks, such as Percival B. Lord's *Popular Physiology* (1834) and John Fletcher's *Rudiments of Physiology* (1835–7). Lord's re-capitulation theory merged natural historical and ethnographic paradigms in noting the way in which the human embryo progressed through stages resembling a fish, a reptile, a bird and then a mammal, before moving through the racial hierarchy of Negro, Malay, American and Mongolian types.[39] These theories were integrated into the anonymously published *Vestiges of the Natural History of Creation* which posited a highly controversial theory of species transmutation based on embryological recapitulation, speculating on the 'production of new forms . . . [as] a new stage in the progress in gestation'.[40] *Vestiges* reverently insisted that its theory of transmutation was a consequence of a divinely ordained plan of evolving creation, but that did not prevent it from being constructed as a scandalous example of gutter atheism and infidelity: Adam Sedgwick, Professor of Geology at the University of Cambridge, described it as 'rank materialism'.[41]

The conclusion that can be drawn from this popularisation of embryological language through transmutational speculation is that the products of an increasingly complex and high-status division of scientific labour could also be drawn into the very linguistic marketplace that Coleridge feared and despised. As Coleridge strove to recover a language of reflection and inwardness that would be equal to the mission of culture, that language was always already inscribed with supplements from science and evolutionary speculation which compromised the presumed source and integrity of that inwardness. Coleridge's efforts to create a counter-medicine and a counter-science are strenuous, but it becomes a struggle to fashion from the existing languages of medicine and science a pristine language of organic wholeness that would be adequate to the reflective rigours of self-making.

5. COLONIAL INTERTEXTS IN COLERIDGE'S IDEA OF CULTURE

The concept of the colony provided Coleridge with another imaginative space through which to invent 'culture'. This is evident in Coleridge's early commitment to Pantisocracy, the ideal community founded in a remote, uncivilised region that would depend for its future on the maintenance of brotherly sympathetic bonds among the colonists, and the labour that they exerted on the cultivation of land. In Robert Southey's letters (1793–4) on the subject, fantasies of colonisation and cultivation are closely linked: 'Fancy me only in America; imagine my ground uncultivated since the creation, and see me wielding the axe.' He went on to imagine that 'when Coleridge and I are sawing down a tree we shall discuss metaphysics . . . and write sonnets while following the plough'. As James C. McKusick has suggested, there is both exhilaration and anxiety in Southey's fantasies of colonisation and cultivation – and both are inseparable from the symbolic material of philosophy and poetry that will be cultivated simultaneously to the earth. McKusick claims that Southey invokes the language of philosophy and art as 'an invincible means of mastery over the colonial Other', but it is surely more complex than that.[42] Pantisocracy was all too fallible, pulled apart by the divisions of status and gender that constituted the 'corruptions' of civilisation; and language, conditioned by both colonial encounters and scientific 'fatalism', could offer only ambivalent projections of mastery in the service of culture.

Even after the collapse of the Pantisocracy, ethnographic writing from the colonies helped Coleridge to reflect on the social, political and spiritual condition of his own nation, and so helped to shape his conception of culture.[43] In a footnote to *On the Constitution of the Church and State*, Coleridge praises a work that he has read almost by accident, by the surgeon, Orientalist, naturalist, ethnographer and diplomat John Crawfurd, specifically his *History of the Indian Archipelago* (1820), compiled as a result of Crawfurd's posting to the region between 1811 and 1819:

Only a few days ago, an accident placed in my hand a work of which, from my very limited opportunities of seeing new publications, I had never before heard. Mr CRAWFURD's History of the Indian Archipelago – the work of a wise as well as of an able and well-informed man! Need I add, that it was no ordinary gratification to find, that in respect of certain prominent positions, maintained in this volume, I had unconsciously been fighting behind the shield of one whom I deem it an honour to follow. (*Constitution* (89))

The position which Coleridge recognised in Crawfurd's ethnographic work, and which he had 'unconsciously' articulated, was 'that the possession of wealth, derived from a fertile soil, encouraged the progress of absolute power in Java'. Crawfurd had generalised this into the following principle:

The devotion of a people to agricultural industry, by rendering themselves far more tame, and their property more tangible, went still further towards it: for wherever Agriculture is the principal pursuit, there it may certainly be reckoned, that the People will be found living under an absolute government.[44]

Crawfurd also observed that, in the Orient, this 'mode of culture' (1, 346) and the quality of the land that it adapted to produced particular, almost untranslatable, linguistic differences:

The languages of Europe have no terms to express this distinction [up/down, wet/dry], which in the Indian islands is so natural and obvious. The terms marsh-land and up-land are not sufficiently comprehensive or distinct. The lands appropriated by this situation to the wet culture are, in Javanese, and almost all the other languages in the Archipelago, termed *Sawah*, and the dry lands in the Javanese *Tagal*. (1, 344)

Crawfurd's philological perspective thus records the effect of culture – here literally in its agricultural sense – shaping language. Coleridge strives to locate an embryonic copula linking Crawford's observations to the positions that are maintained in his own work on the English church, state, and the idea of culture.

Crawfurd's ethnographic work on the Indian, or 'Malay' Archipelago took as its object either so-called savage or barbarous states of society, and worked within the kind of framework that organised his 'Mission to Ava' article for the *Edinburgh New Philosophical Journal*. He discovers 'primitive' priesthoods at work in the region, and the belief systems of rival cults under particular regimes of colonisation and cultivation are brought sharply into focus. Thus, he observes of the followers of the god Siwa in Bali, adapted to Hindu worship, a primitive division of labour in which its priesthood is one of four great castes (along with soldiery, merchants and serviles) (II, 237). These Brahmins are 'genuine Hindus' and as such distinct from the people, who display savage characteristics by continuing 'the worship of personifications of the elements, and the most natural objects around them' (II, 238). Crawfurd finds in Bali another instance of the relation between agricultural abundance, political authority and the (non)-performance of spiritual distinction in his observation that 'I could discover no religious mendicants. In a fruitful soil, understocked with inhabitants, and where the priesthood possesses valuable temporal authority, there is less occasion to seek for spiritual distinction' (II, 240). The reverse is true among Javanese 'Mahomadan' converts whom Crawfurd sees undertaking pilgrimage to Mecca 'less on account of piety than on account of the distinctions and immunities which the reputation of the pilgrimage confers upon a simple and untaught people' (II, 269). In Crawfurd's ethnography, human inwardness is not a readily accessible region; the regular display and performance of the outward trappings of spiritual distinction is an index of simplicity and primitivism.

Crawfurd's account of belief and worship in the Malay Archipelago recognises the grafted status of Christianity amongst a plurality of religious cults, and the close relation of religion to the politics of colonialism. Crawfurd distinguishes between the power of Christianity and Islam as drivers of colonisation in the region. On the one hand, Western European colonisers (the English and the Dutch) adopted the conversion tactics of the earlier Portuguese and Spanish adventurers: caring little for the 'language, habits and manners of the natives'; their 'intemperance . . . avarice and rapacity . . . brought their religion into odium'. Islam, on the other hand, was 'more popular, because introduced with more skill, and under circumstances more agreeable to the genius of the character, the state of society, and the temporal prosperity' (II, 274). As a consequence, Christianity has been adopted only by the most 'barbaric' populations of the Archipelago, and 'can reasonably be viewed as but little better than one form of superstition distinguished from another' (II, 276). Looking at the more successful variant of Christian religion at work in the Philippines, Crawfurd argues that Christianity still might become more influential if it could learn to imitate the assimilative practices of Islam: although Crawfurd does not presume to 'decide . . . our right to impose our religion' upon the people of the Archipelago, he does think that it will nonetheless be fair 'to view Christianity in its influence as a mere instrument' for 'disseminating civilisation' (II, 278–9).

And yet, a question remains over what, inwardly, can be lastingly touched and fashioned by this 'instrumental dissemination'. Colonial subjectivities are inclined to display an imitative and parodic relationship with the religion in which they have received instruction, as is clear from an anecdote which Crawfurd relates. Observing a party of Javanese labourers who had converted to Islam, Crawfurd recalls how 'one of the party was repeating a verse of the Koran, which he had somehow acquired, and mimicking a preacher of their acquaintance. When he had done, the rest applauded him by a loud shout, and a convulsive roar of laughter. He again repeated the verse.' Religious observance consists of repetition with parodic variation: the possession of civilisation is never assured, because whilst an authoritative text has been disseminated to the labourer, the 'content' on which the enunciated supplement is based has been acquired haphazardly, mysteriously – 'somehow'. Crawfurd remarks that the religious belief he sees imitated displays 'neither bigotry nor austerity . . . and most frequently it has not much solemnity' (II, 268). What Crawfurd discovers is Homi Bhabha's sense of the defamiliarising effects of mimicry, which makes a stable colonial subjectivity a problem rather than a lasting achievement.[45] By implication, an English national self securely shaped by and grounded in culture can, from this perspective, be seen as 'the problem of problems'. The parallel problem underlies Coleridge's theory of the Idea in *On the Constitution of the Church and State*.[46]

'Ideas' evolve, and their 'line of evolution, however sinuous, has still tended to this point, sometimes with, sometimes without, not seldom, perhaps, against the intention of the individual actors, but always as if a power, greater, and better, than the men themselves, had intended it for them' (*Constitution*, 30). The 'Idea' in Coleridge's thought rested on two pillars: first, that it is defined by 'knowledge of *its ultimate aim*' (12), so that ideas are teleological, and have to be understood as evolving entities within a purposive, intentional frame. And secondly, ideas – for example, the idea that persons should never be means but, instead, moral ends in themselves – are more powerful than the individuals whose minds they inhabit. As Coleridge argues, such ideas are present to the minds of agricultural labourers who feel the injustice of having their wages supplemented by parish poor rates, though such men are not conscious of the idea that motivates their sense of injustice, in that they would not be able to present it 'to the minds of others' (*Church and State*, 16). In contrast to Crawfurd's encounter with the Javanese labourer who has 'somehow' acquired the Koran, and is able to mimic it, Coleridge encounters a labourer who 'somehow' articulates the idea of 'man's moral freedom' not in speech, but instead with his 'whole practical being' (*Church and State*, 18). There is clearly a difference between the ambivalent colonial subject with his mimicry, and the English labouring subject who is dignified with an integrated practical (if not intellectual) being. And yet, Coleridge was not able to repress the full implication of the mindless subject and his mimicry from the English 'civilisation' that culture would shore up.

Coleridge's appeal to the language of comparative anatomy and embryology in *Constitution* places England in a hierarchical, developmental relationship to Javan political absolutism and landed 'modes of culture'. Coleridge takes English agriculture, property, and the authority derived from them to be conserving foundations 'for the permanence of the state' (24). But Coleridge also acknowledges highly advanced dynamics which spread civilisation, these being 'the four classes of the mercantile, the manufacturing, the distributive and the professional' (25). In addressing the condition of English modernity, Coleridge draws attention to the malformations that have been shaped by the increasing imbalance between different 'interests' in the body politic, the 'moniyed interest' and 'landed interest' as Coleridge styles them. If 'land' values permanence, 'money' values the circulation of goods and the dissemination of knowledge characteristic of civilisation. Indeed, it is the intensive scale of 'the diffusion of the information and knowledge useful or necessary for all' (25) that marks the main difference between the colonised East and England; the dissemination of information and intellectual traffic is precisely what Coleridge seeks to regulate in England.

The clerisy would be responsible for that regulation. In common with Crawfurd's sense of the functionality of Christianity as disseminator of civilisation in colonial settings, Coleridge assigns a functional role to the National Church in the body of 'THE CLERISY of the nation', which would teach the disciplines of 'law and jurisprudence; of medicine and physiology; of music; of military and civil architecture; of the physical sciences . . . as well as the Theological . . . and the prima scientia . . . PHILOSOPHY, or the doctrine and discipline of *ideas*' (46–7). The clerisy would both map and regulate the intellectual field. Coleridge's ethnographic observations of primitive, colonised societies were related to his interest in the emergence and function of institutions, particularly of worship and organised religion as agents of cultivation. In an unpublished fragment, Coleridge reflected more directly on the origin of the institution of priesthood:

The power of a Priesthood, how {it is} beneficial–In the first place it could not exist but by a splitting of the Savage [?Conqueror/Conjuror] into three parts, the Warrior, the physician, and the priest–2. it could not exist without a certain appropriation of Property, and must of necessity interest a very powerful Class in encouraging more certain modes of production than those of Hunting, or Fishing– 3.–Conjuring abstracted or refined, the Priesthood must support their influence by external order & splendor which could not but forward arts, & the division of Labor–the introduction of abstract ideas and general terms–

Coleridge lists seven originary functions of priesthood, the remainder of which were: that it formed a bulwark against military despotism; it consti- tuted a repository of ritual (despite these having their origins in blood and violence); priesthoods gave rise to property laws.[47] Coleridge's fragment is notable for its materialist functionialism, particularly its insistence on the principle of the division of labour, and the way in which the priesthood emerged as a class fraction encouraging new human productive and colonis- ing capacities including 'the appropriation of Property', an appropriation that sought legitimacy through the performance of distinctions through external displays of splendour and authority. Crucial to this legitimacy was the identity of priests as custodians of a repository of 'civilised arts' which could generate further 'inventions'. This was linked to 'the introduction of abstract ideas and general terms', for Coleridge sought to place limits on the extent of intellectual invention. It is significant that Coleridge's frag- ment on priesthood observes a fundamental division of labour between the priest and the physician. For Coleridge, this was a division that, in the early nineteenth century, was being increasingly breached: the problem was the inventiveness of the languages of medicine and science, and their dissemination by the 'mechanic dogmatists', especially in the way in which this language had come to inhabit theology.

For Coleridge, the effects of the conflict between theology and materi- alist science were recorded in etymologies. In the *Constitution*, Coleridge points to the evolution of the idea of the *person* as moral subject and end in itself 'in contradistinction from thing' (15), by providing the reader with an etymology of *parson*, linking it to the Latin *persona*, 'the representative and exemplar of the *personal* character of the community of the parish; of their duties and rights, of their hopes, privileges and requisite qualifications, as moral *persons*, and not merely living things' (52–3). When Coleridge came to deal with the word 'Idea' itself, certain inflections of usage, mediated by mechanistic materialism, were in danger of rendering speakers 'merely living things'. The institutional and intellectual warfare recognised in the work of Adrian Desmond added a particular edge to Coleridge's etymological arguments. Coleridge imagines his antagonist reader as 'a young Liberal, fresh from Edinburgh or Hackney or the Hospitals'. Coleridge imagines that in speaking to him 'of Free-will, as implied in Free-agency, he will perhaps confess to you with a smile, that he is Necessitarian . . .' (17). Among Coleridge's named targets were the surgeon and comparative anatomist William Lawrence (17), regarded as a materialist and atheist, and one who attacked John Hunter's vitalist theories (to which Coleridge was more inclined, though with reservations).[48] Materialism marked the debasement of the articulation of the Idea, as illustrated in Coleridge's philological account of this key word. Coleridge is concerned with the 'remarkable contrast between the acceptation of the word, Idea, *before* the Restoration, and the *present* use of the same word':

Before 1660, the magnificent SON OF COSMO was wont to discourse with FICINO, POLITIAN, and the PRINCELY MIRANDULA on the IDEAS of Will, God, Freedom. SIR PHILIP SIDNEY, the star of serenest brilliance in the glorious constellation of Elizabeth's court, communed with SPENSER, on the IDEA of the beautiful; and the younger ALGERNON—Soldier, Patriot and Statesman—with HARRINGTON, MILTON and NEVIL on the IDEA of the STATE: and in what sense it may be more truly affirmed, that the people (*i.e.* the component particles of the body politic, at any moment exisiting as such) are in order to the state, than that the state exists for the sake of the people.

Present use of the word.

DR. HOLOFERNES, in a lecture on metaphysics, delivered at one of the Mechanics Institutions, explodes all *ideas* but those of sensation; and his friend DEPUTY COSTARD, has no *idea* of a better flavoured haunch of venison, than he dined off at the London Tavern last week. He admits, (for the deputy has travelled) that the French have an excellent *idea* of cooking in general; but holds that their most accomplished *Maitres de Cuisine* have no more *idea* of dressing a turtle, than the Parisian Gourmands themselves have any real *idea* of the true *taste* and *colour* of the fat. (64–6)

What emerges from this contrast between uses of *idea* pre-1660 and in the present is the way in which the popular scientific sensationalism of the present – satirised in the figures of Holofernes and Costard, their Mechanics Institute and the French-inspired obsession with appetite – can be read in relation to Crawfurd's encounter with the Javanese labourer, mimicking the Koran. For Coleridge represents present-day use of the word ('no idea, no idea') as mere fatuous and repetitive mimicry of an earlier Platonised ideal of the Idea and its high-intellectual institutional embodiment. Coleridge's theory of the clerisy re-works Crawfurd's colonial observations, Platonising them and placing them in a 'home' setting. Furthermore, Coleridge focuses his anxieties about scientific sensationalism, and the medical intellectuals who articulate it, upon his opposition to transmutation, exemplified in his resistance to an 'Ouran Outang theology of the origin of the human race, substituted for the book of Genesis, ch.I. – x' (66). Coleridge's determination to preserve 'the SCIENCE of Theology' was an attempt to steer the science of evolution in a Platonic direction (47).

Coleridge's interventions were rhetorical and textual; yet his 'symbolical' concerns became institutionally embodied in significant ways. In October 1832, J. H. Green addressed the new Medical School of King's College, London, as its Professor of Surgery. Green was a Coleridge disciple, and the Preface to his address directly appealed to Coleridge's ideas about the clerisy.[49] Green upheld Coleridge's defence of theology as the unifying discipline of the Christian university, and he also held theology to be the custodian of the base material of the intellectual field, that is language itself. For Green, the theology of the medieval schoolmen was responsible for 'casting the common mould for all the languages of Europe in all their forms of connexion, and sequences of thought' (6). Philology linked to theology, in the manner proposed by Coleridge, would be an important tool in regulating scientific speculation. And the cultivation of intellectual pursuits had to be regulated, as Green asserted by appealing to a field metaphor: 'the field must be fenced, and cleared of obstructive or noxious growths, before it can be cultivated and sown, or planted for human uses' (4). What Green feared was the random dissemination of materialist speculation. Such growths, 'arising like weeds, the growth of accident', would, for Green, undo 'the English gentleman' (42–3).

King's College was founded to counter the Benthamite influence of the newly established University College. At the opening of King's College on 8 October 1831, Charles James, the Bishop of London, preached in the chapel on 'The Duty of Combining Religious Instruction with Intellectual Culture'. Focusing on comparative anatomy, James warned that 'the Creator should not be superseded by the creature, as an object of enquiry and desire'.[50] To prevent this happening James articulated 'our desire . . . to erect the shrine of science and literature' in order to fulfil 'the pious designs of the founders, and diffuse the benefits of a holy and useful education, through a far wider circle than that which will of necessity bound its first exertions' (29).

Charles Darwin's sisters hoped earnestly that their brother would begin to worship at a more fitting 'shrine' to literature and science. In January of 1826, Caroline and Susan Darwin wrote to their brother: 'We have had no more new books, but have just ordered Coleridg's [sic] 'Aids to reflection,' which I hear very highly spoken of by several people'.[51] The reference to Coleridge's *Aids* was apposite, given where Darwin was studying and the company he was about to keep. For in October 1825, Charles Darwin had gone up to Edinburgh, which, along with Hackney, was identified by Coleridge as one of the hotbeds of radical materialist philosophy, to begin the study of medicine. In the years 1826–7, Darwin was to mix in circles frequented by Robert E. Grant, a doctor by training, but a naturalist of independent means with an interest in the natural history of marine life, and a convinced transmutationist. In 1827, Grant was appointed to the Chair of Comparative Anatomy at the Benthamite University College, London.[52] Coleridge was well known to the Darwin–Wedgwood circle because of the patronage given to the poet and philosopher by the wealthy industrialists. Caroline was nudging her brother to become more reflective and Coleridgean on matters spiritual. Darwin did not take the bait; at least, not at this point. As Adrian Desmond and James Moore record in their biography of Darwin, he did eventually read Coleridge's prose in 1840, when his father, Dr Robert Darwin, was dying: at this time of loss, Darwin read *The Friend* and *Aids to Reflection* for intimations of immortality. But as Desmond and Moore put it, 'Darwin was unmoved, even as he watched his father subside. There was no cure in Coleridge's books.'[53] Neither was there a clear way forward through John Stuart Mill's essay on Coleridge, also written in 1840, the note on which was set aside among the 'Old and Useless Notes'. Darwin would worship at the shrine of literature and science erected by William Wordsworth.

CHAPTER 2

'Our origin, what matters it?': Wordsworth's excursive portmanteau of culture

I. WORDSWORTH AND SCIENCE, CHARLES DARWIN'S POETICAL 'BOAST'

When J. A. Symonds wrote his essay on 'Culture: Its Meaning and Uses' in 1893, he offered a riposte to a reviewer who sneered at the man of letters apparently 'travelling round Europe with a portmanteau full of culture on my back'.[1] Staggering under the burdensome knowledge of the arts, crafts, sciences, literature, and manners and mores of other places, as though such knowledge were a 'pedlar's pack', was, for Symonds, a misconception of 'culture'. Yet William Wordsworth's *The Excursion* (1814) dramatised 'culture' in precisely this manner, as though knowledge and the affective power that builds sympathy were the contents of a pedlar's pack, carried between geographical regions by the migrant figure, the Wanderer at the centre of the poem. Wordsworth's poem itself 'transports' knowledge through a range of lengthy endnotes reflecting variously on peddling and colonisation; travelling and self-cultivation; religious sentiments concerning death and epitaphs as markers of immortality and 'sympathy'; and education as a mode of 'simple engineering'. When combined with the poetry, this knowledge produced, I argue, an unstable discursive mix, an instability that Wordsworth was alert to in his unpublished reflections on language as 'counter-spirit', or another version of that supplementarity that would mark the practice of the 'literary' following encounters with discourses of science. For Wordsworth's writing was a compelling mix for those who were beginning to fashion science as an important source of mental culture. Wordsworth's poem and its transported philosophical reflections participated, over a long period, in the formation of that slowly woven magic garment, consisting of humane and scientific knowledge, that was to be imaged by Symonds as 'culture' in 1893.

Wordsworth's *Excursion* remains a neglected part of the Wordsworth canon, though the recent work of Sally Bushell has done a great deal to remind scholars of the dramatic and polyphonic qualities that shaped the poem, and that, through these, Wordsworth was consciously shaping a role for the 'active' reader.[2] Wordsworth enjoyed an enduring but contested legacy as a reading experience in the nineteenth-century intellectual field. His poetry became a remarkable source of authority among intellectuals who contributed to the formation of a literature of science. The popular scientific journal *Nature*, founded in November 1869, carried a line from Wordsworth's sonnet 'A volant tribe of bards' ('Miscellaneous Sonnets', 1827) on its masthead: 'To the solid ground / Of nature trusts the Mind that builds for aye.' In 1874, John Tyndall's controversial assertion of scientific materialism as the basis for life, addressed to the British Association for the Advancement of Science in Belfast (*The Belfast Address*), concluded by citing the 'spirit' invoked in the closing lines of Wordsworth's 'Tintern Abbey': 'A motion and a spirit, that impels / All thinking things, all objects of all thought, / And rolls through all things'.[3] If scientific materialists could appropriate Wordsworth's appeals to spirit, perhaps there had always been a latent and subversive strain of materialism in Wordsworth. In 1814, *The Excursion* was famously attacked by Francis Jeffrey in the *Edinburgh Review*, who found in it 'a tissue of moral and devotional ravings . . . a kind of mystical morality' practised at 'the shrine of those paltry idols . . . set up . . . among his lakes and mountains'.[4] This materialist idolatory of the landscape was part of the 'tissue' of Wordsworth that would interest the later nineteenth-century aesthetician Walter Pater as he rethought the relation between the discourses of literature and science from the 1860s.

However, the dominant view of Wordsworth among the emergent profession of scientists in the 1820s and 1830s was that his poetry re-inforced science's support for Christian revelation. The Cambridge philosopher of science William Whewell, and the geologist Adam Sedgwick, expressed this view powerfully. As John Wyatt puts it, 'for the new generation of Cambridge fellows the voice of the great poet of Nature harmonized with their own appropriation of the natural landscape'; *The Excursion* was both a dramatisation of a natural order in which hardship, death and destruction predominated, and an 'apologia for an orderly world with a benevolent intention'.[5] In a letter of 1820 to J. C. Hare about the vacant Mastership of Trinity, Whewell remarked that 'The general opinion gives it to [Christopher] Wordsworth. If this turns out so, he shall invite his brother [William] here and you shall come and meet him, and we will be the most poetical and psychological college in the universe.'[6] It did turn out so, and William Wordsworth did indeed become attached to these Cambridge savants upon the appointment of his cleric brother to the Mastership of

Trinity. Whewell's sense of the symbolic capital that the poet Wordsworth would endow upon the intellectual and moral authority of Cambridge science is striking.

Harriet Martineau's work on science also looked to Wordsworth's writing as symbolic capital that would support and enhance the shaping of a human science. Her *How to Observe: Morals and Manners* (1838) aimed to school its readers in the refined observational skills necessary for grasping the 'infinite . . . diversities in man'.[7] Martineau's second chapter, entitled 'Moral Requisites', opens with the epigraph 'He was alive / To all that was enjoyed where'er he went, / And all that was endured', which is Wordsworth's account, in the *Excursion*, of the Wanderer's field of celebratory and stoical observation.[8] Christopher Herbert has described Martineau's text, which she addressed to 'travellers and students', as perhaps the first to explore 'the interconnection of the vocation of fieldwork and the still uncodified idea of culture'.[9] Martineau's epigraph suggests that Wordsworth's poetry shaped the relation between 'fieldwork' and 'culture' in two senses: first, by validating the language of fieldwork as a refined contribution to travel writing, observation, and the cultivation of self; secondly, by endowing science with a position of dignity in the intellectual field.

Charles Darwin would be touched by both senses, and recorded reading Martineau's book in June 1838, in the same notebook as, and some four months before, he recorded his reading of Malthus on population.[10] Darwin also read Wordsworth. Cambridge educated after his abortive experiment with medicine in Edinburgh, Darwin was exposed to the tastes of Whewell, Sedgwick and their circle. He later remarked in his *Autobiography* that, on returning home to England from his *Beagle* voyage, he read the poetry of Wordsworth and Coleridge with 'great pleasure'. He above all 'boasted' that he read *The Excursion* 'twice through'.[11] The position of this 'boast' in the autobiography is striking as it occurs just before Darwin's discussion of the erosion of his religious belief, whereby 'the rate was so slow that I felt no distress, but was at last complete', like a landscape worn down by the material elements (50). Darwin's recollection that he gained pleasure from reading Wordsworth and Coleridge is followed by the admission that, in later life, his mind has lost its taste for poetry, and has become 'a kind of machine for grinding out general laws' (84). Something that was once pleasurable and vital has become mechanical. This is a conceptual and discursive tension that is also at play in *The Excursion*. It is a tension that has deeper implications for both the emergence of Darwin's evolutionary theory and the complex make-up of 'culture' in the nineteenth century as a keyword for debating the authority and value attached to the sources of material reality.

In his Preface to *The Excursion*, Wordsworth announced his withdrawal from battles and crowds, writing of himself retiring to his 'native mountains, with the hope of writing a literary work that might live'. This notion of 'living literature' can be situated in the scientific and philosophical battle over meanings of 'life'. The common view of Wordsworth, articulated by the philosopher Henry Sidgwick in the late nineteenth century, is that he was writing at too early a stage to be hit by the main stream of evolutionary speculation that impacted so dramatically on Tennyson. But as Stephen Gill has observed, new trends in the intellectual history of evolutionary theory urge a re-thinking of that view.[12] Coleridge's reaction provides some sense of context. As discussed in the previous chapter, Coleridge alludes to Erasmus Darwin's transformist speculations in a letter to Wordsworth of May 1815, in which Coleridge guardedly expresses disappointment with *The Excursion*. Coleridge had eagerly anticipated *The Recluse*, of which *The Excursion* was the 'intermediate part' (Preface), as 'the *first* and *only* true Phil. Poem in existence'. By 'a philosophical poem' Coleridge understood a work which would devise 'the Totality of a System' for meditating on 'the faculties of Man in the abstract' which, in establishing a 'solid and immovable foundation', would shift aside the 'sandy Sophisms of Locke and the Mechanic Dogmatists'. Coleridge also expected the true philosophical poem to 'have exploded the absurd notion of Pope's Essay on Man, Darwin, and the countless Believers . . . of Man's having progressed from an Ouran Outang state'.[13] In Coleridge's view such a speculation remained undefeated by *The Excursion*.

Coleridge's references to Erasmus Darwin and the tradition of the philosophical poem indicate that, to Coleridge's mind at least, Wordsworth was contesting a place in the intellectual field that had previously been occupied by Erasmus Darwin. The grounds for this supposition are not immediately apparent. *The Excursion* is generically modelled on symposia, autobiographical narration and embedded story-telling. A dramatic poem in nine books featuring the talk that takes place during the wanderings (excursions) among the Cumbrian mountains and Lakes of the Wanderer, the Solitary, the Pastor and the poet-narrator, its make-up is very different from the Augustan machinery comprising Erasmus Darwin's *Temple of Nature*. Yet Wordsworth continued to follow the tradition of the philosophical poem by using notes to anchor his position intellectually, and provide direction for the reader. These notes included Wordsworth's own 'Essay Upon Epitaphs', re-published from Coleridge's *Friend*; a commentary on Robert Heron's account of his tour of Scotland, and on the place of pedlars in the circulation and dissemination of goods and knowledge; an account of the 'mechanics' of colonial education, and fragments from William Gilbert's commentary on his own philosophical poem of 1796, 'The Hurricane'. Indeed, anxieties about materialist speculations are articulated in the philosophical apparatus appended to *The Excursion*, endnotes which, along with the poetic narrative itself, were making claims for the work as a contribution to 'culture' as a complex of intellectual and affective symbols.

2. PEDDLING CULTURE: MIGRATION AND COLONISATION

How does *The Excursion*, this imaginary pedlar's pack, contribute to the formation of this complex of symbols? In his Preface to *The Excursion* Wordsworth cites lines from the incomplete *Recluse* which situate his poetic project in the context of the question of audience, and its division between the many and the few ('fit audience let me find though few!'). 'Cultivation' and 'culture' are important words in the poem: they testify to the etymological shift from agricultural process to mental formation. But in being dramatised and personified, in particular through the figure of the Wanderer, they are materials that are aimed at constructing sympathetic bonds between reader and poem. The Wanderer thus reflects on the '*moral things*' (IV, 806) that humans can learn when immersed in nature 'on the mountain-top / Or in the cultured field' (IV, 827–8). At the same time, 'culture' is associated with valued, scholarly learning: in the course of one of his moral tales about the lives and deaths of his flock, the Pastor says of a couple: 'In powers of mind, / In scale of culture, few among my flock / Hold lower rank' (v, 716–17). This is far from devaluing the couple, for when the Wanderer is introduced by the narrator, he is presented as one of the 'many' poets 'sown / By Nature' – that is to say, 'wanting the accomplishment of verse' which their youth 'denied them to acquire, through lack / Of culture and the improving aid of books' (I, 76–83).

The Wanderer utters a distinctive kind of poetic wisdom. He discourses on the proper way to behold nature and science, and he is also an ethnographic curator, preserving knowledge of archaic customs and traditions. In Book II, as the narrator and the Wanderer encounter in the mountains a funeral procession advancing to the sound of a hymn, the Wanderer remarks that the sound is 'more than human!', and though

> Many precious rites
> And customs of our rural ancestry
> Are gone, or stealing from us; this, I hope,
> Will last for ever.   (550–3)

In the Wanderer's elaborate account of the ritual of the funeral procession which follows, the 'senseless weight' of the corpse on the way to burial in the 'open grave' is represented as an object which naturally commands reverence and honour; the Wanderer's stress on the importance of the preservation of customs and traditions surrounding death is thus bound up with another root sense of 'culture'. The Wanderer is, accordingly, a figure who embodies the early nineteenth-century emergence of 'culture' as a keyword. For he is an unlettered representative of the many at the heart of a highly literate poetic project which seeks to align itself in relation to the few, or a select audience.

It is in this sense that the Wanderer's occupation as a pedlar becomes important, so important that after the lines describing the way in which the Wanderer's peripatetic occupation has given him access to and knowledge of the ethnographic variants comprising the 'manners', 'enjoyments', 'pursuits', 'passions' and 'feelings' of diverse men (i, 340–4), Wordsworth points the reader towards an endnote in which he accounts for the validity of his representation of the Wanderer, which otherwise might shock 'the prejudices of artificial society'.[14] Wordsworth's note consists of a long quotation from a work of travel writing and observation, Robert Heron's *Journey in Scotland* (1793). Wordsworth italicises the text in which Heron lends 'factual' support to his portrait of the peddling Wanderer as a reflective, contemplative poet-figure (*'as they wander, each alone, through thinly inhabited districts, they form habits of reflection and of sublime contemplation'*).

Wordsworth's appeal to Heron can be seen in the context of late eighteenth-century representations of travel to Scotland, and their contribution to the formation of an ethnographic meaning of culture. Mary Poovey has argued that Samuel Johnson's *A Journey to the Western Islands of Scotland* (1775) was an early contributor to this development. Although Johnson's writing clearly makes claims for the improvement of the observer,[15] the extent to which Johnson's travel writing contributed to Poovey's claims for the emergence of 'cultural relativism' are more questionable.[16] Perhaps of greater relevance is Heron's claim about the significance of migrant pedlars as agents of cultivation, compared to Johnson's insistence on the prerequisite of 'useful violence' as the military precursor to the introduction of the 'arts of peace' in Scotland.[17] The quotation from Heron's work is resonant because of the way in which it constructs pedlars as migrant agents of circulation, a process bound up, as Heron makes clear, with the ancient and modern histories of imperial conquest and colonisation:

We learn from Caesar and other Roman Writers, that the travelling merchants who frequented Gaul and other barbarous countries, either newly conquered by the Roman arms, or bordering on the Roman conquests, were ever the first to make inhabitants of those countries familiarly acquainted with Roman modes of life, and to inspire them with an inclination to follow Roman fashions, and to enjoy Roman conveniences. In North America, travelling merchants from the Settlements have done and continue to do much more towards civilizing the Indian natives, than all the missionaries, papist or protestant, who have ever been sent among them.[18]

Thus, pedlars circulated the fruits of classical civilisation in concert with the process of colonisation. Indeed, according to Heron's observation of the North American experience – an experience that was important to Wordsworth in even his earliest *Lyrical Ballads* poetry – mercantile circulation is more effective than organised missionary work. For Heron's point about the reflective inwardness of pedlars is linked to their function within an economy of colonial practices, and a much more ambitious contention regarding the circulation of specific modes of self-fashioning or (to employ Bourdieu's term) *habitus*, which would have had particular resonance for Wordsworth:

This most useful class of men commonly contribute . . . by their personal manners, no less than by the sale of their wares, to the refinement of the people among whom they travel . . . With all these qualifications, no wonder that they should often be, in remote parts of the country, the best mirrors of fashion, and censors of manners; and should contribute much to polish the roughness, and soften the rusticity of our peasantry.[19]

Heron concludes his account of pedlars with the observation that, after a life of travelling, a pedlar can return to his native country to be regarded as a 'gentleman'. There are two points which follow from this note. First, the gentlemanly status and reflective disposition of Heron's rustic pedlar is not simply the real-life alibi for Wordsworth's Wanderer.[20] More precisely, the endnote, in presenting a discourse on circulation which balances refinement and rusticity, exclusivity and commonness, rhetorically performs a sense of position and mission for the work that the poem aspires to perform in the intellectual field. Second, and in relation to the intellectual field, the type of material which Wordsworth cites in his notes is different from that presented by, for instance, Erasmus Darwin in *The Temple of Nature*; while Darwin alluded to anthropological generalities about the arts and sciences of civilisation, Wordsworth cites ethnographic material which is more obviously observational and experiential. The Wanderer, and the poem in which he figures, are conceived as refined circulators of human sympathy.

3. THE 'EXCURSIVE POWER' OF MIND AND CAMBRIDGE SCIENCE

The Preface to the poem provides readers with a kind of prospectus which suggests that a 'high' philosophical statement about man, his adaptive power and the creativity of the faculty of mind, will be forthcoming:

> while my voice proclaims
> How exquisitely the individual Mind
> (And the progressive powers perhaps no less
> Of the whole species) to the external World
> Is fitted:—and how exquisitely, too—
> Theme this but little heard of among men—
> The external World is fitted to the Mind;
> And the creation (by no lower name
> Can it be called) which they with blended might
> Accomplish:—this is our high argument.
>
> (62–71)

In the same Preface, Wordsworth warns readers that they will find no explicitly articulated system in *The Excursion* ('It is not the Author's intention formally to announce a system'), though, he adds, if they attend to the 'lively images, and strong feelings' comprising the dramatic structure of the poem, then 'the Reader will have no difficulty in extracting the system for himself'. However, the question of what, if any, philosophical system the reader will take away from Wordsworth's *Excursion* is complex: 'system' will have to be extracted from 'lively images' of natural history, the geology of the earth, the cultivation and colonisation of land, and the anthropology of 'marking' death through epitaphs and customs of worship. The system will be apprehended through sympathetic reflection on the language constructing these representations.

In its role as philosophical poem, *The Excursion* reflects on science as an intellectual practice; and, at these moments, the position adopted is vigorously opposed to materialism and a mechanistic conception of science. In Book IV, the Wanderer declaims on the just ambitions that ought to underpin study of nature, man and science:

> Happy is he who lives to understand,
> Not human nature only, but explores
> All natures,—to the end that he may find
> The law that governs each; and where begins
> The union, the partition where, that makes
> Kind and degree, among all visible Beings;
> The constitutions, powers and faculties,

Which they inherit,—cannot step beyond,—
And cannot fall beneath; that do assign
To every class its station and its office,
Through all the mighty commonwealth of things;
Up from the creeping plant to sovereign Man . . .

(332–43)

. . . Science then
Shall be a precious visitant; and then
And only then, be worthy of her name:
For then her heart shall kindle; her dull eye,
Dull and inanimate, no more shall hang
Chained to its object in brute slavery;
But taught with patient interest to watch
The processes of things, and serve the cause
Of order and distinctness, not for this
Shall it forget that its most noble use,
Its most illustrious province, must be found
In furnishing clear guidance, a support
Not treacherous, to the mind's *excursive* power.

(1251–63)

The Wanderer's discourse on the true understanding of human nature in the economy of nature contemplates those 'partitions', based on laws of inheritance and innate aptitude, which arrange 'visible Beings' into hierarchical orders ('Up from the creeping plant to sovereign Man'). At the same time, the Wanderer contemplates the origins ('where begins') and extent of 'union' between a plurality of distinct 'natures.' A liberated 'Science' will 'serve the cause / Of order and distinctness', and offer 'support / Not treacherous, to the mind's *excursive* power.' Here Wordsworth plays on the title of his poem by using the adjectival sense of the term, employed extensively in the eighteenth century (*OED*) to describe desultory habits of seeing or reading (indisciplined running around), which escape from confinement and fixed limits. The whole point of true science is to discipline the excursive power of mind, which is likely to mislead when confronted with the plenitude of nature, and the (false) counsel of a science of mechanics ('the mind's repose / On evidence is not to be ensured / By act of naked reason. Moral truth / Is no mechanic structure . . .' (v, 560–3)). However, the complex syntax of the Wanderer's lines articulating the relation between 'partition' and 'union' in understanding the relations between living beings is, strikingly, a poetic enactment of the excursive mind in free movement.

The problem of the mind captivated by a science enslaved to mechanism is explored through the voice of the Solitary, a widowed and misanthropic

man who is first seen by the narrator and the Wanderer as he approaches
them from 'the enclosure of green fields / Into the rough uncultivated
ground' (II, 495–6) in which his dwelling is situated. His cottage contains
the text of *Candide*, Voltaire's attack on complacent Enlightenment optimism symbolically ravaged by 'the injurious elements' (II, 440–3), and the
objects of a science that can no longer be assembled into coherence: 'fossils,
withered plants and flowers . . . Mechanic tools / Lay intermixed with scraps
of paper, some / Scribbled with verse.' Thus, Erasmus Darwin's attempt
to blend speculative natural history and poetry into ideological support
for a society energised by manufacture, machinery and progress finds its
image in this and the Solitary's 'shattered telescope' (II, 663–7). For the
Solitary can no longer use science reliably to see. Whereas the narrator and
the Wanderer look upon rock formations 'That with united shoulders bore
aloft / A fragment, like an altar, flat and smooth' (III, 59–60), the Solitary is
undone by the excursive power of mind which prevents him from reading
divine design and significance in the landscape that surrounds him:

> The shapes before our eyes
> And their arrangement, doubtless must be deemed
> The sport of Nature, aided by blind Chance
> Rudely to mock the works of toiling Man.
>
> (III, 124–7)

Accordingly, the Solitary is unable to see the work of Creation and a Creator
revealed before him, so that the question of human origins becomes a matter
of speculative explanations:

> Our origin, what matters it? In lack
> Of worthier explanation, say at once
> With the American (a thought which suits
> The place where we now stand) that certain men
> Leapt out together from a rocky cave;
> And these were the first parents of mankind
>
> (III, 238–43)

In considering the origins of man, Wordsworth's Solitary treats the question in a manner that settles arbitrarily on a mythic image advanced by
a primitive belief system. Wordsworth's Wanderer and narrator, by contrast, see in 'The place where we now stand' the triumph of God's creative
act revealed in the presence of an embryonic altar, fragmentarily glimpsed
in the rock formations of the locale. Wordsworth's *Excursion* defends the
natural theology of God's creation against the 'blind chance' implied by self-
directed matter and the 'excursive mind's' enslavement to it. Despite being

an apologia for order and divine governance, the dialogic, symposium-like structure of the poem rehearses discourses that ask questions about the origins of human life; 'what matters it' as the Solitary puts it? Of course this asks 'to what extent does the question matter?' But to, put it another way, and to exploit an excursive and elliptical reading of the line, re-inventing 'matter' and giving it the force of a verb: 'what matters it?', or what material agency lies at the basis of human origins?

Such questions about origins and mind, and how they might and might not be formulated, were at the heart of William Whewell's later construction of what he called 'palaetiological science'. Whewell's neologism, a hybrid term blending the Greek for causation and knowledge of beings which formerly existed, played a key role in his influential *History of the Inductive Sciences* (1837). For Whewell, geology forms

one of the palaetiological class of sciences, which trace back the history of the earth and its inhabitants on philosophical grounds, [and] is thus associated with a number of other kinds of research, which are concerned about language, law, art, and consequently about the internal faculties of man, his thoughts, his social habits, his conception of right, his love of beauty . . . It is more than a mere fanciful description, to say that in languages, customs, forms of society, political institutions, we see a number of formations superimposed upon one another, each of which is, for the most part, an assemblage of fragments and results of the preceding condition.[21]

The fossil extracted from a geological formation was the paradigmatic object for the palaetiological sciences: it constituted a trace of objects or organisms that had formerly existed, and this trace might contain evidence of some causal relation to existing objects and organisms in the present. The history of geology that Whewell narrates in his *History* (vol. 3, Book xviii) tells a story about the way in which fossils of organic matter became more and more significant to researchers, culminating in the connections that Cuvier forged between research into the mutually illuminating temporalities of geological formations, the extinction of species and developments in comparative anatomy.

For Whewell, geology also authorised philosophical and historical research into past and successive formations of human language, law, morality and modes of inwardness – the thoughts and aesthetic experiences comprising Mill's 'problem of problems' – which together might be said to accumulate into a genetic understanding of 'culture'. It was characteristic of Whewell that, prior to mapping the science, he should name it: Whewell was profoundly aware of the linguistic tools he inherited, and the tradition of Cambridge philology that enabled his coining of nomenclature.[22]

Coleridgean arguments about language and the clerisy were at the heart of palaetiological science.

The inner workings of mind are accorded an important value in Whewell's *History*: they act as a bulwark against some of the more troubling consequences of a search for origins. For Whewell acknowledges that there may be a temptation, in thinking about the origins of inorganic rock, to begin to consider the origins of vegetable and animal life, language and arts, rationality itself, and law and order (III, 484–5). But for Whewell, the 'mysteries' of creation and evolution were 'not within the range of [science's] legitimate territory; she says nothing, but she points upwards' (III, 488). Gazing upwards, the 'real philosopher' will find 'a source of order and law, and intellectual beauty' located in

> a living Mind, a power which aims as well as acts. To us this doctrine appears like the natural cadence of the tones to which we have so long been listening; and without such a final strain our ears would have been left craving and unsatisfied. We have been lingering long amid the harmonies of law and symmetry, constancy and development; and these notes, though their music was sweet and deep, must too often have sounded to the ear of our moral nature, as vague and unmeaning melodies, floating in the air around us, but conveying no intelligible announcement. But one passage which we have again and again caught by snatches, though sometimes interrupted and lost, at last swells in our ears full, clear and decided; and the religious 'Hymn in honour of the Creator', to which Galen so gladly lent his voice, and in which the best physiologists of succeeding times have ever joined, is filled into a richer and deeper harmony by the greatest philosophers of these later days, and will roll on hereafter the 'perpetual song' of the temple of science. (III, 392–3)

It is directive mind which organises the 'harmonies of law, symmetry, constancy and development' in nature. Whewell's affirmative song about the 'temple of science' rhetorically contests the materialist aetiology of origins sung in Erasmus Darwin's *Temple of Nature*.

Adam Sedgwick, the professor of geology, also opposed transformism in his *Discourse on the Studies of the University* (1833), addressed to the Master of Trinity, Christopher Wordsworth. Again, echoes of *The Excursion*'s concern with the relationship between mind, nature, design, expressiveness, death and the distinctiveness of the human occur in Sedgwick's *Discourse*. Originally a sermon, Sedgwick's address justifies the study at Cambridge of classical languages and literature, moral philosophy and, above all, natural science. In particular Sedgwick makes a claim for the way in which science can fix the mind upon a legitimate object when confronted with a material dynamism of sublime proportions:

The mind becomes bewildered among the countless movements continually going on, and the perpetual changes produced by material actions, of which we see neither the beginning nor the end: but we find repose in the study of animated nature. Every being possessing life may first be considered apart from the rest of nature. Its bodily organs are produced by powers of vast complexity, and understood only in the effects – confined in the operation to the individual being, and entirely separate from the ordinary modes of atomic action. Yet these organisms, thus elaborated, exhibit throughout a perfect mechanism, in all its parts (as far as we can comprehend them) exactly fitted to the vital functions of the being. Contrivance proves design: in every organic being we survey (and how countless are the forms and functions of such beings) we see a new instance of contrivance and a new manifestation of an intelligent, super-intending power.[23]

Sedgwick presents another perspective on the excursive movements of mind overwhelmed by the proliferation of material interactions comprising the natural world. 'Repose' from this condition is experienced when 'animated nature' or 'life' is separated off from the rest of nature. For 'life' is the very essence of the argument against the apparently ceaseless order of change that the mind can perceive in the materialities of nature, in so far as 'life' is clearly mechanical contrivance perfectly designed to allow organisms to fulfil their 'vital functions'. In other words, the vitality of life is a quasi-aesthetic argument from design, proving the existence of an 'intelligent, super-intending power', acknowledgement of which imposes order on the 'countless . . . forms and functions' comprising living beings, a profuseness which otherwise might stimulate further excursive movements of mind.

Wordsworth's defence of God's design and purpose in nature were asserted in his endnotes to *The Excursion*; and yet these endnotes, and the poem that generated them, could be read against the grain of the defence that they upheld – something that Wordsworth feared and reflected upon.

4. ENDNOTES TOWARDS AN UNDERSTANDING OF SYMPATHY AND A DEFINITION OF CULTURE

The Biblical myth of human origins was conventionally recorded in Erasmus Darwin's *Temple of Nature*.

> WHERE EDEN'S sacred bowers triumphant sprung,
> By angels guarded, and by prophets sung,
> Wav'd oer the east in purple pride unfurl'd
> And rock'd the golden cradle of the World.
>
> (1, ll. 33–6)

But these poeticised narratives were then re-cast into speculative notes. Thus, poetic discourse representing man's Edenic origins emerges as an allusive and mythic encoding of archaeological and historical evidence recording the origins, common descent and progress of civilisation. The 'golden cradle of the World' is 'translated' accordingly in the apparatus of a footnote:

The nations which possess Europe and a part of Africa appear to have had their origin near the banks of the Mediterranean, as probably in Syria, the site of Paradise, according to the Mosaic history. This seems highly probable from the structure of the languages of these nations, and from the early possession of similar religions, customs and arts, as well as from the most ancient histories extant . . . The use of iron tools, of the bow and arrow, of earthen vessels to boil water in, of wheels for carriage, and the arts of cultivating wheat, of coagulating milk for cheese, and of spinning vegetable fibres for clothing, have been known in all European countries for as long as their histories have existed. (1, 5)

Thus, whilst the Biblical Eden is seen as the poetic rendition of the 'cradle of the World', material indicators of common descent are language, religion and custom, and the arts of civilisation. In Canto II (entitled 'Reproduction'), Eve's temptation is re-written sensuously as a scene of erotic self-recognition, desire for the other, and consummation (ll. 134–58); the Fall is presented later in the poem (III, 'The Progress of Mind', ll. 445–60) as the symbolic origin of conscience within a sensationalist account of the cultivation of moral sympathies.

The sensations promoting sympathy between humans were central to a materialist account of the origins of the ethical bonds that sustained society, such as Erasmus Darwin's mythic and philosophic narrative in *The Temple of Nature*. Wordsworth appended to *The Excursion* his 'Essay Upon Epitaphs', first published in Coleridge's periodical *The Friend* in 1810, as a comment on the workings of sympathy and an implicit contestation of the consequences of materialist transmutation and the sciences of life. Wordsworth directs the reader to his essay at the end of Book V of the poem, where the Pastor reflects upon impulses for honouring the graves of the dead: impulses which reside not in 'the naked *Heart* alone of Man', nor 'in the vital seat / Of feeling', but in

> The other that empowers him to perceive
> The voice of Deity, on height and plain,
> Whispering those truths in stillness, which the WORD
> To the four quarters of the winds, proclaims.
>
> (ll. 990–3)

The Pastor goes on:

> And by the care prospective of our wise
> Forefathers, who, to guard against the shocks,
> The fluctuation and decay of things,
> Embodied and established these high truths
> In solemn institutions:—men convinced
> That life is love and immortality,
> The being one, and one the element.
>
> (ll. 997–1003)

The Pastor's invocation of the Logos honours the Word which will guard against fluctuation and decay, enshrined in institutions. Wordsworth's 'living literature' promotes itself as one such institution, but the writing and language upon which it is founded is, as Wordsworth acknowledged, a complex disseminatory force.

In the statement framing the annexed 'Essay Upon Epitaphs', Wordsworth addresses 'the sympathising reader' whom he conjectures will 'not be displeased to see the Essay'. So it is significant that Wordsworth constructs 'the sympathising reader' as one who will identify with the authority of the Pastor's injunction to peer beyond 'the naked *Heart* alone of Man', and 'the vital seat / Of feeling' – that is, mere sensationalist sympathising and feeling – and towards a sympathy which identifies with the Deity and the 'intimations of immortality' that it bestows. This is the very subject matter of Wordsworth's essay.

Wordsworth's essay begins with an appeal to antiquity through works of eighteenth-century archaeology and anthropology which argue that even 'savage tribes unacquainted with letters' bury their dead and mark the place of their burial.[24] Thus, Wordsworth demonstrates an anthropological awareness of the common basis of human customs. However, whereas for Erasmus Darwin these customs and arts were indicators of a common human origin, and a descent which could be traced to the conjunction of tactile capacity and idea-generating power acquired arbitrarily by bestial (simian) ancestors, Wordsworth interprets evidence of the common urge to bury and commemorate the dead within a framework of divine revelation. By asserting his claim for the presence of a 'consciousness of a principle of immortality in the human soul', Wordsworth finds a new way to insist on the essential nature of the boundary-line separating man from beast:

The dog or horse perishes in the field, or in the stall, by the side of his companions, and is incapable of anticipating the sorrow with which his surrounding associates shall bemoan his death, or pine for his loss; he cannot pre-conceive this regret, he can form no thought of it; and therefore cannot possibly have a desire to leave such a regret or remembrance behind him. Add to the principle of love which exists in the inferior animals, the faculty of reason which exists in Man alone; will the conjunction of these account for the desire? Doubtless it is a necessary consequence of this conjunction; yet not I think as a direct result, but only to be come at through an intermediate thought, viz. that of an intimation or assurance within us, that some part of our nature is imperishable.[25]

Although beasts, as sentient beings, are capable of sympathetic affections, Erasmus Darwin's *Temple of Nature* holds that the faculty of reason distinguishes humans from beasts: 'Where REASON's empire o'er the world presides, / And man from brute, and man from man divides' (III, ll. 401–2). Wordsworth accepts this ('the principle of love . . . exists in the lower animals'), and assigns the need to be commemorated by friends and loved ones to the '*social* feelings' of 'Reason'.[26] However, in Darwin's scheme, the empire of reason which separates the human from the bestial is built on the contingent transmutational principle of gradual emergence: in a footnote to the phrase 'REASON's empire', Darwin defines it as 'the faculty of the use of voluntary power, which is owing to the possession of the clear ideas acquired by our superior sense of touch, and afterwards vision, which distinguishes man from brutes' (III, 117–18). Wordsworth, in contrast, holds intimations of immortality to be the new, unbreachable barrier separating the human from the bestial, which he places beyond the humanly pre-eminent, yet socially orientated, edifice of reason. For Wordsworth holds here – as he does in his 'Immortality Ode' – that these intimations 'or assurances' of immortality are innate even in the unsocialised child. Thus, burial sites are placed 'in close connection with our places of worship' (731), and the epitaphs are written on monuments to the dead: both are institutionalised expressions of this basic, yet divine, intimation.

The significance of the epitaphic to a conception of culture is confirmed in the way in which Wordsworth interweaves commemoration, worship and institutionalised expressiveness with literacy and the value of symbolic capital: 'the writer who would excite sympathy' by inscribing an epitaph has to strike an appropriate balance between universality and specificity in honour both of the immortal soul and the particular memories associated with the dead subject. Consequently 'an epitaph is not a proud writing shut up for the studious' – a formulation which, simultaneously, serves the self-consecrated status of *The Excursion* as valuable, sympathy-building capital in the intellectual field.[27]

In appending his own previous writings to his poem, Wordsworth enacts the prehistory and exhumation of his poem's formation. Something of this is suggested in the allusion to geological science in the original introduction to the 'Essay Upon Epitaphs', which framed the text when it appeared first in Coleridge's *The Friend*, and was probably written by Coleridge (though omitted by Wordsworth when he appended the essay to *The Excursion*). In that original framing statement, the 'labour' of writing the essay 'may be likened to that of a Teacher of Geology, who, to awaken the curiosity of his Pupils, and to induce them to prepare for the study of the inner constitution of the planet, lectures with a few specimens of fossils and minerals in his hands'.[28] Writing about examples of epitaphic writing is thus compared to a science which can read the secret historicity and 'inner constitution' of the planet on the basis of rock specimens and exhumed fossils. By analogy, the inner workings of the cultivated human mind can be understood in the same way. And yet, the 'excursive' mind might use such language to draw very different and dangerously materialist conclusions about its historicity and descent.

This danger was glimpsed by Sedgwick in his *Discourse* of 1833, in which he contends that hierarchies have to be observed within the order of living things, and insists on a firm dividing line between humans and beasts through the distinctly Wordsworthian notion of the imagination: 'it is by the imagination, more perhaps than by any other faculty of the soul, that man is raised above the condition of the beast'. For Sedgwick, the imagination enables men to 'mount up from earth to heaven' – to glimpse immortality – for 'all that is refined in civilised life, all that is lofty in poetry or ennobling in art, flows chiefly from this one fountain' (*Discourse*, 42). Sedgwick continues to work through Wordsworthian and Coleridgean concepts in acknowledging that science can be seen as 'a repulsive language, which rejecting both the senses and the imagination, speaks only to the understanding' (9).

However, Sedgwick insists on the ontological status of science as a language, and advances a naturalistic view of language, for it is 'never formed by a convention of learned men . . . it is the offspring of our intellectual nature, and bears the image of such ideas as rise up of necessity in the mind, from our relation to the things around us' (11), and is thus 'the connected natural signs of internal thoughts' (26). And because 'the laws by which God has thought good to govern the universe are surely subjects of lofty contemplation' (10), even the 'symbolical language' of natural science enables its practitioners to reach lofty imaginative heights, in so far as it 'gives the mind a domination over many parts of the material world' whilst 'keep[ing] down a spirit of arrogance and intellectual pride' (9).

Accordingly, the clerisy of natural science, the custodians of scientific language such as Bacon and Newton, are presented by Sedgwick as geniuses of science who 'speak to us from their tombs' (3). This epitaphic language of death and the tomb pervades Sedgwick's account of his own discipline, geology. Despite being a new science, 'the very name of which has been but a few years engrafted on our language', it can be presented in reassuring terms, for the geologist sees

a long succession of monuments each of which may have required a thousand ages for its elaboration. He arranges them in chronological order; observes on them the marks of skill and wisdom, and finds within them the tombs of the ancient inhabitants of the earth. He finds in them strange and unlooked for changes in the forms and fashions of organic life during each of the long periods he contemplates. (22)

The geologist's object of study is expressed in the language of the monument and the tomb. Amidst geological 'monuments' will be signs of meaningful intervention, the 'skill and wisdom' of the creator. Yet the entombed remains of organic life from the distant past also present 'strange and unlooked for fashions' in organisation and patterns of adaptation. Fossil remains of extinct forms of organic life were used as evidence by naturalists with Lamarckian tendencies to argue the case for the transmutation of species over a time vastly exceeding a Mosaic chronology. Though Charles Lyell's new geology required an expanded time-frame for his uniformitarian theory of subsidence and elevation, he resisted the deduction of species transmutation from fossil evidence. Sedgwick's *Discourse* also vehemently resists transmutation, especially its implications for humanity: 'man . . . was called into being within a few thousand years of the days in which we live – not by a transmutation of species (a theory no better than a phrensied dream), but by a provident continuing power' (23). After 1844 and the publication of Chambers's *Vestiges*, Sedgwick issued new editions of his *Discourse* which expanded considerably upon this refutation of the 'phrensied dream' of transmutational speculation.

If Sedgwick was on the defensive against very obviously articulated 'phrensied dreams' of transmutation, Wordsworth, in his third essay on Epitaphs, destined for *The Friend* but never published in his lifetime, reflected on the more subtle ways in which subversion could be effected:

Words are too awful an instrument for good and evil to be trifled with: they hold above all other external powers a dominion over thoughts. If words be not (recurring to a metaphor before used) an incarceration of the thought but only a clothing for it, then surely will they prove an ill gift; such a one as these poisoned vestments, read of in the stories of superstitious times, which had power to consume and to alienate from his right mind the victim who put them on. Language, if it do not uphold, and feed, and leave in quiet like the power of gratification, or the air we breathe, is a counter-spirit, unremittingly and noiselessly at work to derange, to subvert, to lay waste, to vitiate, and to dissolve.[29]

Whilst Wordsworth conceives of 'good' language as a form of nourishment, or spirit-sustaining breath, there is also a disseminatory 'counter-spirit' in language, a force 'unremittingly and noiselessly at work to derange, to subvert, to lay waste' which Wordsworth finds 'evil'. Counter-spirit resides in the possibility of counter-readings that could work 'noiselessly', without ever clearly signposting that the subversion has occurred.

Counter-significations and the force of linguistic supplementarity intrude into *The Excursion* at precisely those moments when human sympathy in the face of death is expected to be most active: thus in Book VII when the Pastor reflects on what remains of the dead man when, in the passage of time, 'of his course remain / No cognizable vestiges' (ll. 357–8). His epitaph will 'perchance' stimulate memory in the following century when people 'hear his name pronounced, / With images attendant on the sound' (ll. 354–5). However, in this reflection on images and their relations to the materiality of sound and the lapse of time, the very detailed pursuit of the sound–image relation makes the desired resolution of the point open to dissolution: it is not clear how securely images remain attached to sound; nor, therefore, is the extent to which language is imbued with presence, especially when the breath that utters the words that speak of the dead 'instantly dissolves' as surely as the decaying corpse (l. 360).

The problem of presence is also manifest in the concluding book of *The Excursion* as the Pastor delivers a closing sermon in a natural setting, amidst the lakes and moutains. The Pastor reminds his congregation that the land in which they listen to him was once inhabited by primitive savages. The Pastor, raising his eyes to 'Heaven', reflects on a time when

> Once, while the Name, Jehovah, was a sound
> Within the circuit of this sea-girt isle
> Unheard, the savage nations bowed the head
> To Gods delighting in remorseless deeds.
>
> (IX, 681)

Wordsworth's Pastor here moves away from the language of the Logos, which was a prominent feature at the conclusion of Book v of the poem (where the reader is referred to the 'Essay Upon Epitaphs'), and on the basis of which 'solemn institutions' such as the veneration of the dead would be

built. When the Name of God, Jehovah, is articulated, it is described as
a 'sound' rather than a presence; a sound, moreover, within a 'circuit',
meaning a circumscribed space (a 'sea-girt isle'). Yet, 'circuit' is an unusual
term in so far as it is shared between a number of domains of discourse,
including legal and ecclesiastical governance, but also the science of energy.
The name 'Jehovah' – the name of the unnameable – will be disseminated
through the channels of this circuit in the way that pedlars circulate the
goods and civilised mores of colonial conquest.

The avowed aim of the Pastor's sermon is to mark how 'wide [is] the difference' (l. 715) between the savage tribes that had once colonised this lush,
lakeland spot, and the present, in which the history of the Fall has seemingly been reversed, and 'paradise, the lost abode of man / Was raised again'
(ll. 717–18). Yet, the site where the personae of the poem find themselves is
characterised by a mingling of human and natural histories in which nature
imitates a human site of worship, where

> bare columns of those lofty firs,
> Supporting gracefully a massy dome
> Of sombre foliage, seem to imitate
> A Grecian temple rising from the Deep.
>
> (ll. 599–602)

Wordsworth celebrates a heathen temple of nature: whereas Erasmus
Darwin's 'Temple of Nature' was part of the figurative machinery of his
poem, a motif allegorising the fecundity of life (see Canto I), Wordsworth's
is more troublingly present in a tangible landscape of the romantic sublime
which had once sustained savagery and was now Edenic. This puts into context the anxieties expressed by Francis Jeffrey as he objected to Wordsworth's
idolatory of landscape in his critical condemnation of the poem in the
Edinburgh Review. Monuments and remains could generate troubling
meanings, as well as reassurances.

Wordsworth's anxieties about 'counter-spirit' in language are also manifest in images of childhood and mimicry in *The Excursion*. In his dialogue
with the Pastor (Book VII), the Solitary asks his listeners to 'mark the babe
/ Not long accustomed to this breathing world' (ll. 261–2). The Solitary's
image of the baby contrasts with the meaning that childhood acquires in
the 'Essay Upon Epitaphs'. If the child's inner intimations of immortality
assure against the bleakness of consignment to 'a subterraneous magazine
of bones' (VII, l. 345), then the Solitary's smiling, grasping, crying baby
is disarming precisely because it is 'irrational of soul', or to all appearances lacking in the very assurances of immortality that can offer comfort

against the 'hollowness' which otherwise 'would pervade the whole system of things'.[30] Indeed, the baby's movements and gestures are troubling because of their disturbing similarity to 'puppetry' (vii, l. 270), 'bemocking, as might seem / The outward functions of intelligent man' (ll. 267–8).

Wordsworth's Solitary sees the baby's mimicry as a ludic indicator of the lurking emptiness which haunts the spread even of apparently sacred rites, such as the Baptism which will convert the babe from an automaton tainted with the animalistic 'original stain' to one assured of a home in 'the fair land of everlasting life' (vii, l. 285). Erasmus Darwin's 'Muse of Mimicry' was the poetic encoding of the principle of the dissemination of 'animal action' and, alongside sympathy, a building block for civilisation and progress. For Wordsworth, by contrast, imitation was haunted by the dangers of language's counter-spirit.

In the final book of the poem, the Wanderer advances a vision of a new society which seeks to answer, once and for all, the debates and doubts that have been voiced in the course of the poem's dramatic structure. Above all, this envisions the importance of England as a leading colonial power in the present and the future, the spirit of the Pedlar Wanderer writ large. For the Wanderer, colonisation should be linked to pedagogy as a mode of cultivation. 'This imperial Realm', he declares

> While she exacts allegiance, shall admit
> An obligation, on her part, to *teach*
> Them who are born to serve her and obey;
> Binding herself by statute to secure
> For all the children whom her soil maintains
> The rudiments of letters, and inform
> The mind with moral and religious truth,
> Both understood and practised,—so that none,
> However destitute, be left to droop
> By timely culture unsustained; or run
> Into a wild disorder; or be forced
> To drudge through a weary life without the help
> Of intellectual implements and tools;
> A savage horde amongst the civilised,
> A servile band amongst the lordly free!
> This sacred right, the lisping babe proclaims
> To be inherent in him, by Heaven's will,
> For the protection of his innocence . . .
>
> (ix, ll. 295–313)

This passage includes the very lines that, in 1879, during a more intensive period of imperial expansion, Matthew Arnold would disparage as being a kind of 'dull' language that might be heard 'quoted at a Social Science Congress'.[31] Nonetheless, the lines, and Arnold's reaction, provide insight into the ways in which Wordsworth's many voices could be appropriated to justify a science of cultivation which was increasingly confident in its imperial and moral claims. If we recall that Charles Darwin boasted in his *Autobiography* of reading *The Excursion* twice through in the 1830s, while later lamenting that his mind had become a kind of machine for grinding out general laws, then contact with *The Excursion* might unobtrusively have accelerated the source of the lament.

In the passage, Wordsworth returns to the image of a 'babe'. However, unlike the Solitary's troubling image of the Baptised, mimicking puppet-babe, the Wanderer's babe 'lisps' a speech proclaiming his right to 'timely culture'. This will protect, in the manner of Baptism, but also, perhaps, as a replacement for that rite, the babe's innocence. The imperial realm's binding obligation to bring 'culture' – 'intellectual implements and tools' – to the 'savage horde' is affirmed again by one final endnote, referring to the success of the Bell system of monitorial elementary education. The Reverend Andrew Bell's system, outlined in *An Experiment in Education Made at the Male Asylum at Madras* (1797), was devised in the Indian colonies. A monitorial system, it was based on the principle of imitation and emulation in the sense that the pupil aspired to be like, and even to excel, the instructing monitor, and the master who monitored the monitor.[32] 'It is impossible', Wordsworth enthuses, 'to overrate the benefit which might accrue to humanity from the universal application of this simple engine under an enlightened and conscientious government.'[33] Accordingly, Wordsworth's apparatus grafts the language of cultivation onto an alliance with the Anglican church as a branch of the circulatory and governmental systems of the modern, imperial English state. The striking point about Wordsworth's support for the Bell system is the mechanistic language which is used to endorse it. Having acknowledged the organic tools supporting cultivation – 'intellectual tools and implements' – Wordsworth imagines the delivery of the process through a simple, yet universal, 'engine'.

Wordsworth imagines his poem as a work of literature 'which might live', and it lives precisely as a contrivance of cultivation which imitates, emulates and, given the trope of peddling on which it is premised, trades already-uttered languages. In being traded, those languages could be counter-read, counter-signed, and further invested to accumulate supplementary values. This applies to Wordsworth's poetic appropriation and inflection of Malthus' population theory. The Wanderer's sense of a colonial mission is the justification for an anxiety about an exploding domestic population which is liable to exhaust the cultivation of 'native soil'; for the Wanderer's discourse takes a Malthusian turn, inflecting Malthusian pessimism with a Paleyite optimism:

> With such foundations laid, avaunt the fear
> Of numbers crowded on their native soil,
> To the prevention of all healthful growth
> Through mutual injury! Rather in the law
> Of increase and the mandate from above
> Rejoice! — and ye have special cause for joy.
> — For, as the element of air affords
> An easy passage to the industrious bees
> Fraught with their burthens; and a way as smooth
> For those ordained to take their sounding flight
> From the thronged hive, and settle where they list
> In fresh abodes—their labour to renew;
> So the wide waters, open to the power,
> The will, the instincts and appointed needs
> Of Britain, do invite her to cast off
> Her swarms, and in succession send them forth;
> Bound to establish new communities
> On every shore whose aspect favours hope
> Or bold adventure; promising to skill
> And perseverance their deserved reward.
>
> (IX, ll. 364–82)

While population increase and scarcity at home is a pressing source of anxiety, the solution is to colonise overseas territories, an early articulation of Edward Gibbon Wakefield's evangelising account of the 'art' of colonisation.[34] While Malthus elaborated a specifically human theory of population, Wordsworth looks into the 'Book of Nature' to sanction this solution: an easy equivalence is posited between swarms of bees flying from an overcrowded hive, and excess labouring populations sailing overseas. Indeed 'wide waters' 'invite' Albion to release her colonising 'swarms', invoking a tradition of colonial imagery which J. R. Seeley's influential *Expansion of England* would recognise in 1883.[35]

The implications of this for the politics of Wordsworth's intellectual affiliations are very complex. Wordsworth professed anti-Malthusian sentiments, in line with his Tory protests against the 'dismal science' of political economy, but he also invoked Malthus in unacknowledged ways that amounted to a theology of colonialism.[36] A positive, Paleyite sense of creatures taking pleasure in their sheer abundance is at work in Wordsworth's use of 'swarms', confirmed in the way that they are presented as a source of joy; the Wanderer's listeners are asked to see Malthus' law of geometric increase as a God-given 'mandate from above' to colonise. It is striking that in turning a Malthusian imperative to advantage, so to speak, Wordsworth's poetic symbolism should turn away from Malthus' predominantly human frame of reference, and focus on meanings borrowed from the animal world. Strangely, in writing against Malthus by applying his principle with Paleyite benevolence to animal 'swarms' or populations, Wordsworth initiates the very move that Darwin would later make in his Malthusian moment of October 1838; that is to say, recognising the population principle at work in the wider and indeed lower domains of nature. Darwin would of course re-instate the universal recognition of parsimony, and the waste of life, in formulating natural selection. But as the next chapter will argue, Darwin looked to the idea of migration, or 'stray colonists', to help shape that theory. To that extent, Darwin's own words would build on the 'counter-spirit' generated by Wordsworth in *The Excursion*. Continuing to focus on the bee-hive as a colony under construction, Darwin would of course go much further along the road of counter-reading and inscription in the *Origin of Species*: the instinct of different hive-building techniques would be presented as evidence of species differentiation, and the gradual workings of the mechanism of natural selection.

For Wordsworth, travel was a source of self-culture. In an endnote to the North American episode of *The Excursion*, in which the Solitary recalls travelling in search of 'Primeval Nature's child' (III, l. 919), Wordsworth reflected on the importance of travel by referring the reader to a passage of commentary from William Gilbert's work *The Hurricane*, subtitled 'A Theosophical and Western Ecologue' (1796). Describing the overall effect of this obscure poetical work as 'strange', Wordsworth nonetheless praises the commentary extravagantly as 'one of the finest passages of modern English prose'; though – in the tradition of Pope and Erasmus Darwin – it functioned as part of the textual apparatus of Gilbert's poem:

A man is supposed to improve by going out into the *World*, by visiting *London*. Artificial man does; he extends with his sphere; but, alas! that sphere is microscopic; it is formed of minutiae, and he surrenders his genuine vision to the artist, in order to embrace it in his ken. His bodily senses grow acute, even to barren and inhuman pruriency; while his mental become proportionally obtuse. The reverse is the Man of Mind: he who is placed in the sphere of Nature and of God, might be a mock at Tattersall's and Brooks's, and a sneer at St James's: he would certainly be swallowed alive by the first *Pizarro* that crossed him:—But when he walks along the river of

Amazons; when he rests his eye on the unrivalled Andes; when he measures the long
and watered savannah; or contemplates, from a sudden promontory, the distant
vast Pacific—and feels himself a freeman in this vast theatre, and commanding
each ready produced fruit of this wilderness, and each progeny of this stream—his
exaltation is not less than imperial. He is as gentle, too, as he is great: his emotions
keep pace with his elevation of sentiment; for he says, 'These were made by a good
Being, who, unsought by me, placed me here to enjoy them.' He becomes at once
a child and a king. His mind is in himself; from hence he argues, and from hence
he acts, and he argues unerringly, and acts magisterially; his mind in himself is also
in his God; and therefore he loves, and therefore he soars.[37] (Wordsworth, *Poetical
Works*, 727–8)

In this discourse on self-improvement, the social and urban sphere of 'artificial' man finds its field of vision in the image of the microscope, and the
over-indulged body of the senses will consequently lose itself in minutiae.
Opposed to this is the 'Man of Mind', whose sphere is the expansive nature
of exotic, inter-tropical regions in which God is revealed. The mind of a
man communing with the sublimity of nature is alienated neither from
itself nor from God: the Man of Mind possesses a magisterial, even 'imperial' subjectivity. Charles Darwin was an attentive reader of Wordsworth's
citations of other texts, as the following chapter will show. This note is
likely to have produced resonances for one who had recently returned from
exposure to the Andes and the 'vast Pacific' as a consequence of the *Beagle*'s
scientific and colonial exploits. However, Darwin would go on to situate
relations between mind, sensation and environment – and thereby, the
cultivation of self – in a very different framework.

Gilbert's text was published in Bristol in 1796 (Gilbert had arrived
in the city from the West Indies around 1787); one of Coleridge's and
Southey's circle, his poem was an expression of the complex intellectual politics of radicalism from that decade, situated between transcen-
dentalism and materialism.[38] Part millenarian allegory derived from the
same roots as William Blake, the poem figures a 'hurricane' in Antigua
(Gilbert's birth place) which will 'terminate in the subversion of Europe by
America, and the annihilation of the artificial system of society'.[39] Gilbert
thus imagined a terrible fate for the 'artificial' man who failed to look
beyond the fashionable places of London. For the destruction of Europe by
America was, Gilbert claimed, surely determined by 'a primary Law of
Nature, that EVERYONE MUST FALL INTO THE PIT THAT HE DIGS
FOR OTHERS'.[40] Gilbert was concerned that other aspects of his poem
should be similarly congruent with the laws of nature. Thus, Gilbert justifies his use of a mermaid, which figures as a feature of his poetic machinery,
by asserting that

the existence of the MERMAID is now certain; as one was exhibited a long while in Oxford-Street, which I saw two years ago nearly . . . From the loins upwards appeared to have been covered with flesh, and there downward with scales . . . WHY NOT MERMEN and MERMAIDS as well as Ourang-Outangs? Why not Sea men and maids (imperfect animals though they are) as well as Sea Lions, Calves and horses?[41]

Mermaids, as Harriet Ritvo has shown, were regularly presented as spectacles for the public gaze and anatomical analysis in the late eighteenth and early nineteenth centuries.[42] The way in which these fraudulent specimens were cobbled together from the dead bodies of fish, baboons and orangutans perhaps explains the way in which Gilbert was able to assimilate the mermaid to his own variety of transmutational speculation, implied in his defiant association – 'why not?' – between the orang-utan as an exemplar of the transformist imagination, and the mermaid. In Gilbert's transcendental vision, the transmutational possibilities evinced in the mermaid replicated the laws that would transform a corrupt and unequal state of society; inequalities and moral corruptions which the relatively privileged Gilbert (son of a lawyer and member of the Antiguan Assembly) would have been touched by as a (probably) mixed-race subject of a British former slave colony. In contesting inequality, as Gilbert's eclectic, not to say mad, notes to his allegorical poem indicate, he too appealed to certain of Erasmus Darwin's observations of the material laws of nature.[43] This is, as it were, the endnoted underground of Wordsworth's *Excursion*; its counter-spiritual transmutationist unconscious.

Transformist images would be reflected back to Charles Darwin as he experienced, first hand, the cultivating power of travel, and received, second hand, news of political conflict from home. In April 1832 he arrived in Brazil after five months on the *Beagle*. J. M. Herbert, a friend from Cambridge and Fellow of St John's College, wrote to him from home:

You will of course be anxious to hear how the Reform Bill is going on; the Second Reading passed the Lords on Friday after a debate of four days; majority nine . . . it is quite glorious to find how fast men are ratting; you I think are amongst a Tory Crew; just put one of them in Pickle as by the time you return home, he will be more valuable as a specimen for the Cabinet of the Antiquarian, than your Fungi & Coleoptera for that of the Naturalist; if you can get hold of one with Monboddo's Tail, or with its ears prolongated, it will be a doubly-interesting specimen.

Herbert addressed Darwin as the inheritor of his family's Whiggish traditions, contrasting his own predilection for reformism with the views of the reactionary 'Tory crew' of the *Beagle* led by the aristocratic Captain FitzRoy. Herbert's playful account of radical change in the polity, and the extinction of the Tory cause, is notably punctuated by an image of transmutational speculation on the simian origins of humans.[44] His letter goes on to connect these national trends with the politics of knowledge-advancement in Cambridge: 'We are getting quite liberal at St John's; I've just been asked to subscribe for Portraits of our two great Luminaries in Science & Literature – Herschel & Wordsworth – both of this College – Science is at present certainly on the Advance.' Herbert places Wordsworth and Herschel side by side, one the representative of Literature, the other of Science. Science is held to be 'on the Advance', an unequivocal contribution to an apparently forward-marching liberal hegemony. Yet, Wordsworth, despite his initial enthusiasm for revolutionary France, was no liberal. And in practice, scientific theories of life, particularly Charles Darwin's emerging species theory, advanced by drawing on a multiplicity of sources. This would include the 'literature' of Wordsworth, and some of his thinking on 'cultivation'. It would also include complex encounters with the practice of colonialism on the one hand, and 'primitive' people on the other. It would be hard to identify unequivocally the political affiliation of the theory of evolution that would emerge.

CHAPTER 3

Charles Darwin's entanglements with stray colonists: cultivation and the species question

I. COLONIAL AND HOME AND THE 'MYSTERY OF MYSTERIES'

Charles Darwin's influential account of his *Beagle* voyage, the *Journal of Researches*, was published in 1839; *The Origin of Species* was not published until 1859. Between these two events, Darwin published a second edition of his *Journal* in 1845, a year after he had written his private sketch on the solution to the species question ('the Essay of 1844'), an essay that was produced out of his experience of the voyage, as well as the voluminous reading that Darwin recorded in his private speculative notebooks. Indeed, it was difficult to draw a definitive boundary between private and public forms of inscription among the gentlemen of science who took possession of the species question in the 1830s and 1840s. Sir John Herschel, in a private letter to Roderick Murchison and Charles Lyell, referred to the appearance of new species tantalisingly as 'the mystery of mysteries'. Such a formulation invited ambitious speculation towards a solution. Herschel's letter was published by Charles Babbage as an appendix to his *Ninth Bridgewater: A Fragment* (1837). Darwin read the published version of this letter, and marked the occasion in his notebook: 'Babbage, 2nd Edit. p. 226 – Herschel calls the appearance of new species the mystery of mysteries & has grand passage upon problem! Hurrah – "intermediate causes".'[1] The second edition of Darwin's *Journal* contained bolder, if carefully coded, speculations on transformism; it was itself a kind of 'intermediate cause' between the private speculations and the case for transmutation by natural selection set out in *The Origin of Species*.

These intermediate speculations were given respectability by a publishing project aimed at colonial intellectual cultivation: the second, revised edition of Darwin's *Journal* was published in John Murray's 'Colonial and Home Library'. As Angus Fraser's study of Murray's initiative has shown, the project was designed to provide colonial readers with improving, inexpensive literary works that were not pirated editions of an original. Colonial

84

readers looking for reading matter might easily lay their hands on some stray import that had landed upon an island territory from some larger continental landmass, usually the Americas. The Copyright Act of 1842 sought to outlaw this practice in British overseas territories, but it left unsatisfied a desire for reading matter at reasonable cost.[2] Murray's 'Colonial and Home Library', consisting principally of biographies and works of travel literature, was designed to satisfy the desire while improving the reader.

Darwin's *Journal of Researches* was a perfectly formed recruit for the series. At the conclusion of the first edition of his work, unchanged in the second, Charles Darwin reflected on travel and the observation of nature as sources of cultivation and self-improvement:

[admiring beauty] depends chiefly on an acquaintance with the individual parts of each view: I am strongly induced to believe that, as in music, the person who understands every note will, if he also possesses a proper taste, more thoroughly enjoy the whole, so he who examines each part of a fine view, may also thoroughly comprehend the full and combined effect. Hence, a traveller should be a botanist, for in all views plants form the chief embellishment. Group masses of naked rock even in the wildest forms, and they may for a time afford a sublime spectacle, but they will soon grow monotonous. Paint them with bright and varied colours, as in northern Chile, they will become fantastic; clothe them with vegetation, they must form a decent, if not a beautiful picture. . . .

Nothing can be more improving to a young naturalist, than a journey to distant countries. It both sharpens, and partly allays that want and craving, which, as Sir J. Herschel remarks, a man experiences although every corporeal sense be fully satisfied. The excitement from the novelty of objects, and the chance of success, stimulate him to increased activity. Moreover, as a number of isolated facts soon become uninteresting, the habit of comparison leads to generalisation. On the other hand, as the traveller stays but a short time in each place, his descriptions must generally consist of mere sketches, instead of detailed observations. Hence arises, as I have found to my cost, a constant tendency to fill up the wide gaps of knowledge, by inaccurate and superficial hypotheses.[3] (*Journal* 1845, 476, 479–80)

Darwin draws on the language of taste and cultivation in music to guide the reader in the appreciation of nature. The reading of cultural inscriptions serves as a powerful analogy here in the sense that Darwin stresses the importance of an aesthetic understanding that strives to unify part and whole: it is important for the botanist to understand the whole picture created by coloured floras and entangled vegetation. Darwin also reflects on the desire for self-improving knowledge in ways that directly appeal to science as an intellectual pursuit. For Darwin, self-improvement is founded upon sensation and desire: seeing nature in 'distant countries' is a means of allaying a 'craving' for mental satisfaction, even though the bodily senses be satiated. But the excitement and novelty of nature also sharpen the desire for mental satisfaction, which looks beyond 'the fact' and towards the speculative building of generalised theories. 'The chance of success', or ambition in constructing new knowledge, is an important motivator in travelling to distant countries to discover the secrets of nature.

Darwin cites Sir John Herschel as the authoritative theorist of controlled intellectual desire. Herschel made this connection between knowledge and desire in his influential *Preliminary Discourse on the Study of Natural Philosophy* (1830), which Darwin later described as having stirred in him 'a burning zeal to add even the most humble contribution to the noble structure of Natural Science'.[4] Herschel's account of 'the mind of man' held that 'his views enlarge, and his desires and wants increase, in the full proportion of the faculties afforded to their gratification'.[5] Herschel's view of the mind cultivated by science continued to uphold mind as a divine gift. Herschel's discourse indeed warned of the dangers of atheism attendant on materialism that might 'foster in its cultivators an overweaning self-conceit' which might lead them 'to doubt the immortality of the soul and to scoff at revealed religion'.[6] Such warnings were issued especially in connection with the question of the transmutation of species, where the ambitious, over-reaching mind might deny its dependence on its divine origins – though as we have seen, Herschel himself was utterly transfixed by this 'mystery of mysteries'.

For Herschel, mind was the only faculty which gave humanity an advantage in, as Foucault put it in his formulation of the anthropological turn in western thought, 'that perilous region where life is in confrontation with death'.[7] For Herschel opens his account of the principles of natural philosophy by stressing the maladapted nature of man: physically, man is 'remarkable only for the absence of those powers and qualities which obtain for other animals a degree of security and respect'. Without mind man would

be disregarded by some, and hunted down by others, till after a few generations his species would become altogether extinct, or, at best, would be restricted to a few islands in tropical regions, where the warmth of the climate, the paucity of enemies, and the abundance of vegetable food, might permit it to linger.[8]

Herschel's nature is an arena of limits, scarcity and threats from competitors; the extinction of the human species lurks as the ultimate expression of finitude. Without mind, the limited capacities of the human body might allow the species to 'linger' as, at best, isolated inhabitants upon tropical islands. It was a capacity for imitation, reflectiveness and aesthetic appreciation that enabled humans to become colonists who cultivated more than 'the crude productions of the soil'. Man 'approves and feels the highest admiration for the harmony of . . . [nature's] parts, the skill and efficiency of its contrivances. Some of these which he can best trace and understand he attempts to imitate, and finds that to a certain extent, though rudely and imperfectly, he can succeed'.[9] In one sense, Darwin's *Journal of Researches* validates this narrative. But Darwin's writing also supplements it, turning Herschel's narrative on its head, and finds unfamiliar sources of meaning in images of mimicry, as well as lingering, stray colonists. And it locates new ways of explaining the laws of life through encounters with some very differently constituted, yet in their way highly effective, inhabitants of tropical islands.

How did Darwin's writing validate Herschel's narrative of human mental supremacy? Another way in which Darwin's *Journal of Researches* was a promising recruit for Murray's series was because 'colonial' and 'home' were the conceptual polarities around which many of his travel observations, and presumptions about cultivation and improvement, were organised. Darwin's whiggish liberalism was compatible with the apologia for colonialism articulated by activists such as Edward Gibbon Wakefield. Darwin thoroughly approved of the energy and purposefulness that went into the creation of settler 'property', as it contrasted so markedly with the egalitarian forms of organisation that 'retarded' the civilisation of native tribes, whose failure to recognise a 'chief' rendered the land on which they lived mere 'waste' in the eyes of colonists. Darwin could not 'understand how a chief can arise till there is property of some sort by which he might manifest his superiority and increase his power' (*Journal* 1845, 219). In his account of New Zealand, Darwin writes about an 'excursion to Waimate', near to the Bay of Islands, and his stay at a fecund missionary farmstead, which is contrasted with the 'useless' country which Darwin has traversed to reach the missionary colonists. Darwin finds himself as though at an 'English farm-house' cultivating 'every fruit and vegetable which England produces' and 'that happy mixture of pigs and poultry, lying comfortably together, as in every English farm-yard'. While Darwin believes that this vision has been brought before him 'as if by an enchanter's wand', he goes on to assert that in reality, 'the lesson of the missionary is the enchanter's wand'. The imported arts of domesticity elide racial difference, so that 'a New Zealander was seen powdered white with flour, like his brother miller in England': the colony in fact becomes home, inspiring 'high hopes . . . for the future progress of this fine island', even though it was also 'the land of cannibalism, murder and atrocious crimes' (*Journal* 1845, 403–5).

But out of the validation come observations that cannot easily be assimilated to the case for improvement. After all, the elision of racial difference (white flour covering a black face) is an instance of unconscious mimicry, and colonisation could in turn give rise to subtler atrocities, for Darwin also remarks that

It is said that the common Norway rat, in the short space of two years, annihilated in this northern end of the island, the New Zealand species. In many places I noticed several sorts of weeds, which, like the rats, I was forced to own as countrymen. A leek has overrun whole districts, and will prove very troublesome, but it was imported as a favour by a French vessel. The common dock is also widely disseminated, and will, I fear, forever remain a proof of the rascality of an Englishman who sold the seeds for those of a tobacco plant. (*Journal* 1845, 406)

In a whole series of instances of stray colonisations, Darwin is forced to 'own as countrymen' fugitive productions that have been introduced either arbitrarily, or through nefarious human exchanges, and disseminated wildly and uncontrollably. This complicates, indeed defamiliarises, the relationship between the colonial and the home, the fecund and the waste, the cultivated and the natural. Darwin discovers that the language of cultivation and animal husbandry can cross a border to justify atrocities that are far from subtle, and which bring him face to face with a 'dark picture' of colonisation. Speaking to the leader of a 'banditti-like' band of Spanish soldiers who pursue Indian tribes on the Bahia Blanca, Darwin is appalled to hear of the massacre of young native women, and the response to Darwin's sense of shock shocks him more: 'Why, what can be done, they breed so!' (*Journal* 1845, 99).

Charles Darwin's account of his *Beagle* voyage was eventually recruited to Murray's 'Colonial and Home' series in April 1845, on the recommendation of Charles Lyell (to whom the second edition was dedicated), and after securing release from any remaining rights assigned to the original publisher, Colburn. Initially Darwin thought that he would have to shorten his work, but Murray agreed in the end to accommodate its length, publishing it in three monthly parts (June–August 1845), rather than the series norm of two. Darwin was pleased and relieved, informing Murray that he 'shd here and there like to add a sentence'.[10] At the same time as writing to William Darwin Fox about the 'most important news' of his acceptance by Murray, Darwin was enquiring of his second cousin if he had read 'that strange unphilosophical, but capitally-written book, the Vestiges, it has made more talk than any book of late, & has been by some attributed to me. – at which I ought to be much flattered and unflattered'.[11] Above all,

Darwin was unflattered, and he dismissed the transformism of the *Vestiges* in private notes. Drawing on embryology, Chambers asserted that 'in the reproduction of higher animals, the new being passes through stages in which it is successively fish-like and reptile-like. But the resemblance is not to the adult fish or the adult reptile, but to the fish and reptile at a certain point in the foetal progress'.[12] Darwin's private note retorted: 'The idea of a Fish passing into a Reptile (his idea) monstrous'.[13]

Being mistaken for the anonymous author of the *Vestiges*, Darwin sought to make his own, more subtle mark on transformist speculation, and 'stray colonists' from nature would be one of the sources of observation that would help him to mount his argument. Having secured the agreement with Murray to re-issue his revised *Journal*, Darwin wrote to Thomas Bell, professor of zoology at King's College London, and the expert who helped to describe the reptiles from the *Beagle* voyage, enquiring 'whether there may be one more than one species of snake at the Galapagos, & whether such have a S. American physiognomy'.[14] As this chapter will argue, Darwin's contribution to a project of colonial intellectual cultivation contained speculative insights from colonisations in nature that would cast an unfamiliar light on the concept of cultivation itself. In turn, these would eventually impact powerfully on evolutionary speculation, though speculations about monstrosities and descriptions of selected animal 'communities' or colonies would become controversial highlights of the argument structuring *The Origin of Species*. Underpinning this was a strong sense of materialist speculation, aided by a surprising source.

2. 'STRONGLY PRAISED BY WORDSWORTH': DEATH AND THE ILLUSIONS OF IMMORTALITY IN SAVAGE CULTURE

Darwin alluded to his reading of Wordsworth as the second edition of *Journal of Researches* took its place in the 'Colonial and Home' series. In one sense, awareness of Wordsworth marked Darwin out as a man of artistic cultivation; in another sense, Wordsworth perhaps engaged Darwin in a more complex set of readerly reflections on culture, life and death.

Darwin was keen to share the fruits of his reading of Wordsworth with John Murray with a view to extending the 'Colonial and Home Library'. In a letter mainly concerned with the business of obtaining author's copies of the new publication, Darwin concludes with a post-script which urges Murray to think of ways of expanding the list of travel writings published in the series: 'should you ever wish to publish old Books of Travel; I strongly recommend you to think of Hearne's Travels (strongly praised by Wordsworth) they are to my mind admirable and little known'.[15] Darwin recommends Hearne, but Wordsworth is the authority for the recommendation, and this provides a striking sense of Wordsworth's place in Darwin's scheme of reading. As James Secord has observed of Charles Darwin's reading practices, 'books were not for ostentatious display, but tools for use [. . .]. Everything was aimed towards maximum efficiency in constructing and elaborating his theories'. However, '[b]ooks not used for work were read in a very different way . . . some books were read for extraction, others for relaxation or amusement'.[16] Darwin's recommendation suggests that Wordsworth was neither exclusively pleasure, nor exclusively work: Darwin read attentively the apparatus that Wordsworth wrote in support of his poetical texts, in the way that he might have read notes and glosses by a naturalist or ethnographer.

The work was Samuel Hearne's *Journey from Hudson's Bay to the Northern Ocean* (1795). Darwin alludes to it in the *Journal of Researches*, and, subsequently, *The Origin of Species*. Darwin's recommendation to Murray is launched on the back of what he describes as Wordsworth's strong praise; this styles Wordsworth as an authoritative guide to reading not only in matters of poetry, but also in writing about travel in colonised regions, and the ethnographic observations which such travel and settlement generated.[17] For Darwin is here recollecting Wordsworth's headnote to his dramatic monologue 'The Complaint of a Forsaken Indian Woman', first published in *The Lyrical Ballads*, but which Darwin would have encountered grouped as one of Wordsworth's 'Poems Founded on the Affections'. Wordsworth's headnote alludes to Hearne's 'interesting work' and its description of how 'in high northern latitudes . . . when the northern lights vary their position in the air, they make a rustling and a crackling noise'.[18] Wordsworth's poem dramatises the forsaken Indian woman's perception of the Northern Lights as an aural and visual phenomenon in the sky. It imagines the effects that the sensations of sight and sound might have on a state of mind left to wrestle with the consequences of that harsh human survival strategy which Hearne observed of nomadic native Americans in the Arctic regions.[19] Gazing into the sky as the visual and aural sensation of the Northern Lights floods over her, the abandoned and dying woman hopes that she will 'see another day' after her body has 'died away'. For Wordsworth, the forsaken savage woman, though bereft of formalised doctrines of religion, nonetheless experiences God through an intimation of immortality.

For Darwin, however, the poem's account of natural 'affections' and its headnote may have initiated more complex and radically sceptical intimations, given the way in which his own thinking was tending in the late 1830s.

In his third notebook, he writes 'Love of the Deity effect of organisation'. He then adds, part in surprise and part in mock-chiding at his own heterodox daring, 'Oh you Materialist!'[20] The notion that religious sentiment might be a material effect of bodily organisation stimulated by external sensation is a possible counter-reading of Wordsworth's dramatic contention that his forsaken Indian woman has sensed the possibility of a future life in the crackling sound of the Northern Lights. Darwin reflected on 'Savages . . . [who] consider the thunder and lightning the direct will of the God' in Notebook M, devoted to questions of mind and morals. He speculated that 'it would be difficult to prove this innate idea of God in civilised nations has not been improved by culture';[21] in other words, the idea of God originated in primitive sensations, and religious sentiment was an effect of the body in nature, supplemented by culture. To materialise religious sentiments is thus suggestive of much grander insights into a developmental hypothesis. A dramatic monologue, designed to build bonds of sympathy, can also be read against Wordsworth's grain, as a defamiliarising exposure of the ways in which objects of worship are materially constructed.

But this materialist account of culture was not only aired in Darwin's private notes, it was also explored in the second edition of the *Journal of Researches*. Darwin was aware that his 'interviews' with the 'Fuegian savages' would be a powerful centre of interest in his revised narrative of the voyage for Murray's 'Colonial and Home' series, and he proposed to Murray to 'add something' to this material, while recognising that Captain FitzRoy had held an evangelically watchful monopoly of the ethnographic observations.[22] Nonetheless, Darwin added substantially to the journal entry dated 'December 25TH' [1832] from the chapter on Tierra del Fuego. Whereas the first edition of the work merely alluded to 'cannibalism' and 'parricide' as effects of famine (*Journal* 1839, 178), the second edition contained more lurid tales of old women being 'brought back to the slaughterhouse at their own fire-sides!' (*Journal* 1845, 204–5).

Darwin also inserted new material that debated whether the Fuegians manifested any 'distinct belief in a future life', for although they 'sometimes bury their dead in caves, and sometimes in the mountain forests, we do not know what ceremonies they perform' (*Journal* 1845, 205). In an attempt to illustrate belief, Darwin recorded the fears of York Minster, a Fuegian captured from a previous voyage, and on board the *Beagle* during its 1831–6 mission: 'York declared for a long time afterwards storms raged, and much rain and snow fell. As far as we could make out, he seemed to consider the elements themselves as the avenging agents: it is evident in this case, how naturally, in a race a little more advanced in culture, the elements would become personified' (*Journal* 1845, 205). Thus in the 1830s Darwin used the word 'culture' in a sense that is often taken as having been originated by E. B. Tylor in his 1871 publication, *Primitive Culture*, in which the term signifies a principle of hierarchical relations between races at various stages of mental progress and civilisation.

A hierarchical and teleological understanding of 'culture' was thus present in Darwin's emerging speculations on the development of life, though it appears not to have been quite adequate to the entangled relations between overlapping agencies that Darwin needed to plot. To this extent, the Fuegian people were not only a recognisably compelling component of Darwin's voyage narrative, but also figures that generated complex processes of thought as the species question was implicitly broached. 'I could not have believed how wide was the difference between savage and civilised man: it is greater than between a wild and domesticated animal, inasmuch as in man there is a greater power of improvement' (*Journal* 1845, 196). The relationship between change under a regime of domestication, and change under the regime of nature, becomes one of strange mutual illumination. The Fuegians are, when first viewed, 'partly concealed by the entangled forest', and the old man that Darwin sees for the first time has 'entangled hair' and wears feathers around this hair, entangling him further into the animal estate (*Journal* 1845, 195). The old man communicates friendship by patting the breasts of Darwin and the crew and making 'a chuckling kind of noise, as people do when feeding chickens' (*Journal* 1845, 196). This contributes to the curious economy of mimicry, of which the Fuegians are 'excellent' practitioners: by casting the crew of the *Beagle* as chickens, or domestic animals, mimicry destabilises hierarchies, and brings the crew into an estranging contact through intensely sharpened sensations: a deeply strange kind of sympathetic bond is constructed with people who appear to have no home and no cultivated domestic affections.

For Darwin, the early migration undertaken by these people to the southern tip of the Americas was an enigma: they had almost inexplicably colonised an inhospitable environment that had moulded their struggle for life and their patterned response to it, so that 'Nature by making habit omnipotent, and its effects hereditary, has fitted the Fuegian to the climate and the productions of his miserable country' (*Journal* 1845, 206). And yet the putrefying landscape that sustains the Fuegian life yields a meaning. The forested topography of Tierra del Fuego is, for Darwin, an 'entangled mass of the thriving and the fallen [which] reminded me of the forests within the tropics – yet there was a difference: for in these still solitudes, Death, instead of Life, seemed the predominant spirit' (*Journal* 1845, 200).

If the spirit of death haunts these Wordsworthian 'still solitudes', the fact of there being a creative relationship between death and the production of new life was something that Darwin strengthened emphatically in the second edition. In his account of quadruped remains found in the fields of Patagonia (9 January 1834), Darwin had added a sentence drawing attention to the 'wonderful relationship in the same continent between the dead and the living . . . [which] will, I do not doubt, hereafter throw more light on the appearance of organic beings on our earth, and their disappearance from it, than any other class of facts' (*Journal* 1845, 165; cf. *Journal* 1839, 164).

3. REFASHIONING THE EPITAPHIC: FROM PLAINS TO CORAL ATOLLS

At St Helena (July 1836), Darwin remarked on securing accommodation close to Napoleon's tomb. The placement of *The Journal of Researches* in Murray's 'Colonial and Home' series, with its emphasis on travel writing, perhaps explains the removal of Darwin's 'confession' from the first edition, that the tomb held 'little attraction for me' (*Journal* 1839, 360). In both editions, Darwin includes his fascination with the way in which the presence of Napoleon's tomb on St Helena has the effect of inspiring travel writers to describe the island using a variety of synonyms for the word 'tomb': 'grave . . . pyramid, cemetery, sepulchre, catacomb, sarcophagus, minaret and mausoleum': St Helena is transformed into an epitaph, an isle on which multiple grave writings are inscribed.

Darwin consistently writes the landscapes of his *Beagle* narratives in the epitaphic mode, from the plains of Patagonia to coral atolls. This mode draws on the Wordsworthian store represented by *The Excursion*, in particular the poem's preoccupation with 'a subterraneous magazine of bones' (VII, 345); and it has the effect of bringing new relations of causation to bear on William Whewell's palaetiological science. From August 1833, the district around the Río de Plata had started to deliver up to Darwin, its secrets of extinct mammalia including the remains of the toxodon, a giant quadruped. In his 1837 paper for the Geological Society of London, written two years before the first edition of the *Journal of Researches*, Darwin adhered to Lyell's framework, looking for laws and processes working in the present and then applying them retrospectively to evidence from the past embedded in the ground, and palliated it by appealing to epitaphic language: 'the author . . . supposed that the ancient rivers, like those of the present day, carried down the carcasses of land animals, which thus became entombed in the accumulating sediment. Since that period . . . the gradual rising of the land . . . [has] exposed, in many places, the skeletons of those ancient inhabitants.'[23] In describing the secrets yielded by land movement, Darwin uses the language of entombment.

Later, in the *Journal of Researches*, at another discovery of mass destruction, Darwin concludes that 'the whole area of the pampas is one wide sepulchre of these extinct, gigantic quadrupeds' (*Journal* 1845, 149). Extinction is afforded the kind of reverential language of mortality associated with Wordsworth and, latterly, Adam Sedgwick. And Darwin, in common with Sedgwick, finds 'strange . . . forms and fashions of organic life' in the extinct toxodon, described in the *Journal* as 'perhaps one of the strangest animals ever discovered'. Darwin, however, celebrates the strangeness of an animal which blends features of the rodent with the dimensions and structural plan of an elephant: 'how wonderfully are the different orders, at the present time so well separated, blended together in different points of the structure of the toxodon' (*Journal* 1845, 80). Darwin's point was to explain palaeontologically the means by which the strange blend of characteristics evident from the entombed remains of this dead being could be reconciled with the spread and separation of branched orders which characterised the existing plan of nature.

Darwin observed the materials of palaetiological science accumulating before him in Patagonia as he described the patterns of life and death of the guanaco, the 'South American representative of the camel of the East' (*Journal* 1845, 158). The living guanaco confronts Darwin with precisely the rather contradictory, entangled set of dispositions that a living species could manifest. Though 'generally wild and extremely wary' they are also 'very easily domesticated'. If the boundary between the wild and the domesticated is blurred in the case of the guanaco, its actual behaviour under domesticity is 'very bold', so that they 'readily attack a man by striking him behind with both knees'. The guanaco in the wild, by contrast, displays 'no idea of defence' (*Journal* 1845, 158–9). Darwin notes that 'the guanacos appear to have favourite spots for lying down to die', and spots on the banks of the St Cruz river are 'white with bones'. Darwin draws attention to these mass graves 'because in certain cases they might explain the occurrence of a number of uninjured bones . . . buried under alluvial accumulations; and likewise the cause of why certain animals are more commonly embedded than others in sedimentary deposits' (*Journal* 1845, 160). Epitaphic writing needs to proceed carefully in the conclusions that it draws about the contents of graves, and the natural processes that have filled them. In fact, at this point Darwin moves from the language of the epitaph to the language of the romantic sublime. Recounting the expedition of a yawl to find water, Darwin recounts a scene of isolation, seclusion and desolation, punctuated only by a guanaco upon a hill as 'watchful sentinel', and, in descriptive language redolent of *The Excursion*, 'a trickling rill . . . of brackish water'. Darwin 'asks how many ages the plain had thus lasted, and how many more it was doomed thus to continue'; in answer, in the second edition of his narrative, he inserts Shelley's 'Lines on Mont Blanc':

> None can reply—all seems eternal now.
> The wilderness has a mysterious tongue,
> Which teaches awful doubt.
>
> (*Journal* 1845, 161)

Strikingly, Darwin cuts the final line off before the alternative that Shelley's actual line offers – 'or a faith so mild'.[24] Darwin's speculations and observations, palliated though they may be in a sympathetic epitaphic language, conclude in 'awful doubt'.

Darwin discovered a curious blend of life and death in one unique structure, coral. Coral colonies present a strange image of the relationship between the individual living elements of the reef and the dead, hard structure that predominates. Indeed, Howard E. Gruber has argued that Darwin's theory of coral formations was an early 'model theory' of natural selection, even to the extent that it contains a Malthusian principle of population growth and limits, for coral cannot grow beyond some limiting distance from the surface of the sea.[25] In the *Journal of Researches* Darwin records exploring the lagoons of Keeling Island: he wades out first 'as far as the living mounds of coral, on which the swell of the open sea breaks', and later finds himself amidst a forest of delicately branching coral that is all 'dead and rotten' (*Journal* 1845, 435–7). The contrast between the living and dead corals, and their branching tree-like form, come to function suggestively for Darwin, helping him to explain and re-conceptualise radically the relationship between extinction and transmutation. As he states in his first notebook, 'The tree of life should perhaps be called the coral of life, base of branches dead, so that passages cannot be seen.'[26]

Darwin explained coral within a Lyellian geological frame, though in this case, Darwin was more Lyellian than Lyell, who had thought that coral formations grew by encrusting rising volcanic rims. Darwin turned Lyell's theory on its head, arguing that the landmasses forming the islands in the Pacific were gradually subsiding. As the land sinks, the coral accumulates, rising to compensate and keeping itself at optimum depth. The theory of land subsidence fundamentally alters the relationship between the land

and the coral, as Darwin registers in his choice of metaphor in his paper on coral formations for the Geological Society of London (May 1837); these formations are now seen as 'monuments over subsided land' – the land now buried from view beneath the waves, restored to memory. The coral takes on an epitaphic function.[27]

Darwin's description, in the *Journal*, of the view of a coral island presents a challenge to observation and theorising:

A long and brilliantly white beach is capped by a margin of green vegetation; and the strip, looking either way, rapidly narrows away in the distance, and sinks beneath the horizon. From the mast-head a wide expanse of smooth water can be seen within the ring. These low coral islands bear no proportion to the vast ocean out of which they abruptly rise; and it seems wonderful, that such weak invaders are not overwhelmed, by the all-powerful and never-tiring waves of that great sea, miscalled the Pacific. (*Journal* 1845, 282)

Coral atolls present a remarkable aesthetic effect created by nature: sur-rounded by a mighty and moving force of the sea, the atoll constitutes a sharp frame of white and green, which holds within it a smooth and calm expanse of water. It is a picture, but one that is brought about seemingly by great force, and unequal power relations; the Pacific has been misnamed because of the violence that it metes out upon corals, which are seen as 'weak invaders', and 'great fragments scattered over the reef . . . plainly bespeak the unrelenting power of the waves' (*Journal* 1845, 436). And yet, 'wonderfully' for Darwin, the coral formations hold steady, even though they can only continue to form their base in relatively shallow waters. Darwin explores this contest of power further:

It is impossible to behold these waves without feeling a conviction that an island, though built of the hardest rock, let it be porphyry, granite or quartz, would ultimately yield and be demolished by such an irresistible power. Yet these low, insignificant coral-islets stand and are victorious: for here another power, as an antagonist, takes part in the contest. The organic forces separate the atoms of carbonate of lime, one by one, from the foaming breakers, and unite them into a symmetrical structure. Let the hurricane tear up its thousand huge fragments; yet what will that tell against the accumulated labour of myriads of architects at work night and day, month after month? Thus do we see the soft and gelatinous body of a polypus, through the agency of the vital laws, conquering the great mechanical power of the waves of an ocean which neither the arts of man nor the inanimate works of nature could successfully resist. (*Journal* 1845, 436–7)

Darwin perceives a striking chemical agency at work in the interaction between the waves and the small, 'soft and gelatinous body of a poly-pus', which contributes to a theory of life expressed in the metaphor of accumulated labour. A higher 'vital power' is served by this agency, so Darwin works with a familiar romantic opposition, between the mechanism of forceful water and the vitality of the 'soft' body. Significantly, Darwin's vitalism resists established hierarchies and rhetorics of power: the small, soft body is contrasted with the relentlessness of the machine-like sea, and it is the small soft body which is victorious, and the materiality of mechanical force that is overcome.

Yet this was not an opposition that could remain un-entangled and without supplements for Darwin as he was confronted by new natural relations and objects for which to account. In a remarkable passage on the kelp off Tierra del Fuego, Darwin constructs the sea not as a machine, but as a kind of reverse image of barren coastal landscape in its capacity to sustain 'great aquatic forests' supporting 'new and curious structures' (Journal 1845, 228–9). And as Darwin contemplates the natural sandstone spit that forms the harbour at Pernambuco, Brazil, he doubts 'whether in the whole world any other natural structure has so artificial an appearance'. Several miles long, the spit is perfectly straight. At its centre is a few inches' thickness of calcareous matter, including shells, barnacles and nulliporae, which are 'hard, very simply-organised sea-plants'. Darwin's opposition between organic, vital coral-polyp and inert machinate water has been deconstructed; the tissue from which this natural, yet to all appearances artificial, structure is built is explained through myth, a language of primitive culture that points to nature as a process of labour. Darwin sees it as 'a breakwater erected by Cyclopean workmen' (Journal 1845, 472–3). Darwin had referred to the South American continent as 'the great workshop of nature' in his first edition, but later removed the reference (Journal 1839, 158). But in the 'Essay of 1844', Darwin was beginning to articulate the implications of the forces at play in this workshop: 'Nature may be compared to a surface, on which rest ten thousand sharp wedges touching each other and driven inwards by incessant blows'.[28]

Darwin was refining his theory of life. In the first edition of the Journal of Researches, he alluded to Lyell's sense of the relationship between 'the geographical distribution of plants and animals, as consequent upon geological changes.' Because coral reefs were 'monuments' to subsided land, raised by 'infinite numbers of minute architects', Darwin speculated that these compound animals mingling living and dead tissue might hold the key 'to that most mysterious question, whether the series of organised beings peculiar to some isolated points, are the last remnants of a former population, or the first creatures of a new one springing into existence' (Journal 1839, 355). Coral might solve the mystery of the species question. While

Darwin modified this speculation in the second edition (*Journal* 1845, 457), a great deal of his speculative energy was now being invested in the figure of the 'stray colonist'. Though the 'stray colonist' connotes the sense of the isolated migrant, the stray was always over-determined by the overlapping agencies that were shaping the architecture of life. In the *Origin*, Darwin would account systematically for the mechanisms moving stray colonists from one region to another, while all the while observing how those agencies would re-fashion the migrants, and build living colonies with social and aesthetic meanings.

4. STRAY COLONISTS AND THE THEORY OF LIFE'S ARCHITECTURE: VERY LIKE A WHALE

At the opening of his account of Keeling Island, a coral island in the Indian Ocean six hundred miles from Sumatra in the Malay Archipelago, Darwin records the arrivals of colonisers from all orders of nature. On the one hand, there were humans, such as Mr Hare, 'a worthless character', who arrived on the island with a group of Malay slaves, and the British merchant seamen Ross and Liesk, to whom the Malays defect. On the other hand, there were the seedlings that have been washed up to germinate and cover the islands with flora. For as Darwin notes, 'all their terrestrial productions must have been transported here by the waves of the sea', giving the island the appearance of 'a refuge for the destitute' (*Journal* 1845, 429–31).

As Alan Bewell has pointed out in connection with the Enlightenment roots of Wordsworth's poetry, its subject matter often collects images of destitute, marginal individuals and races.[29] This perhaps provided Darwin with a framework for appreciating the significance and value of apparently stray, destitute beings encountered during the voyage of the *Beagle*. It certainly had an impact on socially marginal readers at home. Alfred Russel Wallace, a struggling land surveyor, yet with a strong desire for self-improvement, read *The Journal of Researches* in 1842. Wallace's activities and peripatetic early life during the 1830s took him from Wales to London, where he mixed in Owenite and working-class circles. He had frequented the 'Hall of Science' off Tottenham Court Road, a practical embodiment of the kind of educational reform which the Benthamite W. J. Fox had called for (and which Coleridge abhorred). As James Moore has argued, Wallace's subsequent experiences as a land surveyor in Wales – a demand created by the imposition of the Tithe Commutation Act (1836), which played a role in setting off the Rebecca disturbances – gave him an insight into the web of relations that could be mapped between land occupation and ownership, specific patterns and expectations of life, material privation, and a sense of social injustice.[30]

Wallace specifically transcribed Darwin's passage on the analogy between the appreciation of music and the appreciation of botany (quoted at the beginning of this chapter).[31] In 1847, he was reading Darwin's *Journal* again, alongside Chambers's *Vestiges*. For Wallace, the *Vestiges* 'serves both as an incitement to the collection of facts, and an object to which they can be applied when collected', whereas Darwin's work 'is second only to Humboldt's "Personal Narrative"' as the journal of a scientific traveller, and 'as a work of general interest, perhaps superior to it'.[32] It is striking that while Darwin revised the second edition of his *Journal* to meet subtly the challenge of the *Vestiges*, informed and ambitious readers like Wallace were already reading Darwin's concerns with distribution in his travel narrative in the light cast by Chambers and the species question. In 1858 Wallace would have cause to write to Darwin from the Malay Archipelago, outlining his own Malthusian answer to the species question. Darwin would see an independently conceived version of his own theory of natural selection articulated back to him, and this resulted in the dash to complete *The Origin of Species* in 1859.

But Darwin's theory was in a real sense present by the time of the second edition of the *Journal*, and, through the figure of the stray colonist, gesturing towards what would become the argument of the *Origin*.[33] In the first edition of the *Journal of Researches* Darwin describes the Galapagos archipelago as 'a little world within itself; the greater number of its inhabitants, both vegetable and animal, being found nowhere else' (*Journal* 1839, 269). From this account, the archipelago could be viewed as almost a unique centre of life stocked by individual acts of creative power. By the time of the second edition of the work, published in Murray's 'Colonial and Home Library', the 'little world' is also described as a 'satellite attached to America'. Darwin also adds some migrants, a 'few stray colonists'. These 'stray colonists' bring the naturalist 'somewhat near to that great fact – that mystery of mysteries – the first appearance of new beings on this earth' (*Journal* 1845, 359). For in looking at the population of finches, originating on the American continent, Darwin remarks that 'seeing this gradation and diversity of structure in one small, intimately related group of birds, one might really fancy that from an original paucity of birds in the archipelago, one species had been taken and modified for different ends' (*Journal* 1845, 361). The theory has been shaped and mediated by reading experiences: Darwin appropriates the phrase 'mystery of mysteries' from Herschel's letter, published in Babbage's *Ninth Bridgewater*. Darwin's notebooks on transmutation record a preoccupation with 'stray' colonisers of land, as in the detail that Darwin extracted from John Crawfurd's account of his Burman mission, recorded in his first note-book (see my introduction):

> account of HAIRY man (**because ancestors hairy**) with one hairy child, and of *albino* DISEASE being banished, and given to Portuguese priest.— In first settling a country.— people very apt to be split up into many isolated races! Are there any instances of peculiar people banished by the rest? —
>
> -----------
>
> ∴ most monstrous form has tendency to propogate as well as diseases.[34]

Darwin's immediate interest is in the further propagation of variation that follows from the isolation of stray colonists. In his 'Essay of 1844', Darwin had theorised in more detail the place of the variable 'stray colonist' in the emergence of new forms of island life, and much of this material was later expanded and absorbed into the *Origin*, in particular its chapters on 'Geographical Distribution'.[35]

Thus, Darwin's particular contribution to Murray's 'Colonial and Home' publishing project, aimed at colonial readers and designed to resist the incursion of pirated material into colonial literary markets, fashioned the 'stray colonist' in nature as an important figure in its theory of life and evolutionary development. Darwin went on to argue in the *Origin* that this principle 'is of the widest application throughout nature'. Most readily visible on oceanic islands, it is also observable 'on every mountain, in every lake and marsh'.[36] In what was to be received as a controversial passage in the *Origin*, Darwin speculated on how the natural selection of a particular feeding peculiarity observed in a species of bear might be preserved and accumulated over generations in a lake, and what might evolve as a result. The Malthusian theory of natural selection led Darwin to write this passage in the first edition, a passage so notorious for its speculative over-reach and ambition that it was toned down in subsequent editions:

> In North America the black bear was seen by Hearne swimming for hours with widely open mouth, thus catching, like a whale, insects in the water. Even in so extreme a case as this, if the supply of insects were constant, and if better competitors did not already exist in the country, I can see no difficulty in a race of bears being rendered, by natural selection, more and more aquatic in their structure and habits, with larger and larger mouths, till a creature was produced as monstrous as a whale.[37]

Darwin had been of course dismissive of Chambers's embryological theory of transformism in his reading of the *Vestiges*: 'The idea of a Fish passing into a Reptile (his idea) monstrous'.[38] And yet, Darwin's speculative imagination was capable of producing its own monstrosity. However, the 'monstrous' bear–whale was not even from his own 'direct' observation, but a passage he had read from Samuel Hearne's narrative of his travels in North America. This was the book read by Darwin and 'strongly praised by Wordsworth', indeed recommended by Darwin, on the authority of Wordsworth's name, to John Murray as a possible contribution to the latter's 'Colonial and Home' series. Moreover, despite Darwin's careful formulation of the argument about transmutation by natural selection, Darwin's defiant sense of 'why not' takes as its object of desire a hybrid aquatic creature – half bear, half 'monstrous' whale – an object every bit as strange and unfamiliar as William Gilbert's mermaid. Darwin deleted much of this passage after the publication of the first edition, leaving the bear swimming and catching insects, 'almost like a whale', and going no further.

In the *Journal of Researches* Darwin suggested that nature selects and cultivates colonists of space over time; they begin as one organism, and, through variable descendants, become something else, the bear that transforms into a whale being a striking example from the *Origin*. 'Culture' is consequently a term that ambiguously straddles a number of conceptual binaries: as he contemplated the religious impulses of the Fuegians, Darwin explicitly placed culture on a sliding scale between the savage and the civilised, the wild and the domestic. But the term would also resonate on the boundary between the animal and the human, the colonial and the home.

The relation between 'colonial' and 'home' can be seen as a frame to account for the researches into the mimetic properties of tropical insects by Alfred Russel Wallace and H. W. Bates in the early 1860s. This work, which was reviewed with interest by Darwin, provided striking evidences of the way in which butterfly colonists of space could become assimilated seamlessly to an environment by 'imitating' the appearance of a 'protected' species suffering from fewer predators. The aping of the habits and coloration of a 'native' was perhaps the most radical way in which a colonised space could be transformed, over time, into a 'home'. And yet, as Darwin, Bates and Wallace argued, this mimicry had no lasting effect on the organism's deeper structures of anatomical organisation and affinity, nor was it 'willed' in Lamarckian fashion by the organism. Instead, they argued, 'mimicry' was the outcome of the blows absorbed by the face of nature from the tightly packed wedges imagined in Darwin's machine of natural selection.[39] Darwin's theory of natural selection thus complicated anew the status of the category of 'imitation' within the discourses of natural history, and human culture, after 1859.

Indeed, some of the most puzzling, alluring and defamiliarising aspects of the *Origin* for its original readers arose in connection with accounts of accumulated variation that move between the overlapping domains of the cultivated and the natural. The material in Darwin's chapter on 'Instincts', with its vividly detailed accounts of the different species of slave-making ants, and the architectural capacities of humble-bees and hive bees in constructing honeycomb, were widely open to appropriation and further citation. We have seen (Introduction) how T. H. Huxley would appeal to Darwin's work on the bees in his 'Prolegomena' to 'Evolution and Ethics' in the 1890s. John Tyndall would also provide an account of Darwin's honeycomb-building bees in his *Belfast Address* of 1874. And Samuel Butler would respond to the slave-making ants, and the bear that might become a whale, in his own complex and ambivalent responses to a latent Lamarckism in Darwin's work (see chapter 5). What perhaps focuses interest on the 'instincts' explored in these accounts of different slave-making practices, and co-operative building techniques, is Darwin's contention that apparently unreflective animal instinct is in practice variable, subject to marginal improvement and selective accumulation. Following the naturalist Pierre Huber, Darwin contends that 'a little dose . . . of judgement or reason often comes into play, even in animals very low in the scale of nature'.[40]

When this is added to the fact that Darwin's chapter on instincts deals with social creatures – creatures that conduct trade, war, and reproduction through communities and colonies – then it is possible to grasp how such knowledge initiated, and fed back into, an intensive debate about 'culture' that was conducted through an expanding cultural field from the 1860s. This debate included familiar discourses on class and order, such as Arnold's discourse on 'culture and anarchy'. But it also embraced arguments about the best forms of mental culture; who should exercise the intellectual authority that could apprehend and interpret the material world; and the impact of the economies of nature and the material world upon politics. Different images of the 'colony' would enter into social and political dialogue, as would migration, colonisation and the authority of Christian religion, given that comparative work by ethnographers was revealing a set of common codes and practices among apparently varied cults. Indeed the authority of the bonds created by intellectual and affective representations in general would become important focuses of argument. On the one hand, the related questions of evolution and culture generated expanded opportunities for inventive literary practice; on the other, they generated further supplements to meanings that had been, as Walter Pater would recognise, both a source of fear in and, paradoxically, the effect of, writings by Coleridge and Wordsworth since the early decades of the century.

In November 1859 the *Athenaeum* reviewed a number of works, of which one was a new edition of Paley's *A View of the Evidences of Christianity*, annotated by Archbishop Whately. The reviewer remarked on the context that would receive this relic from the earlier nineteenth century: 'old barriers are giving way; religion is becoming a part of literature and a part of science'.[41] In the same number, Darwin's *Origin* was also reviewed, and the reviewer tended to see the cultural field that would receive Darwin's concepts as a theatre of intellectual conflict; natural selection itself would need to fashion itself as 'a successful competitor in the struggle for existence'. And then the reviewer stepped back, and again mapped a complex context of intellectual reception: 'Having introduced the author and his work, we must leave them to the mercies of the Divinity Hall, the College, the Lecture Hall and the Museum'.[42] The reviewer should also have added 'the Periodical'. These were the new institutions of learning and self-improvement that were receiving and disseminating representations, rhetoric and knowledge. It is to the expanding field mapped by these institutions that the next chapter turns.

CHAPTER 4

'In one another's being mingle': biology and the dissemination of 'culture' after 1859

I. COLONISING WORSHIP: RECEIVING EVOLUTION, RE-READING CULTURE

Robert J. C. Young observed of Matthew Arnold's *Culture and Anarchy* that 'it would be difficult to underestimate the importance and influence of this book as a central, indeed, foundational, account of culture for the humanities in Britain and the United States'.[1] But in the decade when Arnold was laying these foundations – in lectures, periodical essays, and eventually a book – there were competing accounts of culture in circulation. The *Athenaeum's* review of Darwin's *Origin* observed that the book's reception would take shape in the lecture hall, the divinity hall, the college and the museum. The same could be said for these other discourses of culture; in some cases, the discourse would be shaped in a lecture hall that sought to mimic the authority of both the divinity hall and the museum. Discourses of evolutionary science made important contributions to the formation of these other discourses of culture.

In January 1866, J. Baxter Langley and the Sunday League instituted a series of secular, morally elevating lectures about scientific knowledge under the title 'Sunday Evenings for the People'. T. H. Huxley delivered the inaugural lecture, the first of what were to become his resonantly titled *Lay Sermons* (1870). Huxley's lecture, delivered at St Martin's Hall and entitled 'On the Advisableness of Improving Natural Knowledge', was introduced with Haydn's *Creation* being played on the organ.[2] Huxley looked back in time two centuries to the London of 1666, to the problems of reading and interpretation that seventeenth-century Londoners would have encountered as they were beset by plague and fire. As Huxley argued, these phenomena gave rise to a contest of supernatural and sectarian interpretations. Plague was God's punishment, while for some the fire was the work of 'republicans', for others the work of 'papists'. Huxley's point was that this sectarian conflict of ill-founded interpretations needed to be settled by an authoritative understanding of natural phenomena. Indeed, it was, in Huxley's phrase presaging the title of Arnold's fifth chapter of *Culture and Anarchy* ('Porro Unum Est Necessarium'), 'the one thing needful'.[3]

The means for establishing such an understanding was the Royal Society for the Improvement of Natural Knowledge, founded in 1666. The Royal Society became, in Huxley's view, above all the custodian of a tradition of scientific texts and a means of enshrining and upholding the best that had been thought, scientifically: 'If all the books in the world, except the Philosophical Transactions, were destroyed, it is safe to say that the foundations of physical science would remain unshaken, and the vast intellectual progress of the last two centuries would be largely, though incompletely, recorded.' What were to become Arnold's mechanistic and wealth-producing objects of satire in *Culture and Anarchy* – 'great ships, these railways, these telegraphs, these factories, these printing presses' – were, for Huxley, products of the 'best that has been thought and said', a tradition of scientific wisdom 'without which the whole fabric of modern English society would collapse into a mass of stagnant, starving pauperism'.[4] To offset the Malthusian nightmare of a pauperised England degenerating into a state of savage static primitivism, Huxley concluded his lecture with another image of books and reading traditions that he melded with an image of savage idolatries. The 'theology of the present', he argued, 'has not only renounced the idols of wood and idols of stone, but begins to see the necessity of breaking in pieces the idols built up of books and traditions of fine-spun ecclesiastical cobwebs'.[5]

J. Baxter Langley's Sunday evening lectures, calculated to compete with the Sabbath offerings from the churches and chapels of revealed religion, had drawn fire from the upholder of the tradition that Huxley attacked, the Lord's Day Observance Society, which threatened legal action. In his narrative history of the events, Langley describes how the lectures were suspended until the winter of 1866, when he and his associates re-launched the series under the auspices of a registered 'religious association . . . having for its object the establishment of a free unsectarian church, in which the teachings of science should be recognised as important to the moral, social and religious culture of man'.[6] This was Langley's 'Church of the Future', in which the 'social and religious culture of man' would be re-interpreted by evolutionary science. More precisely, religion and science were brought into contact and conflict through traffic between the discourses of colonisation, race and worship; in other words, this was the linguistic terrain that continued to witness live contests between the etymological derivatives of 'culture'.

An example of this occurred a year later (January 1867) when John Craw-furd, the veteran Orientalist and colonial administrator, now President of the Ethnological Society, delivered a scientific lecture on the 'Plurality of the Races of Man' to the Church of the Future. Crawfurd's lecture returned to the question that dominated physical anthropology throughout the nine-teenth century: were human races descended from a common progenitor (monogenesis), or were they derived from a multiplicity of different stocks (polygenesis)? Crawfurd's focus on this question, and argument in favour of polygenesis, aligned him with a controversial camp.[7] His lecture also needs to seen in the context of the reception of Darwin's *Origin of Species*, and a historical series of acts of reading, reception and theory building.

In the 1830s (see my Introduction), the young Charles Darwin read Crawfurd's narrative of his travels and observations in Burma, noting with interest the effect that isolated 'monstrous' colonists might have upon the development of new, distinctive populations. In another context of reading and theory building, Crawfurd's observations of Javan land occupation had helped Coleridge to formulate his theory of an endowed clerical class to support 'culture' in ways that might help to resist materialist, transformist speculation. Now, thirty years later, Crawfurd, in the last year of his life, turned again to theories of colonisation to make sense of the implications of Darwin's mature speculations as part of an on-going debate about 'the social and religious culture of man'.

Crawfurd's contention that diverse domestic varieties of species most likely derived from more than one wild species is implicitly directed against Darwin's opening chapter of the *Origin* ('Variation Under Domestica-tion'), and the argument that diverse domestic varieties descend from a common wild ancestor.[8] Thus, Crawfurd constructed an argument for human polygenesis on the basis of his arguments about speciation amongst lower animals. Crawfurd sought to draw 'lessons' from his arguments about polygenesis and animal speciation from the history of human colonisation. Crawfurd was sceptical about what he took to be the 'geographical impossi-bility' of the process of migration required for the offspring of one progen-itor to populate the world. Moving from animal breeding and migration back to human evolution, Crawfurd argued that even the most powerful colonists of the ancient world, the Greeks and the Romans, had been unable to generate the migratory drive that Darwin's monogenesist argument from a single progenitor seemingly required.[9] A corollary of Crawfurd's position was that Darwin's reliance on 'stray colonists' was not a sufficient condi-tion for such grand evolutionary claims about the platform from which life's diversity was built: the illustrious but ultimately ruined vestiges of classical human empires would mark the impossibility of Darwin's evolutionary theory.

Biological research and arguments about colonial governance in the 1860s gave rise to a contestation of meanings associated with colonies and colonisation. On the one hand the fiercely public response to Governor Eyre's brutal suppression of a revolt in Jamaica in 1865 profoundly divided scientific and literary contributors to the intelligentsia: the whiggish Darwin – Wedgwood anti-slavery traditions in his bones – and the liberal Huxley lined up behind John Stuart Mill and the committee set up to prosecute Eyre, whereas John Tyndall followed Carlyle and Ruskin into the committee set up to defend him.[10] On the other hand, Darwin's evolutionary writings, as I have argued, presented more nuanced, estranging approaches to the idea of the colony. The *Origin* presented examples of the complex ways in which distinctive colonies of organisms could be built, sustained and enhanced by natural selection: it embraced the strange relations of reciprocity among slave-making ants, and the variable architectural instincts of bees. As this chapter will argue, other politically resonant meanings of the colony emerged in the scientific writings of George Henry Lewes and, in particular, Alfred Russel Wallace. These meanings looped back into materialist and indeed socialist variants of 'culture' that were premised on a complex interaction between sympathy, estrangement and biological diversity. Such variants of 'culture' were produced in the context of wide-ranging arguments about intellectual authority, and reflections on the nature and dissemination of the symbolic materials from which the discourses of religion, science and literature were made.

J. Baxter Langley's inaugural address to the Church of the Future that assembled on 24 January 1867 is a good example of how diverse those evolutionary speculations could be in creating links between natural history and religion as agents of mental culture. Langley embodied many of the drives and institutional affiliations that had generated hope and conflict around the term 'culture' from the 1830s. He was from Blackburn, and had been active in what Patrick Joyce has termed the 'romance of improvement' that structured the civic life and politics of Manchester during the 1840s. Secretary to the Manchester Athenaeum from 1846, he participated in schemes for popular evening recreations, and lectured on the power and moral influence of the stage and the genius of Milton, while also listening to debates about colonisation in Ireland.[11] Langley had trained originally for the church, but subsequently switched to medicine at King's College, London, the institution from which J. H. Green had articulated a Coleridgean approach to science and the organisation of knowledge during the early 1830s.[12] In the 1860s, Langley contested a Coleridgean reverence for the divine, blending instead narratives of self-cultivation and materialist evolution. The Preface to his miscellany of literary writings (published by subscription in 1855) records how Langley's vocational conversion from cleric to surgeon was expressed through a charged narrative mingling the identity of the colonial traveller with that of the evolving organism:

> Having been educated for the church, and possessed of an ineradicable dislike to its duties, as well as a want of belief in its doctrines, I have found myself in the condition of a man who, being about to go on a journey on land, under a tropical sky, is burdened with the equipments which might be desirable in a marine excursion . . . and a desperate struggle of adaptation has been going on.[13]

Langley's romantic, secular narrative of self remains shaped by Protestantism: the emphasis is on conversion, burdened travel – the self image of the sober, truthful, colonial traveller was important to the establishment of a distinctively scientific literacy – and struggle leading to exhaustion. However, the drama of his own struggle to adapt was translated into a moral narrative of evolution that was relayed to the congregation of the Church of the Future on the same evening as Crawfurd's discourse on 'The Plurality of the Races of Man':

> Every age has its own phase and expression, and the character of each is as distinct and well marked as that of an individual man. The geological strata in the planet on which we stand record a history of physical progress, each chapter of which preserves some monuments of existences impossible under the present conditions of things, or indicates such conditions as would render life as we now see it as impossible. Human history has parallel records of the onward progress of our race, and each era has its well-marked characteristics. Empires may rise, increase in power, extent and in wealth, but they will as surely decay and die, as the extinct animals have done, when they cease to adapt themselves to the progress of the human mind, and the demands or the conditions of the age. So far as we can comprehend the natural and moral laws of the Universe, the object and purpose of these laws seem to be to minister to a never ending progression and improvement in all things, to afford new possibilities to growth, and as certainly to remove that which is dead, decaying, or which has fulfilled its purpose and become obsolete.[14]

Langley's story of human history finds its originating analogies in material transformations, though it is ultimately couched in a mind-driven idealism. Geological strata are presented as the analogy for understanding successive differing phases and expressions of human history, which echoes Whewell's sense of palaetiological science, and the paradigmatic status of geology to 'reading' time and dynamism in apparently inert matter. In the same way as the geologist reads the story of the earth in rock formations, the historian will read the story of human progress in the different formations of discourse which express successive phases of human culture, each of which is as distinct, whole and as individuated as a person. In contemplating the 'natural and moral' laws of evolution which organise the universe and, thereby, the progress and degeneration of races, Langley invokes historical narratives of colonisation, in so far as the decline of empires finds its analogy in the extinction of animal species which fail to adapt. Langley's sense of a progressive series and succession in evolution thus owes more to the teleology of Chambers's *Vestiges* than to Darwin's *Origin of Species*. And although extinctions are brought about in part by environmental factors, extinction is also a consequence of the failure of an organic being, or a social structure, to adapt adequately to an idealist vision of the growing human mind. Again, this idealism follows Malthus' and Whewell's insistence on a mind-governed universe, which infuses the genius and 'culture' of select human minds with a purpose that can direct history in accordance with divine providence. Langley's evolutionary discourse is a hybrid formation drawn from vocabularies of romantic-idealist palaetiological science, and progressive transmutationism.

Langley also drew upon the Protestant support for print and private reading, applying this to science that had been 'nursed in the dark ages in the cradle of Catholicism'.[15] 'It has been the character of priesthoods', Langley claimed,

that they laid great stress upon the fulfilment of ceremonials – the performance of absolutions, sacrifices, and external occasional acts – ceremonials which could be seen or perhaps enforced, and which were the only means of testing the obedience and sincerity of the worshipper . . . most of them were instructed with the special intent of providing material support to the hierarchy, and maintaining its ascendancy over the people . . . So long as the people were grossly ignorant, and the hierarchies highly cultured in these sciences which seemed most mysterious to the untaught, the priest was ruler, and his courts were filled with trusting worshippers; but the discovery of printing, which placed knowledge within the reach of all, was the downfall of such authority, and destroyed the exclusive aristocracy of learning.[16]

In challenging the monopoly of 'highly cultured' clerisies, Langley thus developed an anthropological, materialist and historical perspective on theology that rendered the orthodox denominations of nineteenth-century Britain the descendants of so many primitive cults, in much the same way as E. B. Tylor was to analyse nineteenth-century theologies as survivals of the past in *Primitive Culture*.[17] Langley's analysis of the situation in the 1860s identified amongst the 'people' a mood of 'indifference towards theological organisation', particularly amongst those possessing 'cultivated minds'.[18] Langley's attempt to speak for the 'cultivated mind' serves as a reminder that the reformation of religion was an important part of Arnold's elaboration of 'culture' (*Literature and Dogma* [1871] and *God and the Bible* [1875] were integrally linked to the argument of *Culture and Anarchy*). At times Langley's discourse pre-empts the vocabulary of *Culture and Anarchy*, as when Langley proposes to replace worship grounded in theology with 'material for thought from the best sources . . . [thus] stimulating the taste for the truth', a formulation that is congruent with Arnold's construction of 'culture' as 'the best knowledge and thought of the time, and a true source, therefore, of sweetness and light'.[19]

Indeed, Langley tropes religion by making a striking conceptual connection between this aspiration and the practice of critical reading that takes its lead from a philological method. In claiming to uncover a forgotten, unfamiliar origin, Langley looks back to the practice of Coleridge and forward to Raymond Williams's etymological archaeologies: 'Here', Langley opines, 'we can claim to have a *religious* function, taking the word from its original sense as indicated by Cicero – derived from *re*, again, and *legio*, to read.'[20] Although the *OED* suggests that this was probably a false etymology, it strengthened Langley's rhetorical purpose: 'culture' could be re-thought by imagining religion as 're-legion', or critical re-reading that had assimilated the lessons of science. Langley's philological understanding of the sign of religion, and its relations to science and the field of culture, is emblematic of discourse that drew upon the expanded range of interpretive devices derived from scientific speculation and observation. These devices could be deployed in the interrogation of politics and society under the banner of 'culture' and its etymological derivatives.

2. CRITICISING LIFE, MINGLING WRITINGS: DISSEMINATING DEVICES AND THE CULTURE OF MIND

Matthew Arnold's 'essay in political and social criticism' conducted its argument through a range of by now familiar rhetorical devices: it was for 'sweetness and light', and against 'doing as one likes'. If society was to be reformed, it first had to be seen in less familiar terms: 'we are sure that the detaching ourselves from our "stock notions and habits", that a more free play of consciousness, an increased desire for sweetness and light, and all the bent which we call Hellenising, is the master-impulse now of our nation and of humanity' (*Culture and Anarchy*, 229). 'Culture', through its attachment to the Hellenising tendencies of the intellectual traditions and racial impulses of classical Greece, would, for Arnold, detach or productively estrange his countrymen from the stock notions and habits to which they had become so thoughtlessly enslaved. 'Culture' as 'free play' could speak for the nation and indeed humanity; the perfection of inwardness that it would stimulate through the approved symbolic materials of poetry and a reformed religion would assist in 'conquering the obvious faults of our animality' (99). At bottom, Arnold's argument was a response to the trespassing upon land by working-class protestors who failed to master 'the animality of their nature', and turned Hyde Park into 'a bear garden' (122). Having mastered the animal element in his own nature, the many-sided 'cultured' man could discourage the narrow men of 'action' from sectarian political aims. Robert Young's re-assessment of *Culture and Anarchy* has been particularly important for the way in which it has returned Arnold's discourse on animal impulse, class and order to the context of mid-nineteenth-century anthropological and racial science. Young's re-reading establishes that 'the struggles between what, for Arnold are in effect four classes [barbarian, philistines, populace, minority] . . . are subsumed into the struggles of racial history'.[21]

There were earlier attempts to locate Arnold's construction of culture in a wider field of intellectual debate that included ethnographic science. In 1963, George W. Stocking argued that Arnold and E. B. Tylor, the ethnologist and writer of *Primitive Culture*, were engaged in an argument over the meanings of 'culture' in the late 1860s and early 1870s. Tylor stated that 'Culture or Civilization, taken in its wide ethnographic sense, is that complex whole which includes knowledge, belief, art, morals, law, custom, and any other capabilities and habits acquired by man as a member of society.'[22] For Stocking, Tylor's use of the term 'culture' where 'civilisation' might conventionally, and more recognisably, have been used (Tylor's tactic of synonymy in his definition of culture – 'culture or civilisation' – is notable) was a direct contestation of Arnold's degenerationist thesis about English civilisation ravaged by sectarian religious conflict and a misplaced faith in mechanistic materialism. Stocking argued that Tylor's 'culture' included beliefs and practical skills ('habits and capabilities') which cumulatively amounted to a scale of material progress through which all populations and races would ascend, from primitive savages to civilized subjects.[23]

Stocking's work remains important because of the productive way it sought to locate nineteenth-century concepts of culture within what he self-consciously described as 'ever-broadening circles of context'.[24] Young broadened the context for understanding Arnold's culture by acknowledging the racial dimension in Arnold's account of class. But in establishing an ethnographic and evolutionary context for Arnold in the first instance, Stocking made it possible to appreciate the way in which Tylor's contestatory account of culture included a defence of material progress and mechanical contrivance; 'culture' is mingled again with materialism, and with the manifold ways in which evolutionary and scientific discourses dialogised culture and many of the keywords with which it had become associated.

For instance, when T. H. Huxley lectured on 'Science and Culture' at the opening of Sir Josiah Mason Science College, Birmingham, in 1880, he focused on Arnold's description of culture as a 'criticism of life'. For Huxley, 'life' was inconceivable outside the conceptual frameworks established by 'natural knowledge' since the formation of the Royal Society in the seventeenth century, for '[n]ot only is our daily life shaped by it, not only does the prosperity of millions depend upon it, but our whole theory of life has been influenced, consciously or unconsciously, by the general conceptions of the universe which have been forced on us by physical science'.[25] In the same year, Huxley lectured on 'The Coming of Age of *The Origin of Species*', and contended that Darwin's 'small green-covered book' provided biology, or the science of life, with 'a firm base of operations whence it might conduct its conquest of the whole realm of nature'.[26] Huxley thus drew Darwin's work into a debate about enhancing the critical powers of mind that placed science in the position of conquering intellectual coloniser. And, as demonstrated at the very beginning of this book, Arnold's *Culture and Anarchy* registered, through its satirisation of Robert Buchanan, a Malthusian perspective on life's expansion and distribution that, unconsciously, echoed Darwin.

Circles of context also need to be broadened to take account of proliferating opportunities for disseminating opinion. As Huxley celebrated the twenty-first birthday of the *Origin*, he held a copy of the first edition in his hand; he could display the book because he was lecturing, at the Royal Institution in London (April 1880). The record of his holding the book survives because the lecture was then published in the weekly magazine that Huxley had helped to form in 1869 to popularise science, *Nature*.[27] Book, lecture, serial publication: all of these dissemination formats were resoundingly active in the debates that this chapter traces, and were a crucial part of the massive expansion of the intellectual field that coincided with the publication of the *Origin*.

In his lecture on the coming of age of the *Origin*, Huxley recalled his own role as public controversialist seeking to keep Darwin's text alive as a 'vital' contribution to science, stating that he 'acted for some time in the capacity of a sort of under-nurse, and thus came in for my fair share of the storms which threatened the very life of the young creature'.[28] In fact, Huxley was an active reviewer of the *Origin* for established periodicals such as the *Westminster Review* and new periodicals such as *Macmillan's Magazine*; these were publications that were generalist in coverage, but served different readerships. As Ruth Barton has observed, scientific intellectuals such as Huxley and John Tyndall preferred to publish work in these periodicals, rather than in specialist organs such as *Nature*.[29]

Huxley reviewed the *Origin* for the *Westminster Review* in 1860. The *Westminster* had a long established reputation as an intellectually heavy-weight, radical organ (Mill published his essays on Bentham and Coleridge in its initial incarnation). The title had been purchased and regenerated by John Chapman in 1851. Huxley's review in the new *Westminster* champi-oned what he took to be the liberal, ideological orientation of Darwin's *Origin*, stating that 'every philosophical thinker hails it as a veritable Whitworth gun in the armoury of liberalism'.[30] The prospectus to the new *Westminster*, written by its sub-editor-to-be, Marian Evans (George-Eliot-to-be), declared that 'the fundamental principle of the work will be the recognition of the Law of Progress . . . it will not be forgotten, that the institutions of man, no less than the products of nature, are strong and durable in proportion as they are the results of gradual development'. The possibility of progress and development would be measured in relation to 'the actual character and culture of the people'.[31] In their biography of Darwin, Adrian Desmond and James Moore point to the re-launch of the *Westminster* as a watershed moment in evolutionary thought, in that 'for the first time, progressive science had collective middle-class support'. What artisan agitators had risked gaol to proclaim now became 'the fundamental principle' of one of the nation's leading literary reviews.[32]

Huxley also reviewed the *Origin* for the new popular family monthly, *Macmillan's Magazine*, in December 1859. *Macmillan's Magazine*, along with *Cornhill Magazine*, represented a new departure in publishing, mixing fiction, general literature and criticism. The format was attractive, and in the later 1860s, Arnold would publish his *Essays in Criticism* in *Macmillan's*, and the chapters comprising *Culture and Anarchy* and *Literature and Dogma* in *Cornhill*. *Macmillan's* was the first periodical to carry signatures; consequently, Huxley's review drew attention to the author's professorial authority, and his scientific affiliations ('Professor Huxley, F. R.S.'). The review consisted of two parts. The first part was an account of the relation between recent geological theory, palaeontology and the species question, originally delivered as a lecture to the Royal Institution.[33] In the second part of the article, Huxley reviewed Darwin's work, pointing out the importance of Darwin's analogy between domestic cultivation and 'Death' in the guise of natural selection as a solution to the species question.[34] In dismissing the earlier speculations of Lamarck and the *Vestiges*, Huxley made the review turn on the question of scientific and intellectual authority. It concludes by arguing that the principle of natural selection will be visited upon Darwin's theory itself, making it a law of intellectual as well as natural life: 'if Mr Darwin has erred, either in fact or reasoning, his fellow-workers will find out the weak point in his doctrines, and their extinction by some nearer approximation to the truth will exemplify his own principle of natural selection'. Huxley's final point is a plea for acceptance of the investigative authority possessed by 'painstaking, truth-loving . . . skilled naturalists', and an exhortation to 'the general public' that it is their 'duty . . . to await the result in patience'.[35]

Huxley's review for *Macmillan's* thus attempted to establish a new relationship between scientific expertise and cultivated public opinion – a theme to which this chapter will return in its conclusion. However, the varied magazine content of *Macmillan's* employed other genres to articulate alternative perspectives on this emerging re-negotiation of the relations between the public and critical intellectuals. In one of those pleasurable, ludic juxtapositions that occur frequently in nineteenth-century magazines, the piece that follows Huxley's review of Darwin, entitled 'Colloquy of the Round Table', meditated humorously on the problem of literary authority, past and present. The dialogue is a comic inquisition into the activities of a round table of writers, led by 'Serious William' and Sir John, who are charged by the 'Inquisitors for the Public' with 'having got up a secret society here, in imitation of the *Noctes Ambrosianae* of Christopher North'. If an imitation of the great energy and success of Christopher North's distinctive contributions to *Blackwood's Edinburgh Magazine* during the 1820s and 1830s is held to be against the public's interest, then the reason for desiring such a return to the 'mother tongue' purity of the *Noctes* is strikingly linked to the increasing power and proliferation of scientific discourse: 'our very babbies are getting so scientific, it's a mercy you ought to be thankful for . . .' And yet, as 'Serious William' defends his imitations of Christopher North's colloquies ('a form as old as time itself'), his defence is cast in the very scientific discourse that the revived style of the *Noctes* set itself against: 'can a set of men meet together . . . exchange words and thoughts . . . without becoming for the time a compound organism?'[36] In his essay on 'Style' (1889), Walter Pater would observe that the condition of English intellectual language in the nineteenth century was marked by its complex absorption of specialist vocabularies (pictorial art, German metaphysics). Following such assimilations and field crossings, Pater predicted that for 'many years to come [scholarly] enterprise may well lie in the naturalisation of the vocabulary of science'.[37] As we shall see, George Henry Lewes mingled the biological vocabulary of the 'compound organism' with the language of literary art and sympathy, while productively suspending the naturalisation effect.

Pater was also concerned with the origins of this process, which he located in the early decades of the nineteenth century. He focused his concerns on Coleridge's elaboration of a concept of culture through the confrontation between philology and science dramatised in *The Friend* and *Aids to Reflection*. In Pater's essay on 'Coleridge's Writings' in the *Westminster Review* for January 1866, 'evolution', 'life' and 'culture' are words that are interrogated, and as Laurel Brake points out, Pater 'silently' enters into a dialogue with Arnold's recently published *Essays in Criticism* (1866).[38] Pater's essay sets in play various meanings of 'culture', including, in the first sentence, the contention that forms of 'intellectual and spiritual culture often exercise their subtlest and most artful charm when life is already passing from them'. Contained in this formulation are two senses of 'culture': on the one hand, there are 'ideas, moralities, modes of inward life', and on the other, 'culture' in its 'palaetiological' sense as an evolutionary 'passing stage', or systems of knowledge and practice, transforming between historical epochs. The particular transformation that fascinates Pater is the change from 'ancient philosophy' to 'modern thought', the latter characterised 'by its cultivation of the "relative" spirit in place of the "absolute"'.[39] Pater silently cites and inflects Arnold's vocabulary in stating that 'the literary life of Coleridge was a disinterested struggle against the application of the relative spirit to moral and religious questions . . . [though he] failed in that attempt' (3). Coleridge's desire for the absolute would always be frustrated by the modern realisation that 'scientific truth is something fugitive, relative, full of fine gradations'; thus, against Arnold's view of disinterested classicism, Pater presents disinterested absolutism defeated by modern relativism (10).

Pater drew on evolutionary theory in arguing that 'the idea of "the relative" has been fecundated in modern times by the influences of the sciences of life. These sciences reveal types of life evanescing into each other by inexpressible refinements of change' (2). In contrast to Coleridge's insistence on the absolute and corrective force of '*Ideas*', Pater emphasises 'the idea of "the relative"'. Whereas for Coleridge the 'cultivating' powers of a theological clerisy would preserve Ideas from an error born of sensational materialism, for Pater it was modern scientific observation that would 'fecundate' the relativity of interpretative frames: 'for the individual, there are [now] a thousand intermediate shades of opinion, a thousand resting-places for the religious spirit' (10). From 'cultivation' to 'fecundation', the metaphors of intellectual endeavour continue to figure through a material, naturalistic sense of tillage, though Pater's metaphor of fecundity suggests a multiplication and dissemination.

Coleridge's approach to 'scientific truth' is exemplified for Pater in *The Friend* and *Aids to Reflection*; in particular, Coleridge's strenuous efforts to use writing 'to fix it in absolute formulas'. Yet, Pater is alert to the complex, self-conscious and contradictory form of these texts that produces supplements in the very desire to fix absolutely:

These books came from one whose vocation was in the world of art; and yet, perhaps, of all books that have been influential in modern times, they are farthest from the classical form – bundles of notes, the original matter inseparably mixed up with that borrowed from others . . . The 'Aids to Reflection', or 'The Friend', is an effort to propagate the volatile spirit of conversation into the less ethereal fabric of a written book; and it is only here that the poorer matter becomes vibrant, is really lifted by the spirit. ('Coleridge', 10)

The classical approach to truth is challenged by a fragmentary modernity of form in which other voices, other texts, are ceaselessly echoed. Moreover, for Pater, Coleridge's texts on science and morality from the 1830s were prophetic of the modernity they sought to arrest, precisely because of the way in which they attempted to fix the volatile variety of utterance into the 'fabric' or matter of publication. It is possible to use Pater's thoughts on Coleridge's writerly, discursive 'conversations' to reflect on the increasingly fluid boundaries between spoken performance and published work, the means by which symbolic material – matter, 'fabric' – is exchanged between economies of communication and dissemination between genres, and indeed between different domains of the intellectual field. The kind of post-1850 periodical in which Pater reflected on the distinctive tensions of Coleridge's writings on culture and the sciences of life from the 1830s was precisely the context of publication that accelerated the blurring of generic boundaries and demarcations of discourse domains.

A good example of the mingling of generic boundaries occurs in George Henry Lewes's 'Studies in Animal Life', which appeared in the first volume of the new monthly *Cornhill* in 1860. Consisting of six chapters appearing between January and June, Lewes's writing moved between the genres of educational polemic (biology was explored as a mode of mental culture), review (the appearance of Darwin's *Origin* was noted), and even biography (reflections on the career of Georges Cuvier). Lewes's self-conscious literariness alluded back to an earlier nineteenth-century poetic of science; each of his chapters begins with the same epigraph taken from Wordsworth's *Excursion* proclaiming 'Authentic tidings of invisible things; — / Of ebb and flow, and ever-during power, / And central peace subsisting at the heart / Of endless agitation'. Lewes's first chapter expands on the epigraph by urging its readers to 'Avert your eyes from our human world, with its ceaseless anxieties . . . [and] contemplate the calmer attitude of that other world with which we are so mysteriously related', for human life 'forms but one grand illustration of the Biology – the science of Life'.[40] Lewes proposes to satisfy the intellectual curiosity of readers by giving them access to the otherness of the animal world, enabling them to acquire a new perspective on the world of human concerns, detaching them from habitual ways of seeing. 'Biology' will provide this productively estranging perspective by uncovering 'mysterious' links between the reader's own world and an animal world customarily conceived as 'other'. Thus, Lewes promotes biology as an educative source of reflection on life, mediated by literary materials: he breaks down the etymological structure of biology precisely to indicate the way in which 'bios' (life) is mediated by 'logos' (discourse) (61).

Linguistic parallels are important to the argument of 'Studies in Animal Life'. In the April number (ch. 4), Lewes appeals to analogies of library classification to explain the classification of genera and species (439). This brings him to the species question, where he notes the radical argument about descent advanced in Darwin's *Origin*, published in the previous October. Lewes draws attention to the importance of Darwin's arguments about the descent of domestic varieties of pigeons from a single wild progenitor (445). But for Lewes, the clinching argument from analogy is linguistic and philological. As Stephen Alter has demonstrated, this was a deeply embedded intellectual parallel, and Darwin drew upon philological analogies in advancing the argument of the *Origin*.[41] In fact, Lewes appeals to Friedrich Max Müller's theories of the descent of Romance languages from an extinct progenitor in urging that 'in the same way we are justified in supposing that all the classes of vertebrate animals point to the existence of some elder type, now extinct, from which they were all developed' (447). In fact, Müller's philological theory would itself make a contribution to extending debate about the reach and applicability of Darwin's natural selection through Müller's *Lectures on the Science of Language*, delivered at the Royal Institution in 1861–2 (and published subsequently).[42]

The complexities of descent and affinity that biology uncovers qualifies it, in Lewes's eyes, for recognition as a source of intellectual cultivation and improvement, an office traditionally reserved for the study of classical languages: 'the one reason why, of all sciences, Biology is pre-eminent as a means of culture, is, that, owing to the great complexity of its investigations, it familiarises the mind with the necessity of attending to *all* the conditions, and it keeps the mind alert' (290). Lewes's advocacy of biology as a complex stimulus to 'mental culture' can be seen as an alternative version of Arnold's interest in the many-sidedness that his own version of 'culture' claimed to develop. For Lewes, however, biological 'many-sidedness' was less about realising the 'master impulse of humanity' (Arnold), and more about the interpretive act of re-locating humanity within a more complex web of relations. Lewes saw that biology paradoxically involved 'familiarising the mind' with the unfamiliar, placing humanity in paradoxical touch with a world in which animals are not 'alien but akin' to humans.

In the final chapter of Lewes's 'Studies', the concept of the colony emerges as a crucial concept for expanding 'mental culture'. Lewes followed Darwin's fascination, in his *Journal of Researches*, for compound animals such as coral polyps. Lewes applied the concept of the colony to living organisms as a basis for exploring principles of cooperation, interdependency and the limits of individuality. 'Formerly', he notes, 'the coral-branch was regarded as one animal – an individual . . . But no zoologist is now unaware of the fact that each polype on the branch is a distinct individual, inspite of its connections with the rest; and philosophic botanists are agreed that the tree is a colony of individual plants'. Lewes draws a political conclusion from his observation of the organisms comprising this colony: 'They are all actively engaged in securing food, and the labours of each enrich all. It is animal Socialism of the purest kind – there are no rich and no poor, neither are there any idlers' (683). Although Lewes begins by informing the reader that he is dealing with 'the simpler forms of Life to make the lesson easier', his narrative powers, structured by the imagined gaze of the microscope, discover complexity in the colony: where identity of task and function was assumed to be the organising principle, as Lewes looks more closely, he notes '*differentiation*', or a division of labour that creates slightly different functions, and thus obligations and rights of reciprocal 'care' to the different organisms or material 'instruments' comprising the colony. Lewes reminds readers of the original Greek meaning of 'organic', much as Raymond Williams would later in *Culture and Society*.[43] Lewes's 'animal socialist' colony persists as a means of registering surprise at strangeness, finding the unfamiliar in the seemingly familiar, establishing kinship where otherness was assumed to reign: in short, and to use Victor Shklovsky's later term, of defamiliarising stock knowledge.[44]

This revelation enables Lewes to push his exploration of the 'animal socialist' colony further by focusing on a new 'case' of 'higher' animals, 'the group of jelly-fish called *Siphonophora* (siphonbearers)'. In his account of the organic components comprising these life forms, Lewes notes 'that there are distinct individuals to feed the colony, individuals to float it through the water . . . reproductive individuals'; 'only' he adds, crucially, 'no one calls the Organism a colony' (684). Thus, Lewes invites his readers to consider problems of linguistic convention in scientific description, and the way in which literary devices can productively expose their workings. Lewes has rhetorically prepared his readers for this moment by telling them at the beginning of his chapter that 'Natural history is full of paradoxes . . . the word meaning simply, "contrary to what is thought" – a meaning by no means equivalent to "contrary to what is the fact." It is paradoxical to call an animal an aggregate of individuals; but it is so because our thoughts are not very precise on the subject of individuality' (682).

Lewes's essay then apparently swerves away from the full, potentially unsettling, implications of this imprecision. After its discussion of compound organisms and 'animal socialism', the essay performs a generic shift that restores and reinforces the familiar parameters of human individuality. It concludes with a heroic, romantic biographical account of the early scientific career of the young Georges Cuvier. But what binds this biography into the rest of Lewes's writing on biology as mental culture is a complex biological re-thinking of the concept of sympathy. As Lewes meditates on the early career of the struggling and obscure Cuvier, he expresses the great sympathy aroused in him by reading letters about Cuvier's youthful and impulsive desire to 'systematically display' the 'universal interdependence' of nature (685) – a sympathy that is not, by contrast, stimulated by reading accounts of the older Cuvier when he had become the powerful and politically preoccupied grand savant of imperial France (690). For Lewes, sympathy is also the sensation that is stimulated by the very activity of uncovering the complex interdependencies at work in and between the organisms of nature, or the sense of 'mingling' that he turns to Shelley's 'Love's Philosophy' to articulate: 'Nothing in this world is single; / All things, by a law divine, / In one another's being mingle'. According to Lewes, the 'thoughts of others, the sympathies of others, the needs of others, – these too make up our life; without these, we should quickly perish' (685). For Lewes, interpretive sympathising is the difference between living and perishing, but the paradoxical interpretive frame that biology produced would defamiliarise the reader from received 'higher' thought about individuality by discovering in the lower animal world resources of mutuality and social sympathy.

This traffic of discourse between the scientific and the literary, and the 'organic' interdependencies between human and animal that Lewes's 'Studies' seeks to map, helped to produce a widened circle of context for Alfred Russel Wallace's *Malay Archipelago* narrative. If Wallace's early work sought to uphold the validity of Darwinian natural selection, it also articulated a materialist discourse of 'culture' that sought to make an earthily aesthetic contribution to social and political criticism.

3. DESTRUCTION, LAND SHOCKS AND CULTURE SYSTEMS: MAN-LIKE APES AND ESTRANGED SYMPATHY IN THE MALAY ARCHIPELAGO

Wallace's *Malay Archipelago* appeared in 1869. Charles Lyell informed him that 'nothing equal to it has come out since Darwin's "Voyage of the *Beagle*"'.[45] Wallace's travel narrative appeared in the same year as Arnold's *Culture and Anarchy*, and one year after the death of John Crawfurd. As a venerable Orientalist and early authority on the 'Indian Archipelago', it is not surprising that Crawfurd should figure in one of Wallace's appendices to his narrative. And yet the way in which Crawfurd appears casts a bizarre light on the persistently marginal and obscure standing of Wallace as the latter's painstaking research was destroyed and lost, flung upon the dust heap:

During my travels . . . I collected a considerable number of vocabularies, in districts hitherto little visited. These represent about fifty-seven distinct languages (not including the common Malay and Javanese), more than half of which I believe are quite unknown to philologists . . . Unfortunately, nearly half the number have been lost. Some years ago I lent the whole series to the late Mr John Crawford [sic], and having neglected to apply for them for some months, I found that he had in the meantime moved residence, and that the books containing twenty-five of the vocabularies, had been mislaid; and they have never been recovered. Being merely old and much battered copy-books, they probably found their way to the dust-heaps, along with the other waste paper.[46]

Crawfurd's disposal of Wallace's philological researches, in battered copy-books, upon waste heaps, elicits sympathy for Wallace that aligns him with Lewes's image of the struggling young naturalist. Wallace's narrative prompted comparison with Darwin's *Beagle* narrative, and his paper 'On the Tendency of Varieties to Depart Indefinitely from the Original Type' might have been read alongside Darwin's first public outing of the theory of natural selection at the Linnaean Society in 1858. For all this, Wallace, unlike Darwin and Lyell, never belonged unambiguously in the ranks of the scientific elite, and was never cautious in his espousal of radical politics.

Wallace did not publish *The Malay Archipelago* until six years after his return from the region, and eleven years after the public revelation of his contribution to the theory of natural selection. Wallace dedicated his narrative to Darwin, and the narrative made a significant contribution to the selectionist, biogeographical evolutionary theory that Darwin had been elaborating since his *Journal of Researches*. Thus in his opening chapter, Wallace considers the 'definition and boundaries' of the land expanse comprising the Archipelago. In Wallace's exploration of boundaries and relationships, the Malay Archipelago occupies a position between two distinctive geographical regions, and is allied in complex ways to both: one group of islands to the North West is Asian, and thus 'Indo-Malayan'; the other, to the South East, is Australian, or 'Austro-Malayan'. The islands comprising the archipelago are separated by means of wide but shallow troughs of ocean. To Wallace's geological eye, this shallowness indicates relatively (in geological terms) recent separation of the island groupings from their respective continental origins. This had important implications for Wallace's explanation of the origins of the life forms that continued to colonise the territory: life forms on the Indo-Malayan islands bear affinity with life in Asia, whilst Austro-Malayan life forms have a visible Australian origin. Crucially, Wallace came to see that human racial similarities and differences, and the languages that he traced in his philological researches, had been shaped by the same kinds of pressures and geological boundaries as animal speciation (*Malay Archipelago*, 15).

Wallace fashioned his writerly authority carefully: he aimed to write an 'interesting and instructive' reading experience, based on direct and reliable observation, or 'narrative and descriptive portions . . . written on the spot' (ibid., ix, xi). In his earlier account of his travels (with H. W. Bates) on the Amazon and Rio Negro (1848–52), Wallace criticised 'travellers who crowd into one description all the wonders and novelties which it took them months to observe', for 'this must produce an erroneous impression on the reader'.[47] Thus Wallace fashioned his writing as the outcome of sober and patient observation. In so doing, he aligned his narrative with writing that had been validated by Huxley's work on the best that had been seen and said on travel and natural history.

One of the many important but less frequently noted functions that Huxley's seminal anthropological work *Man's Place in Nature* (1863) performed was to shape a context of reception for a tradition of colonial travel and observation narratives that had contributed facts on which evolutionary speculations could be built. Thus Huxley begins *Man's Place* by observing that 'Ancient traditions, when tested by the severe processes of modern investigation, commonly enough fade away into mere dreams: but it is singular how often the dream turns out to have been a half-waking one, presaging a reality', a principle that Huxley applied to the hybrid man/beast figures of 'Centaurs and Satyrs'.[48] Huxley's opening and widely read chapter on 'The Man-Like Apes' places at its centre the question of the faithfulness or otherwise of a seventeenth-century travel narrative, 'The Strange Adventures of Andrew Battell of Leigh, in Angola and the Adjoining Regions' which had appeared in the Rev. Samuel Purchas's *Purchas his Pilgrimes* (1625). Battell's text had re-entered circulation during the nineteenth century when it was printed in 1847 by the Hakluyt Society, an antiquarian organisation founded in 1846 and dedicated to publishing voyage and travel narratives that were deemed to be 'admirable examples of English prose at the stage of its most robust development'.[49] As such, the re-printing of such early texts issued from the very 'exemplar' motive that had led to Murray's publication of the 'Colonial and Home Library'.

Huxley focuses on Battell's description of 'the Ape Monster Pongo', in which two 'monsters' are described, 'the lesser . . . called Engeco' whilst 'the greatest is called Pongo'. Battell blurs the boundary separating species of lower animals from the human: the Pongo is shaped like a human but 'giant' in stature, with super-human strength. Yet the description also alludes to the Pongo's predisposition to 'cover' its own dead, in a practice seemingly parallel to human burial. Ultimately, however, the Pongo remains, in Battell's account, on the bestial side of the species divide.[50] Huxley alludes to a whole range of subsequent travel narratives from the seventeenth and eighteenth centuries, which describe and depict, whilst failing consistently to name and differentiate between, the man-like apes found separately in Africa and Asia. Thus, Huxley reads and reads and invokes a textual tradition in which biogeographic specificity and the identity of natural orders became confused. For Huxley, these confusions persist even into Buffon's influential natural history. The latter's popular dissemination would have stimulated 'vulgar' transmutational speculation, but did a 'good deal more disfigurement to Battell's sober account'.[51]

Huxley's strategy in the opening chapter of *Man's Place* is thus to reinstate Purchas's account of Andrew Battell's travels as an authoritative text of sober, industrious and truthful English colonialism, and to present Purchas as an important contributor to the scientific improvement of mental culture. In his essay on 'A Liberal Education: and Where to Find It', published in *Macmillan's Magazine* (1868), originally delivered as a lecture at South London Working Men's College in the same year, Huxley described the English as 'the greatest voluntary wanderers and colonists the world has ever seen', greater even than the Greek and Roman colonists of the classical era, with a literature to match (*Lay Sermons*, 36–7).

Wallace's narrative also follows in the tradition traced by Huxley in that it contributes to knowledge of 'the man-like apes', something that Wallace signalled in his subtitle to his work: 'The Land of the Orang-Utan'. The title page carried an illustration of the creature, and the frontispiece presented a dramatic image of an orang-utan sinking its teeth into the arm of a Dyak hunter: *The Malay Archipelago* thus placed itself in the cultural field by feeding an appetite for what Susan D. Bernstein has characterised as the 'ape anxiety' of the 1860s.[52] Yet, in feeding that appetite it inflected it in subtle and thoughtful ways: Wallace's frontispiece may represent an aggressive, rampant beast biting and clawing at a man, yet the caption reminds the reader: 'Orang-utan attacked by Dyaks'. This caption is symptomatic of the way in which Wallace's narrative subtly inflects the tradition of English colonial travel narrative upheld by Huxley; Wallace presents a more critical view of English colonialism, and of English political and social relations.

Wallace's narrative is shaped by a land that produces a sense of estrangement in western eyes. Wallace notes that the 'inhabitant of most parts of northern Europe sees in the earth the emblem of stability and repose' (*Malay Archipelago*, 220). But there is order beneath the feet in Europe, whereas the Archipelago is always threatening to unleash anarchic natural force, as Wallace recollects from his experience of running in and out of his dwelling during an earthquake and its aftershocks: 'At intervals of ten minutes to half an hour, slight shocks and tremors were felt, sometimes strong enough to send us all out again. There was a strange mixture of the terrible and the ludicrous in our situation . . . I could not help laughing . . .The sublime and the ridiculous were here literally but a step apart' (192). Boundaries between objects of cognition are always on the verge of being dissolved and mingled in new ways in the Archipelago, making the familiar unfamiliar.

Boundaries that demarcate difference can, paradoxically, lead to conclusions that blur other, sanctified differences: Wallace's original discovery of the biogeographical boundary demarcating lands with different continental origins, which became known as 'Wallace's Line', leads him to infer a common story about patterns of animal and human evolution. The land being a source of common, communal life for animals and humans, Wallace formulates a distinctive materialist discourse on 'culture' and social justice that was reflected back into a Britain preoccupied with such questions. The land produces a securely grasped, earthy discourse on 'culture'.

On his travels in the East Indies, Wallace the Owenite socialist radical encountered colonial institutions supporting 'cultivation'. In the Dutch-controlled regions of the Archipelago Wallace observes and praises colonial management for what he described as 'the culture system' (73). This 'culture system' was a coercive scheme of community agriculture formulated by the Dutch, but put into practice at their behest by indigenous populations 'under the direction of the [community] chiefs'. Comprising an extensive network of terracing for the purpose of irrigation and cultivation, the system was adapted to the rigours of Malthusian population law in that it was extended year by year 'as the population increases'. Wallace concludes that 'it is perhaps by this system of village culture alone' that social and political stability was sustained (86). Wallace's encounter with this 'culture system' thus prompts observations in what Arnold would style 'social criticism'. In one sense, Wallace's advocacy of this 'culture system' can be placed in the context of Stocking's reading of Tylor's ethnographic conception of culture, where 'culture' figures as a progressive but hierarchical ladder. Human culture is organised into stages: Western Europeans are advanced, the Malay races are relatively primitive (the Papuans more so). The 'culture system' would instil important lessons of work discipline and community self-reliance, thus raising 'savage' people in the cultural hierarchy (194–7). But in another sense, Wallace's narrative was cast in the form of a symbolic intellectual capital that was produced as a socialist riposte to his own countrymen.

Wallace's praise for the Dutch 'culture system' was offered as a foil to his assessment of English colonial policy in the Archipelago: a misplaced ideology of free trade, protected in reality by the threat of military violence embodied in 'our fleets and armies' (190, 237, 363). English colonial practices, according to Wallace, bolstered English 'one-sidedness' which refused to look beyond the doctrine of *laissez faire* (73). In his Preface to *Culture and Anarchy*, Arnold criticised English social and spiritual reformers for failing to see salvation as 'a harmonious perfection only to be won by unreservedly cultivating many sides in us' (243). In contrasting one- and many-sidedness, Wallace's *Malay Archipelago* works with an Arnoldian device for interpreting value. This is also demonstrated in the fact that Wallace shares with Arnold a sense of the importance of inwardness. Moreover, both link inwardness to the outward-reaching feeling of sympathy. But whereas for

Arnold it is 'establishments' such as the national church that will provide an informing context for sympathy to work in (243), for Wallace, the full panoply of social life should receive 'the sympathetic feelings and moral faculties of our nature'. While Arnold retreats from legislation and commerce, Wallace's sympathy has to be allowed 'a larger share of influence in our legislation, our commerce, and our social organization . . . [or] we shall never, as regards the whole community, attain any real or important superiority over the better class of savage' (457).

Wallace presents the languages of sympathy as a means of reforming the rapacious one-sidedness of commerce and monopoly, and the end of *Malay Archipelago* decisively switches genre to become 'an essay in political and social criticism'. Wallace takes the concept of culture in a different direction from Arnold's idealism. In the conclusion to his narrative, Wallace urges that 'we should now clearly recognize the fact, that the wealth and knowledge and culture of *the few* do not constitute civilization, and do not of themselves advance us towards the perfect social state' (457). Having seen 'culture' materialised in his account of the Dutch 'culture system' of colonial land management, for Wallace the term was inseparable from the means by which the common wealth could be produced and reproduced. Latterly, Wallace became as renowned for his political campaign for land nationalisation as for his contribution to the theory of evolution.[53] Accordingly, 'culture' as an expression of the 'perfect social state' was conditional upon the collective 'possession of the soil of our country' (457); for only then, Wallace contended in language that echoed Arnoldian social classifications, would 'thickly populated' England be liberated from 'a state of barbarism' (458). Though Wallace's reading of the benefits of the 'culture system' begins in the East Indies, its earthy lessons for the material underpinnings of sympathetic understanding can still be carried back to the sources of protest that led to the dismantling of railings in Hyde Park.

Wallace learned lessons of sympathetic understanding in the Malay Archipelago; but they were estranging lessons for the self to learn. Arnold deplored what he took to be the *laissez faire* subjectivity internalised in working-class English protesters as they 'did as they liked', breaking down the railings of Hyde Park, making it 'a bear garden': he traced this latent 'animality' to a crisis of subjective identification in general. Wallace's subjectivity is represented in his narrative as divided between different impulses; his account of his progress through Borneo as an English explorer in search of orang-utan specimens presents an initially alarming picture of destructiveness and waste of life in the name of market principles. Wallace had no private income; he needed to make money from his expedition, not least in order to continue to finance it. Having shot an abundance of male and female creatures, many of which had to be left to rot in the tree-branches in which they had become entangled, Wallace in his attempts to claim his prizes was alert to the perishable nature of the commodity his shot had invested in, and the practical lessons of political economy that he needed to observe in employing local labour to help him recover the corpses (39–40).

As a sober, scientific observer, Wallace sought to place distance between myths about the orang-utan and its reality as an object of investigation within its environment. Noting the difference in size between its small lower limbs and enormous arm span, Wallace observes that 'the dispro-portion between these limbs is increased by his walking on his knuckles, not on the palm of the hand, as we should do' (45). Wallace goes on to declare that 'representations of its walking with a stick are entirely imagi-nary' (46). He was implicitly refuting the eighteenth- and early nineteenth-century theory that the orang-utan was a primitive man on the road to civilisation.

And yet, at the same time as Wallace seeks to separate animal and human economies, a blurring of the line between human and animal is represented in response to a less controllable event. The third orang-utan that he shoots, a female, is carrying 'a young one' which survives the fall; Wallace retrieves the creature, and in doing so manifests a different dimension of self from that of the hunter that tracks and kills the animals. It is perhaps a 'best self' that gives an account of the parental care that he devotes to his 'young one', including his attempt to make 'an artificial mother, by wrapping up a piece of buffalo-skin into a bundle, and suspending it about a foot from the floor'. At first, Wallace believes that he has 'made the little orphan quite happy', but the creature only manages to fill its mouth with hair and wool, so Wallace 'was obliged to take the imitation mother to pieces again'. Wallace is successful, eventually, in feeding the creature, noting the facial expressions of approval or disapproval that accompany certain diets: distaste for a certain meal would lead the creature to 'scream and kick about violently, exactly like a baby in a passion' (34). It is significant that this 'young one' is found in the very position that the novice European traveller was initially accustomed to occupying. Earlier, Wallace refers to himself as a 'booted European', walking on slippery paths designed for 'bare-footed natives'. Because he is enthralled by the unfamiliar 'objects of interest around', he experiences 'a few tumbles into the bog' (27). As he rescues his 'orphan' he finds it lying 'face down in the bog' (32). The bog becomes common ground between man and beast. As we have also seen, the ground is a source of common wealth; not only has it produced an earthly, explicitly politically formulated materialist discourse on culture, it also produces an incompletely grasped, yet distinctively earthy, grotesque discourse. It begins with the effects of both levelling and reversal.

One can understand these effects of levelling and reversal by looking at the way in which Wallace represents a sense of estrangement from his own identity. In the *Malay Archipelago* narrative, he recalls entering a Dyak village in Borneo: 'On entering the house to which I was invited, a crowd of sixty or seventy men, women and children gathered round me, and I sat for an hour like some strange animal submitted for the first time to the gaze of an inquiring public' (52). Wallace swaps roles to become one of the creatures that in other circumstances he has hunted and observed, with a view to displaying its corpse 'to the gaze of an inquiring public'. Wallace's insight into reversal, levelling and display is important for reading another, more playful – and yet also, in its way, profoundly serious – discourse that he wrote on his experience of 'parenting' the baby orang-utan. As Peter Raby notes, this discourse was originally cast in the form of a letter to his sister (25 June 1855), but Wallace also went on to publish it as a brief article under the title of 'A New Kind of Baby' in *Chambers's Journal* for 1857.[54] Wallace also re-published the discourse in his autobiography *My Life* (1906):

> I must now tell you of the addition to my household of an orphan baby, a curious little half-nigger baby, which I have nursed now more than a month . . . I am afraid you would call it an ugly baby, for it has a dark brown skin and red hair, a very large mouth, but very pretty little hands and feet . . . It has powerful lungs, and sometimes screams tremendously, so I hope it will live.
>
> But I must tell you how I came to take charge of it. Don't be alarmed, I was the cause of the mother's death . . . I was out shooting in the jungle and saw something up a tree which I thought was a large monkey or orang-utan, so I fired at it, and down fell this little baby—in its mother's arms. What she did up in the tree of course I can't imagine, but as she ran about the branches quite easily perhaps she was a 'wild woman of the woods'; so I have preserved her skin and skeleton, and am trying to bring up her only daughter, and hope to introduce her to fashionable society at the Zoological Gardens.[55]

Martin Fichman notes that Wallace was an 'insatiable reader', that his reading included novels and other fictional genres, and that a 'fascination with literature is fundamental to his life and work'.[56] This passage breaks down the boundary between natural historical and fictional writing as well as the species barrier: the hybrid beast/human is expressed in terms of racial hybridity, and grotesque antinomies order the description ('large mouth' / 'pretty little hands and feet'). Fictional, quasi-mythic devices are used. The mother is described as 'the wild woman of the woods', the female counterpart of the mythic 'wild man of the woods' (a play on the meaning of *orang-utan*, 'man of the forest'); but shadowing this is also a sense of the madwoman in the attic released from domestic incarceration. Furthermore, a convention of romantic fiction is the imagined and parodied resolution of the narrative: the 'orphan' will grow into a heroine who will be accepted in fashionable society, except that she will do this as an object or specimen displayed in front of the patrons of the Zoological Gardens. The play on genre here is comical, whilst also exposing the monological operation of genre in more 'homely' contexts: Wallace uses the grotesque to defamiliarise a set of manners and social conventions and so probe more precisely what they are and how they work. Fiction, from the 'silver fork' novel to *Jane Eyre*, did indeed encode the rules relating to the 'display' of women in fashionable society. In this respect, Wallace's discourse works intertextually at a number of levels: it alludes to the conventions of Victorian fiction, but it also resonates in relation to Wallace's subsequent elaborations of the politics of evolutionary progress. For while Wallace was sceptical about Darwin's theory of sexual selection as applied to animals, he came to argue that women would need to be granted principal agency in the process of human sexual selection; economic independence for women would lead to men being displayed before women that only the suitable might be chosen.[57] Wallace uses the bestial-grotesque to defamiliarise, but also to analyse how things are, and, potentially, to suggest how they might be different. This, one might argue, begins to reveal the contours of a radically grotesque discourse on culture in which nineteenth-century scientific and natural historical writing were active, making the discourse curiously applicable to a wide variety of topics and contexts.

To this extent, it was another means of contesting Arnold. Arnold's culture needed its touchstones, its practical manifestations of the best that had been thought and said, in order that those who aspired to culture could read, digest and inwardly grow; 'documents with a side of modern applicability and living interest' was how he put it. Arnold made this remark in his essay on the writings of Marcus Aurelius, or 'the most beautiful figure in history' as he aestheticised the Roman emperor in his concluding contribution to *Essays in Criticism*. Aurelius may have persecuted early Christians: Arnold does not flinch from this, and justifies it on the grounds that the Christians of that era were a subversive cult, a threat to the empire in their being constituted as 'a vast secret society' comparable to the Jesuits. And yet, Arnold's Aurelius is in touch with the affective and emotional kernel of Christian morality; moreover, in his veneration of nature in the *Meditations*, Arnold sees in Aurelius an early anticipation of Wordsworth: 'Figs, when they are quite ripe, gape open . . .[they] have a beauty in them . . . a deeper insight with respect to things . . . in the universe'.[58]

Carlo Ginzburg has offered a different reading of Aurelius' legacy. Ginzburg focuses instead on those moments from the *Meditations* in which the familiar is rendered unfamiliar in almost riddle-like form: 'This purple robe, but sheep hairs dyed with the blood of a shellfish . . . gold and silver, what are they, but as the more gross faeces of the earth'. As Ginzburg argues, these rhetorical tactics, which stress materiality and earthiness in questioning conventions for seeing order and distributing power, entered popular culture; these later instances of the discourse are often spoken by a grotesque, beast-like man, often to a figure of authority.[59] Although Ginzburg traces the prehistory of the device of defamiliarisation to Tolstoy's horse which narrates its own story, it is credible to locate Wallace's riddle-like story of the baby orang-utan (what *is* this creature?) in this tradition.

If Arnold's 'culture', descended from the classical tradition, was a proposed means by which detachment from stock habits and perceptions could be effected, then Wallace's estrangement was also grounded in a complex poetics of symbolic material, though it had descended via a different genealogy, one that sought to re-think social relations on the basis of the strangest that has been thought and said, routed through a distinctively materialist aesthetic. Ironically, Wallace's mature career as an evolutionary speculator on consciousness and spiritualism would lead him to defend human distinctiveness, and to urge against breaching the barrier differentiating humans and beasts. Much to Darwin's distress, even by 1869 Wallace had removed human evolution from the operations of an ever more stringently conceived natural selection, restoring to the former a sense of 'Overruling Intelligence'.[60] And yet, Wallace's early science and his various travel writings produced symbolic material – literary material – that extended the reach of evolutionary theory through a materialist aesthetic. It remains to outline the way in which these materialisms were framed and contested through the discourses on evolution and culture espoused by late Victorian intellectuals, who used them to fashion imagined relationships to audiences, the intellectual field, and the symbolic materials with which they worked.

4. EVOLUTION, AESTHETICS AND THE SYMBOL: CULTURED
MECHANISTIC MATERIALISMS IN THE PIT, BOX AND GALLERY

Reviewing Darwin's *Origin* in 1859, Huxley urged the readers of *Macmillan's Magazine* to wait patiently while scientific expertise settled the questions posed by evolutionary theory. But as the argument between Wallace and Darwin illustrates, little was settled and in practice, newer and ever more 'controverted' questions about science and culture were put before audiences and readers. The question 'what is materialism?' was posed by Leslie Stephen on Sunday, 21 March 1886 in South Place Chapel, London. Stephen's act of intellectual reflection was, following in the tradition of Huxley, a kind of 'lay sermon', a means for advancing self-culture and a symbolic substitute for Christian worship. It adopted the tactics of Baxter Langley's 'Sunday Evenings for the People'. But South Place Chapel, the gathering place of the South Place Religious Society, also invoked a longer established radical tradition originally defined and espoused by W. J. Fox's Unitarianism (see chapter 1).

The lectures which were delivered at South Place explored the relations between culture, materialism and models of intellectual authority. Stephen defines materialism as 'the doctrine that matter is the sole ultimate reality', an answer inseparable from the counter-response urged by its mirror image, idealism, 'the opposite doctrine, that mind is the sole ultimate reality'. Stephen traces this opposition to the historical field of 'letters', and the 'most famous historical representatives of these two theories in English literature', Thomas Hobbes and Bishop Berkeley; in so doing, he advances a definition of materialism that is metaphysical.[61] But Stephen was aware that arguments about 'materialism' during the nineteenth century had passed 'from the philosophic arena into the more heated regions of theological controversy'; indeed, 'they have spread yet further and got into the hands of the gentlemen who expound theories of the universe in articles and lectures'.[62] Stephen added that 'the astonishing power and originality' of Hobbes's materialism had only recently been surpassed by the rise of Darwinism.

Stephen's focus on Darwinian materialism and the gentlemen who expounded it grew out of a context of keynote lectures and articles that sought to re-frame the relations between culture and science in the 1870s and 1880s. John Tyndall's *Belfast Address*, being his Presidential Address to the British Association for the Advancement of Science of 1874, prompted wide-ranging and often heated discussion among churchmen. Tyndall responded by projecting science as a special form of mental cultivation; Catholic youth would be 'leavened . . . however gradually . . . [by] its inward modifying power'.[63] In his exposition of the materialist gradualism of Darwin's theory of natural selection, Tyndall focused on Darwin's example of the various bee-hive colonies, and the variable architectural instincts that had been selected to produce different species of bees.[64] Darwin's bees fascinated public apologists for his science, and in his 'Prolegomena' to 'Evolution and Ethics' (1893/4), Huxley, as we have seen (in my Introduction), would also remark on the gradations that Darwin observed between solitary and hive bees, seeing in 'the latter simply the perfection of an automatic mechanism, hammered out by the blows of the struggle for existence' ('Prolegomena', 25). The tendency to view living bodies as evolved 'perfect mechanisms', or collections of instruments functioning mechanically, was an important dimension of materialist argument. Huxley extended this line of thought in his own lecture to the BAAS Belfast gathering of 1874, 'On the Hypothesis that Animals are Automata and its History', which he attributed to the philosophy of Descartes, and in which he included the possibility that humans, too, were automata, distinguished by the processing of the symbol that constituted consciousness.[65]

Scientific discourse and theory reformulated the concept of the symbol, and accorded it an important but potentially variable function in the processing of consciousness: Tyndall's *Address* asserts that consciousness of the external world was inscribed in symbolic form as a result of the 'myriad blows . . . upon the organism, the depth of the impression depending on the number of the blows'. While Tyndall modelled a cause and effect account of symbolic inscription, Herbert Spencer's notion of 'symbolic conceptions' in *First Principles* (1862) on the other hand mixed the traditional idea of the symbol as substitutive denotation, with the more recent sense, from mathematics and chemistry, of the symbol as a convention of notation. For Spencer, 'symbolic conceptions' marked the point at which established conventions of representation substituted for the hard data of empirical cognition once the limits of the latter had been reached. This led him to acknowledge that within every religious and scientific concept was an element of fiction-making, and a space of representation not fully controllable by its writer.[66] Tyndall's *Address* itself was a blow-by-blow bid to re-make the history of philosophy through the language of mechanistic materialism.

Thus symbols could be used to fictionalise, or make traditions, and in the process contest established ones. Tyndall's *Address* also alluded to Descartes's account of the machinate body, but placed it in the same tradition of materialist, atomistic thought as Giordano Bruno and, from the classical tradition, Epicurus, Democritus, Lucretius and Empedocles. In fact, Empedocles emerges as a contested figure from the classical tradition: tragically depicted in Matthew Arnold's suicide poem 'Empedocles on Etna' (1852) lamenting the dawn of modernity and the 'dialogue of the mind with itself', in Tyndall's *Address* Empedocles' theory of love and hate among atoms becomes the original 'partial enunciation' of 'the doctrine of the "survival of the fittest"'.[67] Tyndall's shift indicates how the dialogic contestation of resonant symbolic capital was at the centre of the argument about the reach of materialist philosophy.

Science's re-articulation of 'culture' and its Arnoldian reference points was extended by figures who contributed to the South Place Lectures. These included the medical journalist Andrew Wilson's *Leisure Time Studies: Chiefly Biological*, a collection of essays which opens with a chapter that originated as a lecture entitled 'Science-Culture for the Masses'. 'Culture', according to Wilson's definition, comprises the 'argument . . . or the means whereby we form large-minded, liberal, and, at the same time, correct, ideas about the universe, and of the relation of ourselves to our neighbors'.[68] John Robertson's discourse tackled the question of 'Culture and Action', and so was a riposte to Arnold, whose account of culture specifically excluded 'men of action' from its sphere of activity. Robertson formulated a wide-ranging, democratic account of cultural activity, arguing that 'culture is no more confined to the study of books than to the use of the microscope or the telescope or geological hammer, the artist's pencil or the musician's instrument; the essence of it, scientifically speaking, being the doing of something which expands the powers and opens the way to new activities'.[69] Robertson's thinking is legitimated by the etymological appeal to 'the root meaning of the word' that J. A. Symonds would later appeal to in 1893; for 'culture is simply the tillage or cultivation of our faculties'.[70] Reaching for the 'root meaning of the word', evolutionists returned culture to its materialist roots.

This was the case in Grant Allen's work. Allen sought the origins of 'the general history of human culture', which he traced in 'The Origin of Cultivation' (1894), published in *The Fortnightly Review*. Allen goes to one of the roots of the culture concept in constructing an, in effect fictional, speculative narrative about the inductive powers of early humans: how did they acquire knowledge of plant and crop growing? In offering an explanation, Allen returns to the concern that had preoccupied Wordsworth: human death rites. Allen contends that the minimal condition for cultivating the earth is turning it over, amounting to unconscious tillage, and he surmises that early humans would have done this when they buried their dead. As they scattered the tilled earth of the grave with offerings of animal meats, fruits and berries, cultivation would have been further enhanced by unconscious fertilisation and seeding. The savage later notices that a luxuriant crop has been produced, but 'he knows nought of seeds, and manures and soils; he would at once conclude, after his kind, that the dreaded and powerful ghost in the barrow, pleased with the gifts of meat and seeds offered to him, had repaid those gifts in kind'.[71] Culture thus had its origins in vegetation cults, ghost worship and the symbolic prac- tices that fashioned knowledge out of both. As Herbert Spencer argued in his speculative account of primitive subjectivity in *Principles of Sociology* (1876), the ghost was precisely a symbolic representation designed to solve breakdowns in the framework of primitive epistemology: savage dreams were 'narrations . . . in imperfect language' generating images of a double life that could only be explained through stories about ghostly, intangible presences. Spencer's 'narrations . . . in imperfect language' were, in a sense, primitive versions of the 'symbolic conceptions' he saw at work in modern scientific speculation.[72]

In another South Place lecture in November 1885, the eugenicist Karl Pearson fashioned Christianity as a materially supersensuous arrangement of symbols and narratives that had failed to absorb a properly philosophical culture; early Christianity, he stated, 'unlike modern freethought . . . was not the outcome of the knowledge and culture of its age. In its neglect of the great Greek systems of philosophy, it was a return to blind emotion, even barbarism.'[73] Christianity is a *cultish* survival sustaining the bonds that hold societies together:

In the earliest form of human society, impulses to certain lines of conduct are transmitted from generation, either by direct contact between old and young, or possibly by some hereditary principle. Upon these impulses the stability of the society depends, and they have been evolved in the race-struggle for existence. Looked at from an outside point of view, they build the social habit and the current morality of that stage of society. Without them the society would decay, and yet no man in that primitive state understands how they have arisen. Viewed on the one side as indispensable to the race, on the other appearing to have no origin in human reason and human power, it is not to be wondered at, if we find morality in these early forms of civilization associated with the superhuman. To give the strongest possible sanction to morality – for on that sanction race-existence depends – it is associated with the supersensuous, it becomes part of a religious cult.[74]

Pearson articulates a tension at the heart of evolutionary accounts of culture: religious sentiment, though the property of irrational, primitive cults, was still necessary for 'race-struggle' and 'race-existence'.[75] Accordingly, in reading the symbolic manifestations of popular sentiment, or 'popular culture', there was a need for authoritative intellectual guidance that could align the different 'survivals' comprising 'culture' with their correct etymological genealogies; that is to say, the origins of 'culture' not only in the material practice of cultivation, but also its material embodiment in cultish practices of worship. Biology, psychology and sociology would constitute the grounds of a new secular religion of sympathy to be preached by intellectuals who could identify the legitimate basis, and the appropriate symbolic expression, of evolving social bonds.

Pearson's lecture was revealingly entitled 'Enthusiasm of the MarketPlace and of the Study', a title which encoded the discriminations that divided the intellectual field into the imagined spaces reserved for so-called lowly and refined pursuits, as well as the styles of intellectual self-culture that would be found in each. Pearson acknowledged the importance of 'popular' artifacts and practices for understanding a nation's political character; 'more may often be learned from folk-songs and broadsheets than from a whole round of foreign campaigns'. And yet, these artifacts have to be read and understood in the correct way, for knowledge is disseminated by 'two types of character', or agency, which Pearson classifies as 'the man of the market place and the man of the study'.[76] The man of the study – a disinterested intellectual, a proponent of 'freethought' – is a member of a minority, whereas the men of the marketplace, 'men of words, prophets and orators may be picked up at every street corner'.[77] The emphasis on disinterested minorities indicates the way in which Pearson works with the categories that Arnold had used to produce his discourse on 'culture'; but it is also important to acknowledge the persistence of Coleridgean preoccupations, from the concern with words to the horror of their debasement in the marketplace. Words, their dissemination and interpretation, are a central problem for Pearson, for 'vague generalities', such as human rights and individual liberty, 'abound in the market place'.

Pearson's determination to divide the intellectual field into imagined discriminatory spaces was shared with Leslie Stephen. Continuing his exploration of the reception of materialism in his last published work, a critical biography of Thomas Hobbes for the English Men of Letters series (1904), Stephen would note the way in which Hobbes's original audiences had been categorised in the seventeenth century through a theatrical metaphor. Hobbes's followers appropriated him from either the pit, the gallery or the box: 'The pit was filled by the sturdy sinners who welcomed him as an ally against morality in general; the gallery by fine gentlemen anxious to show their wit; and the boxes by men of gravity and reputation whose approval was more cautious'.[78] This theatrical metaphor could be trans-posed to produce a map of the intellectual field in which the question of materialism had joined forces with evolutionary discourse. In 1886 from the podium at South Place, Stephen imagined that he was arbitrating on the question of materialism from the position of 'the box', or that place occu-pied by 'men of gravity and reputation whose approval was more cautious'. While such men were no longer born aristocrats, men such as Stephen and Pearson saw themselves as members of an aristocracy of intellect. At the same time, the presence of George Jacob Holyoake as a South Place lecturer in 1886 reminded the audience of the moments in the 1830s and 1840s when 'sturdy sinners' had appropriated Lamarckian materialism for radical ends.[79] Stephen's 'What is Materialism?' could be said to illustrate the way in which the intellectuals in the 'box' had wrested materialism and transmutation away from 'the pit', making them morally respectable.

However, a focus on the disseminators of wit in the gallery produces a more complex assessment of the operation of Pearson's market and Stephen's imagined discriminations. Samuel Butler, the subject of the next chapter, in one sense appears to be the embodiment of the gentleman anxious to show his wit, something he achieved first and foremost through his satire on Darwinism, *Erewhon* (1871). Butler appeared to retain a gentlemanly independence of the market; he often had his heterodox books on evolu-tionary theory published at his own expense. He was also keen to differ-entiate his place in the field from the place occupied by Grant Allen, a prolific journalist and reviewer of other people's books. Turning down the opportunity to review Allen's biography of Darwin (1885), Butler remarked, 'Besides I do not review books. I belong to the reviewed classes, not to the reviewers.'[80] However, while Butler despised Allen's marketability, he also lamented the fact that his own books had to be independently financed in the first instance because of poor sales, and could see that the 'men of science' whose orthodoxy he disputed were in fact shaping a kind of market in intellectual authority, and injuring the sales of his books both by a failure to acknowledge them, and by treating them disparagingly when noticed.[81]

Butler was by no means alone in being ambivalently placed. Grant Allen's career highlights the fallacious thinking that Pearson produced in rigidly separating the virtuously disinterested study from the debased marketplace. Allen was a journalist, novelist and scholar who profited by exploiting the intellectual divisions of labour marked out by the increasingly zoned and specialised markets of the late nineteenth-century intellectual field. Allen was a successful popular novelist, author of scandalous successes such as *The*

Woman Who Did (1895), his contribution to the sexual politics of the New Woman question. But Allen also wrote a vast number of articles for periodicals, ranging from the middle-brow *Cornhill* to the more intellectually self-conscious *Fortnightly*, and again to more specialised 'field' publications such as *Mind* (the 'house journal' of psychology).[82] He also wrote for a scholarly market; he published treatises on science, particularly the evolutionary life sciences, aesthetics, ethnography and comparative religion, and, after the model of J. G. Frazer, whose monumental work of anthropology *The Golden Bough* started to appear in 1890, translated classical texts to advance ethnographic topics of debate (Allen translated the *Attis* of Catullus in an attempt to explain the origin of tree worship).

Allen also jousted with Matthew Arnold. In his essay on 'Evolution' for the *Cornhill* in 1888, Allen recognised the rhetorical role that journalistic accounts of evolutionary science played, and that these contests were waged using symbolically resonant linguistic capital. Intervening in a quarrel between Arnold and Spencer about the meaningfulness of the language of evolutionary theory, Allen defends the legitimacy of the language of evolution against Arnold's condescension in *God and the Bible* (1875):

> In Mr Spencer's perspicuous phrase, evolution . . . is a change from the homogeneous to the heterogeneous, from the incoherent to the coherent, and from the indefinite to the definite condition. Difficult words at first to apprehend, no doubt, and therefore to many people, as to Mr Matthew Arnold, very repellent, but full of meaning, lucidity and suggestiveness, if only we take the trouble fairly and squarely to understand them.[83]

In fact, Allen entered into dialogue with the writings of what would come to assume a central position in Williams's 'culture and society' tradition. In his earliest pieces of journalism on the aesthetics of design and lowly material objects, such as a primitive drinking vessel made from a coconut, Allen cited work by the 'teacher' figures of Ruskin, Morris and Pater.[84]

Allen wrote an evolutionary defence of the centrality of the aesthetic to culture and in doing so appropriated a key phrase from Wilde's *The Picture of Dorian Gray* (1891), and a sentiment from Pater's deeply controversial 'Conclusion' to *The Renaissance* (1873).[85] Allen's 'The New Hedonism' appeared in the *Fortnightly Review* in 1894, and in it he contrasts hedonism with what he describes as 'the old asceticism', which is exemplified in 'the gospel according to Thomas Carlyle – that dismal gospel of a Christless Calvinism'. For Allen, Carlyle's moribund gospel is exemplified in a passage from the famous chapter on 'The Everlasting Yea' (Book II, ch. 10) in *Sartor Resartus* (1831): 'What Act of Legislature was there that *thou* shouldst be Happy? . . . What if thou wert born and predestined not to be happy but to be unhappy? Art thou nothing other than a Vulture, then, that fliest through the universe seeking after somewhat to *eat*, and shrieking dolefully because carrion enough is not given thee?' Allen adds a gloss; 'Vile words, which a vulture might indeed be ashamed of!'[86] Raymond Williams was later to observe that *culture* rhymes with few English words, excepting *sepulture* and *vulture*; in Allen's essay, 'culture' seems initially to function as the binary opposite of Carlyle's metaphoric vulture.[87] If Carlyle imagines the vulturised human being spiritually adrift in a materialist universe scavenging for carrion, Allen presents a fecund materialist vision in the tradition of Erasmus Darwin, Lamarck, and latterly Spencer: an evolving universe incrementally advancing self-development through 'culture', for 'every unit of gain in the aesthetic sense, every diffusion in a wider taste for poetry, for art, for music, for decoration, is to the good of humanity. What measures our distance above the beasts that perish consists in these three things – ethics, intellect, the sense of beauty.' 'Culture' is defined as the property that 'measures our distance above the beasts that perish' (382); it has thus supplanted immortality to become an evolutionary measure of the difference between humans and beasts. Indeed, Allen remarks that the religion which once authorised the concept of immortality has become 'the shadow of which culture is the substance. The one pretends to be what the other is in reality. It will be the task of the new hedonism to restore culture to the place usurped by religion' (382). Yet the boundary that culture marks between humans and beasts is not absolute but an evolving, shifting one. Allen challenges assumptions about relations between the categories of 'higher' and 'lower passions' when he argues, on the basis of Darwin's theory of sexual selection, that there is 'a persistent thread of connection between the aesthetic sense in man and in animals'. For the 'sexual instinct' is common to both, and it is that latter that is the origin of the aesthetic, or 'whatever is purest and most beautiful within us' (384). For Allen, culture and aesthetics are felt first and foremost in the sensory motors of the living body.

Allen's aesthetic education had been shaped by a period of employment as a colonial educator. Before his career in writing and journalism, in 1873 Allen took up the post of Professor of Mental and Moral Philosophy at the Government College, Spanish Town, Jamaica. This was less than ten years after Governor Eyre's brutal suppression of the rebellion at Morant Bay, and Allen, as a radical liberal, was no celebrant of Britain's expanding imperial possessions during the closing decades of the century, as examples of his journalism demonstrate.[88] And yet, colonial encounter sharpened his aesthetic education: the Utilitarian Allen argued that the experience of a tropical colony was felt first in the body, delivered by the pain of insect stings and the sun's heat.[89] Allen reflected on sensations experienced by 'exiles to our tropical dependencies' in his philosophical work entitled *Physiological Aesthetics* (1877):

> I have seen views of the tropics in which I could intellectually recognise all the elements of beauty, so that I gave a verbal adhesion to the proposition that they were lovely, while at the same time they utterly failed to provide in me the faintest thrill of pleasure. Photographs of the same places, seen now under an English sky . . . strike me as exquisitely beautiful.[90]

Allen's philosophy proposes to explain those differences in taste manifest as 'the Aesthetic Feelings' by means of a universal evolutionary framework which posits a relationship between organism, environment and adaptation founded on difference and variation. 'Every organism', he argues, 'in proportion to the completeness of its adaptation, energetically resists any act which interferes with its efficiency as a working machine; and such interferences are known subjectively as Pains.'[91] Thus, the white, northern European body, adapted to a cool climate, resists its subjection to painful tropical heat brought about by colonial displacement. But its resistance has to be translated into the symbolic language of subjectivity; for Allen, terms such as 'beautiful' and 'ugly' are 'mere symbols', and 'the Aesthetic feelings' are 'an intermediate link between the bodily senses and the higher emotions'.[92] Accordingly, the body responds, or malfunctions, as a machine in the first instance. But as Allen observes in his recollection of his response to the 'beautiful' photograph of the tropics, the machine can be repaired by the mediated symbol. As the next chapter will argue, Samuel Butler's sense of the symbol in culture, and his distinctively playful sense of the place of the machinate human body in evolutionary debate, were shaped by colonial encounters.[93]

    If Leslie Stephen's theatrical 'pit' and 'box' were the imaginary spaces that marked the distance that mechanistic materialism had to travel in order to become respectable, one can conclude by recalling the resurgent power of the 'gallery' as a symbolic space in the *fin de siècle*, and the fact that aesthetic 'culture' was contested by the men of science in the box, and the aesthete wits in the gallery. Stephen makes this connection when he remarks on a certain semantic inflection of

> materialism . . . which comes with the development of luxury, that which finds a vent in mere aesthetic gratification . . . [This] implies isolation from the hopes and fears of mankind at large, and a power of treating even the sympathies to which practical application is refused as merely a means of dreamy self-indulgence. All true moral feeling, briefly, rests on the growth of altruism, or identification of ourselves with the greater organisation to which we belong.[94]

Stephen associates luxury with 'mere aesthetic gratification', or hedonism, and these in turn with immoral sentiments that find no place for altruism. Oscar Wilde could be said to have been playing to the gallery when, in January 1889, he published his dialogue 'The Decay of Lying' in the periodical *The Nineteenth Century*. The piece would parody, but still foreground, attitudes about the relations between sensuous hedonism and ideas of culture, modes of discrimination and senses of cultish belonging and veneration to which they could give rise. As Vivian describes to Cyril his project for reviving a magazine, he announces that this has been initiated by the 'elect.' 'Whom do you mean', Cyril asks, 'by 'the elect''? Vivian replies: 'Oh the Tired Hedonists, of course. It is a club to which I belong. We are supposed to wear faded roses in our buttonholes when we meet, and to have a sort of cult for Domitian.'[95] For Stephen, the dangers of materialism were highlighted in the existence of minority aesthetic cults that promoted 'a means of dreamy self-indulgence'; in 1894 T. H. Huxley would express the same anxiety about ennui in 'Evolution and Ethics' in his account of the development of the 'intellectual field' as a two-millennia-old 'hothouse' of culture (see my Introduction). In order to hold such dangers at bay, Stephen invokes a literature that would promote sympathy and altruism. He approvingly cites Wordsworth, 'the greatest of poetical moralists', whose moral correctness is exemplified in the lines 'we live by Admiration, Hope and Love', 'And even as these are well and wisely fixed / In dignity of being we ascend.' The lines that Stephen selects are taken from *The Excursion*, the fourth book, entitled 'Despondency Corrected' (ll. 761–4).[96] Thus Wordsworth's poem of 1814, which had served the intellectual elite of science in the 1830s and 1840s, remained a touchstone text for the intellectuals who made evolutionary materialism respectable. And Wordsworth remained an iconic figure of reference. John Tyndall's *Belfast Address* concluded with the closing lines of 'Tintern Abbey', with its invocation of 'The still, sad music of humanity', and, italicised by Tyndall, its identification of *'A motion and a spirit, that impels / All thinking things, all objects of all thought, / And rolls through all things.'*[97]

Yet the animating 'spirit' to which Wordsworth's lines appealed could be a 'counter-spirit', as Wordsworth himself had feared in the unpublished 'Essay Upon Epitaphs'. Stephen did not always find that Wordsworth provided grounds for correcting despondency and intellectual unease. When Stephen wrote the introduction to his *History of English Thought in the Eighteenth Century* (1876) he found his own conviction about the necessity of evolutionary cultural progress towards reason challenged by the poet's wish that he were still 'a Pagan suckled in some creed outworn'.[98] Stephen recalled this line from Wordsworth's sonnet 'The world is too much with us', published in 1807, and significantly juxtaposed, under Wordsworth's 'mutual illustration' principle of 1827, the science-affirming sonnet 'A volant tribe of bards', lines from which appeared on the masthead of *Nature*. The 'world is too much' for the speaker because he is enmeshed in cycles of acquisition and expenditure ('getting and spending'):

> . . . we lay waste our powers:
> Little we see in Nature that is ours:
> We have given our hearts away, a sordid boon!

The cycles of exchange that waste human power lead to a more profound and terminal loss: alienation of the heart from nature. In representing lost nature, the poet draws upon the kind of materially sensuous imagery that Stephen would later note in his account of the 'survivals' that underpinned 'vulgar' Christian beliefs: Stephen used contemporary anthropologists of animism to point to analogies between 'savage' beliefs about the after-life, and the pictures and addresses revered by 'ignorant Catholics and Protestants' that are suffused with 'sensuous imagery' implying 'the materialistic nature of the soul'.[99] Wordsworth writes of 'the Sea that bares her bosom to the moon', anticipating the image of 'suckling' that is so crucial to articulating the Pagan desire expressed in the sestet:

> — Great God! I'd rather be
> A Pagan suckled in a creed outworn;
> So might I, standing on this plesant lea,
> Have forlorn glimpses that would make me less forlorn;
> Have sight of Proteus rising from the sea;
> Or hear old Triton blow his wreathèd horn.[100]

Pagan desire inhabits *The Excursion* along with the 'higher' altruistic thoughts that Stephen praised in his discourse on materialism of 1886. A later generation of intellectuals, caught between the currents of evolutionary theory, discourses of social order and aestheticism, had to come to terms with the complexities of Wordsworth's poetry and its philosophic and discursive legacy.[101]

Walter Pater, in his essay on Coleridge for the *Westminster Review* in 1866, also commented on Wordsworth. Citing the 'Preface' to *The Excursion* ('. . . how exquisitely, too, / The external world is fitted to the mind'), Pater observed that Wordsworth was 'distinguished by a joyful and penetrative conviction of the existence of certain latent affinities between nature and the human mind' which led him to 'a reflective, but altogether unformulated' representation of 'the transitions of nature'.[102] Eight years later, in 1874 (two years before Stephen's reflections on Wordsworth's pagan rejection of modernity in his *History of English Thought*), Pater wrote specifically about Wordsworth in an essay for *The Fortnightly Review*. For Pater, Wordsworth's poetry was preoccupied with 'that physical connection of our nature with the actual lime and clay of the soil'. The poetry was, moreover, 'like a 'survival',

in the peculiar intellectual temperament of a man of letters at the end of the eighteenth century, of that primitive condition, which some philosophers have traced in the general history of human culture, wherein all outward objects alike, including even the works of men's hands, were believed to be endowed with animation, and the world was 'full of souls' – that mood in which old Greek gods were first begotten, and which had many strange aftergrowths.[103]

Such 'strange aftergrowths' of primitive animist thought would be artificially cultivated in what Huxley styled a 'hothouse' – his image, from 'Evolution and Ethics', of the volatile field of culture. Pater's 'strange aftergrowths' would find a place in the late products of the aesthetic movement, in particular Edmund Gosse's *Father and Son*, a compelling story of self-culture which is also a classic narrative of the confrontation between religion and science. As the final chapter will argue, Gosse's 'hybrid' text produced estranging literary effects out of the supplements that were generated by the exchanges between scientific and artistic discourse. Samuel Butler's work was, in its own day, considered as somewhat marginal to the dominant trends in science and art, having been spun initially from materials received and read in the colonial margins of New Zealand. Yet, Butler's interrogation of habits and the conventions of scientific, religious and artistic discourse enabled his 'marginal' writings to produce some new and inventive symbolic 'machines', as the following, penultimate chapter will show.

CHAPTER 5

Samuel Butler's symbolic offensives:
colonies and mechanical devices in the margins of evolutionary writing

I. CULTIVATING THE SINS OF WRITING IN THE FIELD OF EVOLUTIONARY SPECULATION

When contemplating the gentlemen of science in Leslie Stephen's metaphoric theatrical 'box', Samuel Butler inclined towards a hermeneutic of suspicion. Writing in 1890 about scientific exposition in the context of what he held to be the theory that 'deadlocked' progress in evolutionary thought – the theory of evolution by natural selection, elaborated by Charles Darwin and Alfred Russel Wallace – Butler remarked that:

we want to know who is doing his best to help us, and who is only trying to make us help him, or to bolster up the system in which his interests are vested. There is nothing that will throw more light upon these points than the way in which a man behaves towards those who have worked in the same field with himself, and, again, than his style.[1]

In looking for the place where the sources of this suspicion were acted out, Butler appealed to the concept of the field; writers worked in fields of intellectual endeavour, synchronically and historically. From the early 1860s, Butler found himself working in the same field as Charles Darwin. In writing about evolution, Butler came to the view that Darwin had failed properly to acknowledge the contributions of those earlier evolutionists who had shaped the common speculative endeavour, in particular Erasmus Darwin, Buffon and Lamarck. Crucially, for Butler, style marked out a writer's distinctive and resonant place in the field. Butler also formed the view that Darwin and his supporters – notably Huxley and Tyndall – took neither the style nor the substance of Butler's writings on evolution seriously.

Butler published *Life and Habit* in 1877. It was not his first foray into evolutionary speculation; the satiric *Erewhon* (1870), and the playful writings that led to it, had marked him out as a distinctive voice, making him one of Leslie Stephen's 'wits'; indeed, likeness and distinctiveness preoccupied Butler, who was intrigued by the fact that one of his name-sakes was a seventeenth-century satiric poet who had mocked scientific learning (his other namesake was a bishop, his grandfather). But *Life and Habit* was his first avowedly 'serious' attempt at evolutionary theory, even if humour inflected the style, and a humour that was hard to control at that; Butler observed that 'the most perfect humour and irony is generally quite unconscious'.[2] And yet, Butler feared that, in his book, he had perhaps failed to treat a fellow fieldworker – older, authoritative and deserving of much greater veneration – with appropriate respect. Butler was on friendly terms with the Darwin family (Butler's grandfather had taught the young Charles Darwin at Shrewsbury School), and he wrote to Francis Darwin fearing that he might have been less than respectful to his father's writing in the *Origin*: 'In only one passage have I been disrespectful – that is when I say that 'domestic productions' may mean anything *from a baby* to an apple dumpling; but I could not resist, and can only say that it was not I that did it, but sin that was working in me.'[3] For Butler, writing is a process in which agencies other than the writer play a role; or, more precisely, an awareness of those other agencies makes it hard to say exactly who or what the writing subject, the 'I', is. Humour and irony can be quite unconscious. 'Sin' drives Butler to make light of Darwin's 'domestic productions'. To be precise, Butler's sinful humour led him to this:

Mr. Darwin tells us, in the preface to his last edition [6th] of the "Origin of Species," that Lamarck was partly led to his [erroneous] conclusions by the analogy of domestic productions. It is rather hard to say what these words imply; they may mean anything from a baby to an apple dumpling, but if they imply that Lamarck drew inspiration from the gradual development of the mechanical inventions of man, and from the progress of man's ideas, I would say that of all sources this would be the safest and the most fertile from which to draw.[4]

In fact, Butler was citing Darwin's 'Historical Sketch', added to the sixth edition of the *Origin*. This is significant because the 'Sketch' represented Darwin's only attempt to 'place' his own theoretical distinctiveness in the historical field of evolutionary speculation – the one departure from the blindness towards his predecessors that Butler would allege against Darwin. It is also significant because Butler focuses on Darwin's somewhat negative evaluation of Lamarck's reliance on the analogy from 'domestic produc-tions', or the fruits of cultivation. Of course, this was precisely the analogy that Darwin would fashion to develop his own theoretical insight into 'natural selection', if only to stress, as Tyndall put it in another context in his *Belfast Address*, that 'Nature in her productions does not imitate the technic of man.'⁵ Butler of course contests this, contending that the cumulative effects of the 'mechanical inventions of man' do indeed imitate the processes of gradual development in nature, making it the key to his Lamarckian view of evolution. To arrive at this point, Butler focuses on the vagueness of 'domestic productions', humorously reflecting on the range that such a generality might cover, from the 'technic' that generates the apple dumpling to the domestic affections that produce a baby.

And yet, Butler's point is to draw the reader's attention to the ambiguous, slippery ground that is covered by the concept of cultivation. It is significant that *Life and Habit* begins with detailed reflections on the advanced 'arts' in which humans can be cultivated – music, writing, reading – and yet still be unconscious of the 'habit' that they have internalised to enable them to perform the art. To that extent, such arts are acquired and developed in a similar manner to the 'natural' properties or instinctual drives that lead to walking and talking. The 'cultivation' of such knowledge about the slippery interface between cultivation and instinct has the capacity to be, above all, critical and estranging; Butler contends that 'Cultivation will breed in any man a certainty of the uncertainty even of his most assured convictions.'⁶ As this chapter will argue, in contesting Charles Darwin's version of evolutionary theory Samuel Butler devised a set of insights into 'culture' as a symbolic practice of investigation that humorously, but critically, interrogated received accounts of human sovereignty and power relations, particularly as manifest in the darker practices of colonisation.

Samuel Butler and Charles Darwin were initially brought together by a shared experience of cultivation in colonial territories. Butler, having lost his faith and abandoned his career path to the church, left England to farm sheep in the Canterbury Settlement of New Zealand. The Canterbury Settlement was founded on a programme of land acquisition: waste land was acquired by the church and sold to farmer colonists. The purchase money was to be used to build roads and, among other things, to form a religious and educational fund (*Memoir*, 1, 72). When Darwin first became aware of Butler's writings about the *Origin* in 1865 he responded positively to Butler's self-image as a colonist sheep farmer. 'with your rare powers of writing you might make a very interesting work descriptive of a colonist's life in New Zealand' (*Memoir*, 1, 125). Butler's new life clearly recalled to Darwin his excursions in New Zealand and Australia when travelling on the *Beagle* in the 1830s. Darwin thought that Butler's article was 'remarkable for being published in a Colony exactly 12 years old, in which it might have been thought that only material interests would have been regarded' (*Memoir*, 1, 100). Darwin was struck by the presence of culture in print where the

exclusive cultivation of the land and sheep might more reasonably have
been expected. In the *Journal of Researches* Darwin had worried that a life
filled with nothing but sheep might kill conversation, or that a deficient
culture would diffuse from the higher classes to the lower; he noted of
New South Wales that 'the whole population, poor and rich, are bent on
acquiring wealth: amongst the higher orders, wool and sheep grazing form
the constant subjects of conversation' (*Journal* 1845, 421).

Samuel Butler had in fact already written the work that Darwin urged
him to write, *A First Year in Canterbury Settlement*; in that work, characteristically, Butler saw a different kind of culture, evident in the everyday
language of the colonial sheep farmers, which dissolved the boundaries of
human identity, so that 'I soon discovered that a person's sheep are himself. If his sheep are clean, he is clean. He does not wash his *sheep* before
shearing, but *he* washes.'[7] This led Butler to the further re-arrangement
of conceptual boundaries that sought to shift received perspectives on cultivation and food consumption. Butler mused in his imaginative reverie
on evolution, *Erewhon*: 'If it seems to us that the plant kills and eats a fly
mechanically, may it not seem to the plant that a man must kill and eat
a sheep mechanically?'[8] The emergence in Butler's writing of this concern
with the re-configuration of conventional boundaries, and role of devices
and machines in effecting it, is important, but it is first necessary to say
something about Butler's sense of propriety in the matter of writing, and
how he passed in his own mind from being a sinner towards Darwin, to
one sinned against by Darwin.

Samuel Butler's response to Darwin's writing was, the story goes, initially rich and imaginative, with the richness seemingly culminating in
Erewhon. Thereafter, it declined: Butler's subsequent forays into evolutionary speculation, and his quarrels with Charles Darwin, can seem like dead
ends in the history of writing about evolution. Gillian Beer has remarked
on how 'Butler's creative response to Darwin is . . . complicated, and to
some extent limited, by his preoccupation with the plagiarism he imputed
to Darwin.'[9] Strictly speaking, Butler accused Charles Darwin of failing
properly to acknowledge the late eighteenth-century 'sources' of evolutionary theory. In 1879 Butler published *Evolution Old and New*, a comparison
between the evolutionary theories of Buffon, Erasmus Darwin, Lamarck
and Charles Darwin. The work located the later Darwin's writings historically in a transforming field of speculation structured by lines of opposition
and forbidden combinations originating in formations of theological and
philosophical discourse, something recognised in Butler's quotation from
Geoffroy St Hilaire: '"whoever," says this author, "holds the doctrine of

final causes, will, if he is consistent, hold also that of the immutability of species; and again, the opponent of the one doctrine will oppose the other also."[10] In fact, the dispute between Butler and Charles Darwin really turned on either acknowledging, or failing to acknowledge, the sophisticated intellectual structures, ethics and unconscious processes driving the writing process. The dispute was multi-layered, making Butler's response less quirky than it might at first appear.

The dispute originated over the translation from the German, and publication in England, of Ernst Krause's critical study *Erasmus Darwin* (1879). Charles Darwin wrote a preface to the English translation of Krause's study, guaranteeing its accuracy; Darwin also wrote a biographical sketch of his grandfather. Samuel Butler objected to the following assessment of Erasmus Darwin's system, apparently voiced by Krause, which appeared on the final page of the work: 'to wish to revive it at the present day, as has been seriously attempted, shows a weakness of thought and a mental anachronism which no one can envy'.[11] Butler objected to these words because he was the writer of the recently published *Evolution Old and New*, a work which Darwin cited in his preface to the work, and which (along with the earlier *Life and Habit*) was clearly committed to the Lamarckian purposefulness to which Erasmus Darwin had also been committed. Butler surmised that the words must allege that his own thoughts were weak and anachronistic, unless they were there in the Krause's original article, published in the German periodical *Kosmos* prior to the appearance of Butler's work. Butler could find no trace of this passage in the original, so he hypothesised that the passage must have been interpolated by Charles Darwin in an attempt to discredit a rival system of thought, and shore up his own. Butler put the charge to Darwin, who denied it. In fact, Darwin later realised that he had sent Butler's *Evolution Old and New* to Krause as the latter revised his article for English publication. Krause read it and inserted the offending phrase; W. S. Dallas translated the revised article, and Darwin's preface originally acknowledged that Krause's piece had been revised, though Darwin's acknowledgement of the revision was cut at proof stage, inadvertently. Although Darwin pieced together his oversight, he remained publicly silent on the advice of Huxley and Leslie Stephen. A lengthy and increasingly acrimonious public spat ensued; letters appeared in periodicals and newspapers, the scientific elite rallied around Darwin. The dispute had not been resolved when Darwin died in 1882. Francis Darwin made the case for innocent oversight on behalf of his dead father, but this never satisfied Butler, who pointed to what he saw as the sleight of hand at work in Darwin's original words in the preface, guaranteeing the accuracy of the Dallas translation, as though it referred to the original article. This violated 'the standard of good faith and gentlemanly conduct which should prevail among Englishmen' (*Memoir*, I, 322–8, and II, Appendix C, 'The Butler–Darwin Quarrel', 446–67, 463).

Butler's dispute with Darwin was a product of the writing process, in so far as it involved revision, translation, deletion at proof stage, publication and complex questions of authorial originality and responsibility – 'gentlemanly conduct' – which impacted on the 'worth' of the writing. If, as James Secord's work on the *Vestiges* has recently demonstrated, there is a need to attend to the publication history of evolutionary thought, and to see the disputes about evolution as bound up with the politics of writing and reading practices and questions of the status of different forms of knowledge, then Butler's dispute with Darwin, instead of being an irrelevant anachronistic dead end, becomes highly relevant.

Secord has written about geographies of reading – the way in which the complex social dynamics of place shape a reading – and the meanings of 'gentility' in the production of scientific controversy.[12] Both were at work in Butler's original reception of Darwin, as well as in their subsequent dispute. Butler's reading of Darwin's *Origin* took place in Canterbury Settlement, New Zealand. It was aided by his reading of periodicals and magazines which, as we saw in the last chapter, were important sites for the reception of Darwin's *Origin*: in a letter to *The Press* (April 1863), the newspaper which served the colony and to which he contributed his earliest writings on evolution, Butler revealed that he had read *The Saturday Review*, *Cornhill Magazine*, *Once a Week*, and *Macmillan's Magazine*, which provided evidence of the way in which 'well-educated men in England' were responding to Darwin's theory (*Canterbury Settlement*, 170).

While the Cambridge-educated Butler could defend his response to the *Origin* by citing the reading habits of educated English men back at his Canterbury Settlement readers, when he wrote to Darwin a kind of colonial deference took over. When Butler revealed his identity to Darwin in 1865 as the author of a number of articles on natural selection published in the colonial newspaper *The Press*, he feared 'you will be shocked at an appeal to the periodicals mentioned in my letter, but they form a very staple article of the bush diet, and we used to get a good deal of superficial knowledge out of them' (153). For Butler, self-culture in the 'bush' was based on a superficial diet, consuming whatever symbolic material was to hand. 'A strange life we lead here' was the verdict of the book-starved Charles John Abraham, an Evangelical Anglican clergyman who in 1850 left his teaching post at Eton to take up a position in a missionary college in Auckland, New Zealand, and part of the circle of colonial intellectuals with whom

Butler would deal.[13] Butler turned that 'strange life' into writings that play-fully engage with the discourses of evolution, Christianity and mechanical contrivance.

2. READING DARWIN AT NIGHT, WITH A DRINK: MIMICRY AND DIALOGICS

Evangelical Anglicanism was part of Butler's make-up, however critically he distanced himself from it in New Zealand. In a letter of August 1861 to a college friend Butler declared he thought he was

a Unitarian now, but don't know and won't say: as for the Trinity I cannot make head nor tail of it, and feel inclined to agree with a negro who was heard in church here the other day repeating the Athanasian creed: "the Father impossible, the Son impossible, and the Holy Ghost impossible. And yet there are not three impossibles, but one impossible". (*Memoir*, I 97)

Butler describes a scene of repetition and mimicry in which he can only report on the overheard outcomes of the established church's teaching, and these are repetitions which are not quite repetitions; for what is repeated sounds a little like, but unconsciously varies from, the orthodox word 'incomprehensible'. Butler identifies with what amounts to an unconscious parody of the mystery of the creed, in which the bluff enunciation of 'impossibility' is substituted for the mystery of 'incomprehensibility'. These questions of imitation and parody are present in Butler's reception of, and response to, Darwin's writings; they re-emerge in Butler's *Erewhon*, and his later contestation of Darwin's contribution to evolutionary theory.

Butler saw that the relationship between evolutionary theory and reli-gious belief was historically complex, and in itself a strange form of rep-etition. When Butler narrated the advance of the Simeonites, or 'Sims' at St John's College, Cambridge (an association of Evangelicals who fol-lowed the teachings of the Cambridge cleric Charles Simeon) in the semi-autobiographical *The Way of All Flesh* (published in 1903), he placed it in a chronology of 'science and faith' publication controversies. Ernest Pontifex, the hero of the novel, matriculates at the University in the year 1858, 'the last of a term during which the peace of the Church of England was singu-larly unbroken', placed as it was between the publication of the *Vestiges of Creation* (1844), and *Essays and Reviews* (1861) and Darwin's *Origin* (1859).[14] Yet, as the narrator, Overton, insists, although the Evangelical movement had become, nationally 'almost a matter of ancient history', at Cambridge the 'Sims' were raising their collective head as a repetition from the past

(215). Butler thus narrates a complex form of history; the *Vestiges* are given due weight, and if a 'Darwinian Revolution' is announced, then the narrator refers to it as a 'digression'. While Evangelicalism nationally is on the wane, in Cambridge it is strong: intellectual history is a process of simultaneities, overlaps and uneven development.

The earnest, dowdy men comprising the 'Sims' were cultivators of the spirit who were selective in whom they sought to cultivate because 'the soil of the more prosperous undergraduates was not suitable for the seed they tried to sow' (*Canterbury Settlement*, 217). For the 'Sims', the essence of Christianity resided in repeated attempts to imitate its early identity as a persecuted cult, confirmed for them when 'they were themselves . . . treated with the ridicule which they reflected proudly had been the lot of true followers of Christ in all ages' (218). In *The Way of All Flesh*, Ernest Pontifex participates in this persecution by parodying the tracts they write. In fact, Butler had actually parodied Simeonite tracts and their mission of cultivation during his residence at St John's:

How far better would it be if each man's own heart was a little University church, the pericardium a little university churchyard, wherein are buried the lust of the flesh, the pomps and vanities of this wicked world; the veins and arteries, little clergymen and bishops ministering them; and the blood a stream of soberness, temperance and chastity flowing into it. (269)

Charles Simeon's ability to minister intimately to small groups and to enquire diligently into the spiritual condition of individuals is parodied here: the entire apparatus of the church is to be inserted into the very organs of the working body to ensure the effectiveness of ministry for the individual. Indeed, bodily organs become the tools of the church in this parody of the Evangelical concern for the inward condition which additionally draws on Paley's natural-theological account of the contrivances of interior bodily design. What is also striking here is the way in which the detailed workings of the parody anticipate preoccupations and tropes that will figure in Butler's later writing, especially *Erewhon*, in those chapters entitled 'The Book of the Machines', which re-write evolutionary discourses from the colonial margins:

It is said by some that our blood is composed of infinite living agents which go up and down the highways and byways of our bodies as people in the streets of a city. When we look down from a high place upon crowded thoroughfares, is it possible not to think of corpuscles of blood travelling through veins and nourishing the heart of the town? No mention shall be made of sewers, nor of the hidden nerves which serve to communicate sensations from one part of the town's body to another; nor of the yawning jaws of the railway stations, whereby the circulation is carried directly into the heart,—which receive the venous lines, and disgorge the arterial, with an eternal pulse of people. And the sleep of a town, how life-like! with its change in the circulation. (*Erewhon*, 245–6)

In both passages, the boundaries between person, organ and contrivance are blurred, and there is a playfulness with scale as the conventionally large is reduced to the small. Such strategies can lead to a re-thinking of the human, reflecting, comparatively, on its capacities and co-dependencies:

[Man] is such a hive and swarm of parasites that it is doubtful whether his body is not more theirs than his, and whether he is anything but another kind of ant-heap after all. May not man himself become a sort of parasite upon the machines? An affectionate machine-tickling aphid? (*Erewhon*, 245)

To see the human reduced in scale to an 'ant-heap' or 'an affectionate, machine-tickling aphid' is to relativise the human, and estrange it from its own sense of superiority in the moral scale.

Butler's route to this strange perspective in New Zealand was dialogic in a number of senses. On 20 December 1862, a short anonymous article in the form of a philosophical dialogue, entitled 'Darwin on the Origin of Species', was published in *The Press*, the colonial newspaper which served Canterbury Settlement, New Zealand. The article commented on Darwin's style and method of argument. Unusually for an early newspaper comment on the *Origin*, the author of the article was aware of the importance of the theory of natural selection. In addition, he was aware of the conceptual importance of Malthus' population theory to natural selection; he went so far as to assert that the validity of this theory could be measured by any observer who had experienced life in a new colony, observing the impact of the introduction of new domestic species by colonisers (*Canterbury Settlement*, 158). Finally, the brief article turned to the question of whether the *Origin* was subversive of religion, and suggested that it was not: 'the impossibility of reconciling them must only be temporary, not real' (162). As we have seen, the article came to Darwin's approving attention at Down House, England.

Butler, on the other hand, was less sure that the dialogue was worthy of approval. Some years later, in the introduction to *Unconscious Memory* (1880), when reflecting on his dispute with Darwin and on the form in which he'd first engaged with Darwin's ideas, Butler remarked that 'a philosophical dialogue [is] . . . the most offensive form, except poetry and books of travel into so-called unknown countries, that even literature can assume'.[15] In a formulation that seems to grant literature a fugitive, lowly status ('even literature'), philosophical dialogues are peculiarly 'offensive'. 'Offensive' is of course dialogic and can be pulled in two semantic directions: it can mean repulsive, but it can also mean aggressive. Butler's initially positive response to Darwin was indeed re-shaped in the course of further dialogue and was, apparently, moved in a more attacking direction by an opposed perspective that he sought to refute.

In January 1863, an article was published in *The Press* which responded to Butler's initial piece on Darwin's *Origin*, published the previous month. The reply, again published anonymously, was entitled 'Barrel-Organs'. The writer elucidates the title with reference to Dugald Stewart's observation (in his *Dissertation on the Progress of Metaphysics*) that 'on reflecting on the repeated reproduction of ancient paradoxes by modern authors one is almost tempted to suppose that human invention is limited, like a barrel-organ, to a specific number of tunes'. Consequently, Darwin's 'invention' of the theory of transmutation by natural selection is a 'mere barrel-organ repetition' of positions that had already been written by Erasmus Darwin, Joseph Priestly, Lord Monboddo, the author of the *Vestiges*, and even Pythagoras in his doctrine of the transmigration of souls. Playfully citing the *Origin* against itself, a Pythagoran reading of the much-cited example from Darwin's chapter on instinct is advanced, so that 'Darwin's slave-making ants . . . would have been formerly Virginian cotton and tobacco growers' (164–5). The piece concludes with 'one word more about barrel-organs' and relates a bizarre anecdote about worship in a church in a 'neighbouring province' in the colony, which serves as an analogy for readerly investments in writings about evolution:

There is a church where the psalms are sung to a barrel-organ, but unfortunately the psalm tunes come in the middle of the set, and the jigs and waltzes have to be played through before the psalm can start. Just so it is with Darwinism and all similar theories. All his fantasias . . . are made to come round at last to religious questions, with which really and truly they have nothing to do; but were it not for their supposed effect upon religion, no one would waste his time reading about the possibility of polar bears swimming about and catching flies so that they at last get the fins they wish for. (166)

In a passage that focuses on one of those resonant moments from the *Origin*, it is argued that readers are compelled by spiritual need to ask religious questions concerning transmutational speculations about bears becoming whales, in the same way as members of the colonial congregation beholden to the barrel-organ are compelled by spiritual need to listen out for the psalms amidst the jigs and the waltzes. The writer of 'Barrel-Organs' makes religion the paradoxical point of evolutionary speculation: though it has nothing whatever to do with the arguments supporting evolution, religion is the only discourse that provides a meaningful framework in which to read about the transmutational 'wishes' of organisms – a notably Lamarckian formulation.

Butler confided to Darwin that the author of the 'contemptuous rejoinder' to his original dialogue had been Charles John Abraham, another educated migrant, formerly master at Eton, and by then elevated to the bishopric of Wellington; Festing Jones, Butler's biographer, identified Abraham as the author of 'Barrel-Organs'.[16] But there must be a suspicion that it was actually Butler who had been the author, penning a rejoinder to himself as it were, given the article's playful use of an image of machinery and its interest in a long intellectual history of evolutionary speculation. Darwin's reply ('I ought to have read the Bishop's letter, which seems to have been very rich') was later annotated by Butler, acknowledging that he had replied in turn to the rejoinder as though 'I were someone else, to keep up the deception attacking myself also' (*Memoir*, I, 125). In the dispute that broke out in *The Press* between correspondents representing the opposing positions, who took to signing themselves 'A.M' (ostensibly Butler), and 'Savoyard' (ostensibly the Bishop) between February and April 1863, the main object of the dispute was Darwin's swimming whale-like bear from the *Origin*, and the force of Darwin's transmutational claims about what it was, and what it might become (see chapter 3). The dispute was apparently resolved in a note from the editor:[17] 'we have heard that it is different in earlier editions . . . the difference between 'A.M' and 'Savoyard' is clearly one of different editions' (*Canterbury Settlement*, 177). Thus, attention is shifted from the object of the philosophical and religious dispute (either a whale-like bear, or the bear that might become a monstrous whale) to the writing and publication process, the appearance and subsequent deletion of printed symbolic material in the public domain. Even if 'Barrel-Organs' was written by Bishop Abraham, as Butler claimed, it seemed to shift Butler's rhetorical response to Darwin from one that respectfully elucidated his theory to one that was highly inventive, and yet more offensive.[18] For playful engagements with the language of machinery, the mechanics and mysteries of the writing and communication process, and evolution are at the heart of Butler's offensive against orthodox Darwinism.

This became apparent in July 1863 when *The Press* published another piece by Butler entitled 'Darwin among the Machines', which playfully applies Darwin's theory of descent from a common type to the 'primordial' mechanisms comprising 'mechanical life'. Thus, the lever, the wedge (the mechanical contrivance at the heart of Darwin's 'face of nature' image), the inclined plane, the screw and the pulley have developed into Brunel's engineering wonder, the *Great Eastern* (179–8). Writing in a progressivist vein, Butler speculates that natural selection will explain the improvement and refinement abroad in the 'machinate world', though human intervention in this world renders it more a case of artificial selection which might in turn lead to the 'domestication' of the selectors:

We are daily adding to the beauty and delicacy of their [machines'] physical organisation; we are daily giving them greater power and supplying by all sorts of ingenious contrivances that self-regulating, self-acting power which will be to them what intellect has been to the human race. In the course of ages we shall find ourselves the inferior race – inferior in power, inferior in that moral quality of self-control . . . No evil passions, no jealousy, no avarice, no impure desires will disturb the serene might of these glorious creatures. (182)

This is written in a discourse on the positive values of culture that Arnold might have recognised, though in this version, the 'obvious faults of our animality' will not be conquered by a remnant of disinterested individuals, but rather by the perfection, sweetness and light, and disinterestedness that had been attained by contrivances designed and refined by humans: machines. But this results in a reversion to animality through the Malthusian principle of struggle in a conclusion which advocates 'that war to the death should be instantly proclaimed against' machines (185). Butler's imaginative speculations on machinery, virtue and evolution did not rest there, however, and he was to refine this conclusion.

   In another playful piece, written in 1865 when he had returned to England, but still submitted to and published in *The Press* (29 July), Butler no longer conceived of an opposition between humans and machines. The piece was significantly entitled 'Lucubratio Ebria' (writing undertaken at night, accompanied by drink), which announces uncertainties surrounding both self-understanding – 'we cannot fully understand our own speech' – and the reception this 'speech' will receive: 'we fear lest there be not a sufficient number of interpreters present to make our utterance edify' (*Canterbury Settlement*, 187). After a rehearsal of Charles Darwin's theory of natural selection, the 'drunken' writer invokes a speculative evolutionary narrative about imitation. This narrative draws upon the idea of mimicry to blur the boundary between beasts and man, and imagines the originary moment of transmutation from simian to human to have been centred on a device: 'It was a wise monkey that first learned to carry a stick, and a useful monkey that mimicked him', thus adding 'extra-corporaneous limbs to the members of his own body', and making the species 'not only a vertebrate mammal, but a vertebrate machinate mammal into the bargain' (187–8). There thus emerges a blurring of boundaries that goes beyond the beast/human distinction: the organic body is extended by the device, but in the process the boundary between body and machine becomes dis-limned. As the writer goes on to suggest, the stick, in being a tool which extends the body, is also an instrument of violence which was present to the imagination as much as the body, for man learned 'to perceive the moral government under which he held the feudal tenure of his life – perceiving it he symbolised it, and to this day our poets and prophets still strive to symbolise it more and more completely' (187–8). The machinate animal is also the symbolising animal whose symbolic practices can be disseminated further by machines, for 'we are children of the extended liberty and knowledge which the printing press has diffused' (*Canterbury Settlement*, 190–1).

For all its emphasis on the advanced technology of print, such Lamarckian thinking on evolution, the symbol and the mechanical contrivance enabled Butler to open up an unusually broad and non-hierarchical theory of symbolic action that enabled, on the one hand, a poetics of convention-breaking, and on the other a positive, materialist recognition of cultural difference. In his much later essay 'Thought and Language' (1890–4), Butler argued that 'language' could positively occur in situations where there was, minimally, a shared and recognised convention, an institutional view of symbolic exchange that enabled him to identify 'effectual language' in a wide variety of contexts, including among humans without speech who constructed alternative codes based on gesture and sign.[19] In addition, Butler's view embraced species-centred, naturalistic varieties of codes and conventions evolved by non-human communicants. To make this point, Butler cites what 'my great namesake [the seventeenth-century wit, Samuel Butler] said some two hundred years ago: "they know what's what, and that's as high as metaphysic wit can fly"' ('Thought and Language', 215–16).[20] Turning to a metaphor of bodily design and organisation, Butler argued that 'our own speech is vertebrated and articulated by means of nouns, verbs, and the rules of grammar. A dog's speech is invertebrate' (212), and for a dog, 'that's as high as metaphysic wit can fly'.

He conceded that language needed ideas before it could be language; but his conception of the 'idea' places him outside the tradition of Coleridgean idealism. For Butler, ideas could be rudimentary and low level, and communicated through bodily – even beastly – activity:

'some ideas crawl, some run, some fly' (187). In other words, the 'ideas' conveyed by a given set of linguistic conventions are embodied in an organic 'device', be it body or institution, in which the language practice takes shape. Moreover, Butler's metaphors for ideas – crawling, running, flying – imagine language as transportation, movement and infinite extension.

In defining language as communicative action, Butler draws attention to its derivation from the French *langue*, or 'tongue', a derivation that privileges the 'self-presence' of speech. However, Butler also sees writing as its own distinct form of language; if 'tonguage' privileges the organ that shapes speech, then writing is also the different material embodiments that enact and convey its inscriptions; Butler describes these as 'handage, inkage and paperage'. In contrast to speech, these material embodiments and contrivances give writing remarkable powers of extension; as Butler acknowledges, 'the written symbol extends infinitely' (198). This emphasis on infinite extension is important in two senses: first, because writing permits the practical 'transportation' of ideas through signs and notations inscribed by 'handage' with 'inkage' on 'paperage'; the results can separate from their author and circulate widely. Secondly, extension also happens by transportation within and between practices of signification: 'scratch the simplest expressions', Butler observes, 'and you will find the metaphor. Written words are handage, inkage and paperage; it is only by metaphor, or substitution and transposition of ideas, that we can call them language . . . it is in what we read between the lines that the profounder meaning of any letter is conveyed' (195). As I shall argue, 'reading between the lines' involves the transposition of significations between 'departments' of thought. For Butler this was the means by which identity and the modes of authority that fixed it were satirically interrogated, dispersed, and re-conceived with new insight. Butler was peculiarly alert to the 'extended' workings of writing as an advanced human symbolic practice in theology and science in which conventions were open to literary modification or a 'sleight of mind' that invites an understanding of 'a new covenant as to the meaning of symbols' – a formulation that echoes with Biblical, theistic connotations. This language is repeated in Butler's contention that 'much lying, and all irony depends on tampering with covenanted symbols' (205).

Even in the early 'Lucubratio Ebria', the interrogation of conventions generated new insights into the material, differentiating effects of what came to be called 'cultures'. The relationship between body and machines is complex and shifting in ways that can be represented through conventions of symbolisation, and, consequently, re-configured by a rearrangement of what he came to call 'covenanted symbols'. Butler 'drunkenly' practises this, meditating on the evolutionary status of the wealthy man 'who can tack a portion of one of the P and O boats onto his identity'. Such a man 'is a much more highly organised being than one who cannot' (*Canterbury Settlement*, 192). Symbols are a product of location and are selected according to context. When Butler inserted a version of this machine/body-identity equation into the famous 'Book of the Machines' section of *Erewhon*, he reflected on one who is able to 'tack on a special train to his identity' (273): boats are adjuncts to the identity of the mobile colonial subject, and Butler was an example of this mobility, writing back to New Zealand from England. On the other hand, trains were adjuncts to the identity of the domesticated, commuting English subject.

'Drunken writing' about evolution enabled Butler to articulate a theory of ethnic corporeal difference which downgraded the authority of data concerning biological racial difference and hierarchy, which was both delivered by late nineteenth-century imperial expansion and legitimated by evolutionists such as Huxley.[21] Thus, whilst E. B. Tylor's influential textbook *Anthropology* (1881) could acknowledge that the white races – which grew ever 'more dominant intellectually, politically, morally' – owed much of this dominance to 'the appliances of culture', he could still insist that 'it must not be supposed that such differences as between an Englishman and a Gold Coast negro are due to slight variations of breed'. On the contrary 'they are of such zoological importance as to have been compared with the differences between animals which naturalists reckon distinct species'.[22] Butler, by contrast, used the idea of the appliances of culture to redefine ethnicity as complex product of the biological, the locational, the linguistic and technological: 'By the institutions and state of science under which a man is born it is determined whether he shall have the limbs of an Australian savage or those of a nineteenth-century Englishman' (191). Butler's account of Ernest Pontifex's politics in *The Way of All Flesh* – 'Conservative so far as his vote and interest are concerned. In all other respects he is an advanced Radical' (429) – probably applied to himself. The advanced Radical in Butler was certainly manifest in his refusal to subscribe uncritically to ideas about racial types and hierarchies, and a particular reading of evolutionary theory was crucial to the critical stance that he developed. Butler's New Zealand responses to Darwin and evolutionary theory prepared the way for his later work on evolutionary theory, but in equal measure it shaped the work for which he became famous, his satire on colonial exploration and exploitation, *Erewhon*.

3. EREWHON: PARODYING 'A LEAVEN OF CULTURE'

'The Book of the Machines' occupies three late chapters of Butler's anonymously published satire on the accidental discovery of a lost society by
a gentleman colonist, the son of a clergyman who goes 'over the range'
from his settler's farm and convinces himself that he has found the lost
ten tribes of Israel. He encounters a world which he experiences as turned,
from the perspective of morals and customs, upside down: illness is treated
as a crime, and embezzlement is treated as an illness; civilisation assisted
by mechanisation is outlawed, and the case for this is set out in 'The Book
of the Machines'. The material comprising these chapters had been largely
worked out in the articles Butler submitted to the Canterbury *Press*. But
whereas in their original format, these writings were articulated through
the voices of anonymous philosophical disputants or an inebriate writer, in
Erewhon they exist in the form of competing books translated into English
by the narrator, who struggles to understand the patterns of thought and
practice to which he has been suddenly exposed. As in the travel narratives
of Darwin and Wallace, the surprises are felt in the body of the narrator
and are articulated through his voice: as a first person narrative, *Erewhon*
qualifies as one of the stranger contributions to the nineteenth-century
literature of self-culture.

'The Book of the Machines', the reader is told, has had a profound impact
on Erewhonian society: its evolutionary philosophy of machinery, which
speculates on the eventual supplanting of humans by machines, had led to
a civil war in which the 'anti-machinist' party had been victorious, and to
the consequent destruction of all machines and knowledge about how
to engineer them (233). And yet, the condition of existence of the book as
an object is grasped in a discourse which opposes this ultimately victorious
point of view. For the alternative point of view understands the book itself as
a contrivance – a kind of a reproductive machine – which extends, whilst
dispersing beyond one centre of control, modes of agency which have
human, organic origins. Reflecting on the points where the machinate and
the human shade into one another the 'memory [of man] goes in his pocket-
book' (272; see also 'Lucubratio Ebria', *Canterbury Settlement*, 192). Butler's
polemically opposed perspectives on machines weave different conclusions
from a common starting point; the 'anti-machinist' author of the 'Book of
the Machines' asks, rhetorically, 'Is not machinery linked with animal life
in an infinite variety of ways?' This generates associated questions about
linkages and the dislimning of boundaries: 'But who can say that the vapour
engine has not a kind of consciousness? Where does consciousness begin,

and where end? Who can draw the line? Who can draw any line? Is not everything interwoven with everything?' (237).

It is significant that Butler should raise the question of boundaries which mark the essence and location of consciousness, precisely in order to blur the presumed clarity of that essence. Although it ends by calling for the destruction of all machines, the argument of 'The Book of the Machines' nonetheless blurs the differences between humans and machines. In an argument which structurally rehearses lines of contestation similar to those surrounding the issue of vitality in the matter of the species question, the proposition is entertained that a machine cannot be like a human because it cannot reproduce itself. To see matters otherwise requires a different method of thinking to that which 'see[s] a machine as a whole', whereby 'we assume that there can be no reproductive action which does not arise from a single centre' (255). Thus, although machines have to be reproduced outside of themselves, as it were, by human intervention, the natural world contains many instances of 'assisted' reproduction, as in those cases of the fertilisation of flowers which depend on insects. Reproduction is a process of multiple, ovelapping agencies which can suspend assumptions latent in the language of 'wholeness'.

The concept of 'organic wholeness' derives from a romantic discourse on vitality which impacted on literary criticism, initially through the critical theory of Coleridge and Wordsworth ('a literature which might live'). Romantic organicism applied the language of wholeness to writings which seemed to embody the principles of vitality and integrity. Rhetorics of 'wholeness' remained active through the nineteenth century – witness their importance to Arnold – and in the late nineteenth century they became important aesthetic justifications for refined forms of prose fiction and the novel. Reflecting on *Erewhon* in a preface written for the revised edition of 1901, just a year before his death, Butler readily conceded that his text 'was not an organic whole' (xvi): this at precisely the moment of the emergence of an 'organic' novelistic aesthetic of unity championed by Henry James and Joseph Conrad. It can be argued that Butler's thoughts about the reproductive capacity of machines loop back into a discourse upon literary practice itself: reflections questioning the concept of 'wholeness', advancing a theory of plural centres of production, can be read as a shadow commentary upon the kind of literary inventiveness that was launched in *Erewhon*.

For *Erewhon* is manifestly hybrid, compendious and discursive rather than organic and unified: it begins as a narrative of travel in colonial waste lands before becoming a satiric fantasy on the model of More's *Utopia*, and this generic hybridity enabled Butler to add to the text that was published as the first edition. In 1901 he extended his account of the higher education system of Erewhon, the so-called 'Colleges of Unreason', by writing an additional chapter (22), as well as adding chapters on Erewhonian arguments about the rights of animals (26) and the rights of vegetables (27). The book thus regenerated itself from a multiplicity of intellectual discourses, and Butler acknowledged in the Preface of 1901 there is 'no central idea underlying' *Erewhon* (xv). In this sense Butler's satire runs counter to the Neoplatonism of Coleridge, which was dedicated to sustaining the 'doctrine and discipline of ideas' (see my chapter 1). Butler's account of the Colleges of Unreason is a satire on theological language, which is presented as an evasive language of so-called 'hypothetics' which was, the narrator informs us, 'originally composed at a time when the country was in a very different state of civilisation to what it is at present' (218). The custodians of this language are a clerisy, responsible for diffusing 'a leaven of culture throughout the country' (85). Whereas for Coleridge the national church and its clerisy would preserve and cultivate the 'organic' ideas sustaining national life, Butler parodies the idea of the church by symbolising and dismantling it into multifarious and defamiliarised components.

Butler's parody on the national church is realised in the Musical Banks, a hybrid invention blending the different forms of symbolic conventions associated with both worship and commerce. The Musical Banks are housed in 'epic' stone and marble buildings with windows 'filled with stained glass descriptive of the principal commercial incidents of the bank for many ages'; the affective impact of the buildings carries 'both imagination and judgement by storm' (149–50). Inside these sites of veneration and edification, music is played to accompany the mercantile transactions that take place. Value is expressed in the material contrivance of currency (147), and the overwhelming effect of the architecture convinces the narrator that 'those responsible for the upraising of so serene a handiwork, were hardly likely to be wrong in the conclusions they might come to upon any subject. My feeling certainly was that the currency of this bank must be the right one' (149). And yet whilst Erewhonians officially recognise the currency of the Musical Banks as the dominant and respectable medium for moral transactions, in practice the Musical Banks play host to very few people, even fewer of whom actually believe in their effectiveness. The exchange values appear to be randomly set (150–2), and 'any one could see that the money given out at these banks was not that with which people bought their bread, meat and clothing' (155). The 'cramped expression' of the 'cashiers and managers', the clerisy who staffed these institutions, was not, the narrator observes, 'that which one would wish to diffuse' (157).

If there 'is no central idea underlying' *Erewhon*, and if the text parodies that Neoplatonic, Coleridgean vision of an organic, evolving Idea vested in the institution of a national church, then the estranging strategy underlying Butler's satire is premised on the invention of a symbolic system of belief and practice which thrives upon incoherence, contradiction and misrecognition. And yet, Butler's construction of an apparently other, quasi-barbaric society is also premised on the reader's ability to recognise those incoherences and contradictions as being very close to home when translated into representations of dissimilar things, such as spiritual solace materialised in the machinery of a currency.

The ambiguous territory between difference and kinship in which recognition is shaped is explored through the text's dramatisation of instances of imitation, mimicry and repetition. The giant, grotesque stone heads that mark the boundary of Erewhon, and which the terrified narrator encounters as he stumbles upon the civilisation, are complex realisations of this drama. On the one hand, imitation appears to be a reliable method of conveying an impression of these objects: the narrator immediately recognises the grotesque stone heads on the basis of his native manservant Chewbok's imitation of their expression at the very beginning of the narrative, before the two have ventured over the range. And yet, the significance of these figures cannot be contained within a precisely delimited field of cultural reference. For the figures are 'barbarous – neither Egyptian, nor Assyrian, nor Japanese – different from any of these, and yet akin to all' (43). These imitations of human heads are primitive machines, functional organ pipes which catch the wind to produce music, which the narrator describes as 'ghostly chanting'. The uncannily affected narrator cannot place this noise, and yet 'almost immediately knew what it was', for the narrator later realises that he has heard something different from, but akin to, Handel's compositions for the harpsichord (44–5). These primitive machines seem to generate a passable imitation of Handel; and yet, perhaps Handel's compositions are a sophisticated 'development' of this primitive survival; or perhaps, again, Handel has unconsciously repeated these structures of sound in his composition?

The imitative movements and repetitions dramatised in *Erewhon* challenge anthropological narratives of evolutionary development and presumed relations of cultural superiority and inferiority. The narrator's manservant Chewbok, like a typical savage Maori, is a good mimic when he conveys to the narrator the image of the grotesque heads. But Chewbok's imitations also border on the fraudulent. He is discovered in London by the narrator, at the very end of the narrative, passing himself off as a native missionary: he has become the Rev William Habbakuk, claiming to be a racial 'specimen' of the lost ten tribes of Israel, who delivers an incoherent and incomprehensible speech (322–3). The narrator, the son of a clergyman, is astonished at the sight of this false evangelist who, scandalously, is imitating the true pioneer colonialist.

Yet there is a deep irony here, because the narrator has just disclosed himself as an exploitative mimic of already invented schemes: the narrator, having returned from Erewhon, has been 'for months at my wit's end, forming plan after plan for the evangelisation' of the land. The plan that he devises involves shipping the Erewhonians to Queensland territory, Australia, to work on sugar plantations which are 'in great want of labour': they will be converted to Christianity, then returned to Erewhon in old age 'to carry the good seed with them'; money for this scheme will be raised by shareholders who will enjoy 'the comfort of reflecting that they were saving souls and filling their pockets at one and the same moment'. The narrator concedes that 'I cannot claim the credit for having originated the above scheme'; instead, his idea is an imitation of a scheme he has read about in a report in *The Times*, in which the Governor of Queensland bestows legitimacy on the 'migration': 'if one can judge by the countenances and manners of the Polynesians, they experience no regret at their position' (322). The enforced shipment of Polynesian labour to work on Queensland sugar plantations was indeed a flourishing mode of colonial exploitation in the South Seas of the 1860s and 1870s. Although it appears that Butler invented the 'report' that he cites from *The Times* at the end of *Erewhon*, the issue of enforced Polynesian labour in Queensland was a controversial issue in the first months of 1872: *The Times* of 23 January (p. 4) reported on the illegal importation of Polynesian labour into Queensland, and identified it as a neo-slave trade.

Human slavery as a continuing colonial practice pointedly returns us to the way in which *Erewhon* plays with scale and the uncertainties of the boundaries delimiting the human from other phenomena in the organic and inorganic worlds: the 'Book of the Machines' asked whether, after all, man is not 'an affectionate machine-tickling aphid?', or perhaps even, 'another kind of ant-heap'? (245). In glimpsing an analogy between the human body as a host site to parasitic, struggling organisms, and an ant colony, one is returned to 'Barrel-Organs', that polemical essay directed against Darwin's theory by the Bishop of Wellington – or was it Butler himself? – in which Darwin's theory of evolution was viewed as a repetition of Pythagoras's doctrine of the transmigration of souls. 'Barrel-Organs' cites the example of Darwin's slave-making ants from the chapter on instinct in the *Origin*; the slave-making ants are imagined as re-incarnated Virginian cotton and tobacco growers (*Canterbury Settlement*, 164–5). Expectations are reversed; the souls of the slavers have passed from the humans to the ants, and this clearly questions the grounds for presuming human superiority and progress: it is the ants which imitate and repeat the instincts of the humans in their practice of slave-making. The reader is jolted into a different perspective on the anthropomorphisms of Darwin's account of the slave-making ants, thus foregrounding the workings of evolutionary speculation as a mode of symbolisation with political and critical implications.

4. BUTLER'S WANDERINGS IN THE MARGINS OF EVOLUTIONARY WRITINGS

Evolution Old and New defended a tradition of evolutionary speculation which, Butler was convinced, had been poorly treated owing to the powerful position achieved by Charles Darwin's theory of evolution by natural selection. The tradition that Butler sought to re-instate was based on the work of Buffon, Lamarck and Erasmus Darwin, a tradition which foregrounded the purposefulness and agency of individual organisms in processes of transmutation. It led Butler to write of organisms as being involved in a 'moral struggle':

> They have seen very little ahead of a present power or need, and have been most moral, when most inclined to pierce a little into futurity, but also when most obstinately declining to pierce too far, and busy mainly with the present . . . Wherever there is life there is a moral government of rewards and punishments understood by the amoeba neither better nor worse than by man. The history of organic development is the history of a moral struggle.[23]

The emphasis on moral struggle, and the pervasiveness of a moral government in which rewards and punishments are distributed is an echo of Butler's evangelical, Simeonite inheritance: Butler continued to draw on this language, even though he parodied it in his Cambridge days. In stating that a moral government applied equally to an amoeba as to man, Butler also implied that slave-making pioneer colonists were subject to this government in just the manner that slave-making ants were.

And yet, for all its commitment to purposefulness and moral agency, *Evolution Old and New* is a very strange text. A book which came into being because Butler was convinced that readers needed to know more about the history of evolutionary speculation – a need which came about because of Butler's sense that Charles Darwin had not acknowledged his debt to the evolutionary writings of the past – might be expected to be extensive in direct quotation. And it is; though, surprisingly for a writer who demanded such precision of his opponent in matters of textual accuracy, Butler could be somewhat lax. In his chapter on Lamarck, for instance, he could write this after an extensive citation: '[This is taken, I believe, from Dr Darwin or Buffon, but I have lost the passage, if, indeed, I ever found it . . .]': or, 'This too is taken from some passage which I have either never seen or lost sight of.'[24] Reading and drives to select and construct significance can generate, Butler seems to acknowledge, fictions of purposefulness, direction and authority built upon more obscure origins. Elsewhere, Butler was inclined to satirise such an effect. Thus, when the narrator of *Erewhon* describes the effect of reading the report describing the scheme of enforced Polynesian labour in Queensland, it is as though his 'eye had been directed' by 'one of those special interpositions which should be a sufficient answer to the sceptic, and make even the most confirmed rationalist irrational' (321). In *Evolution Old and New*, Butler formulates, at times, a very different way of writing about writing, and interventions that reshape a given symbolic practice. He urges recognition of the inevitable marginal 'errors and wanderings' that occur in and between discourses in the intellectual field:

There is a margin in every organic structure (and perhaps more than we imagine in things inorganic also), which will admit of references, as it were, side notes, and glosses upon the original text. It is on this margin that we may err or wander – the greatness of a mistake depending rather upon the extent of the departure from the original text, than on the direction that the departure takes.[25]

My final chapter will explore the cultural evolution of Edmund Gosse as set forth in *Father and Son* – a story about the impact of Darwinism which also reserved a space for error.

CHAPTER 6

Edmund Gosse's cultural evolution: sympathetic magic, imitation and contagious literature

I. HARROWING OF SELF

Edmund Gosse's *Father and Son* (1907) offered itself to its original early twentieth-century readers as a reliable and representative '*document*' and 'record' concluding the nineteenth-century conflict between religion and evolutionary life sciences, and examining its impact upon a particular history of mental cultivation.[1] The narrative of educational development, of self-culture, recalls the young Gosse's relationship with his widowed father, the nineteenth-century popular naturalist Philip Henry Gosse, whose Calvinist theology and insistence on the literal fact of Biblical Creation was challenged by Lyell's geology and Darwin's theory of evolution by natural selection. The narrative also records the way in which Philip Henry Gosse responded to the Darwinian challenge by writing *Omphalos* (1857), an attempt to reconcile geology and Genesis that signally failed to convince anybody on either side of the debate. Gosse's narrative presents this as a decisive conflict, with Darwinism on the side of development against stagnant 'Puritanism': 'of the two human beings here described, one was born to fly backward, the other could not help being carried forward' (31) in the direction of individual, aesthetic self-fashioning (211). It is significant that, in presenting his work as a '*document*', Edmund Gosse should have contrasted it in 'the present hour' with fiction that assumed 'forms so ingenious and so specious' (29). Gosse was responding to an Edwardian vogue for what the contemporary critic Stephen Reynolds described as 'autobiografiction', a hybrid mix of autobiography, social investigation and fiction.[2] But Gosse claimed he had rigorously excluded fiction, and the result was a document, a record, a transparently mimetic literary performance. However, the comprehensive biographical material that Ann Thwaite has published on the Gosses since 1984 suggests how problematic a relationship Edmund Gosse had with 'facts', and how fictional a 'document' *Father and Son* is. Gosse's mimesis, his imitation of past actions, is in practice cunningly opaque.

Gosse's text is more nearly an instance of what Herbert Spencer called a 'symbolic conception': it retrospectively reconstructed a symbolic fiction of knowledge about the moment 'when the theory of the mutability of species was preparing to throw a flood of light upon all departments of human speculation and action' (86). Gosse's narrative was published just one year before the Darwin–Wallace celebration marking the fiftieth anniversary of the reading of their papers on natural selection to the Linnaean Society. *Father and Son* brought evolutionary discourses into a context shaped by late aestheticism and emerging modernist aesthetics.[3] Gosse had moved in the intellectual circles of the aesthetic movement in the 1890s; he knew Walter Pater, and he was J. A. Symonds's literary executor. *Father and Son* is a record of what Symonds described as 'self-tillage' in his essay on 'Culture' in 1893 (see Introduction), which amounted to 'the ploughing and the harrowing of self by use of what ages have transmitted to us from the work of gifted minds' (*In the Key of Blue*, 200). In being a narrative about religion, science, and the possibilities of aesthetic self-realisation, *Father and Son* was poised between 'Humanism and science', and contributed to that cumulative view of 'culture' which Symonds conceived as a 'magic robe, warp and woof combined into one fabric' (206–7). However, 'magic' in Gosse's text does not enchantingly weave a unified fabric: it generates conflict and transgression, and – to use but re-inflect another of Symonds's metaphors of culture – a 'harrowing of self'.

In contributing to the debate about culture, humanism and science, *Father and Son* carried with it a flavour of the discussions that characterised the 1870s and 1880s, in which the voices of Arnold and Huxley had figured so prominently. In fact, it also carried curious traces of a debate from 1886 which was prompted by the exposure of Edmund Gosse's notoriously imaginative scholarship. The 'English Literature and the Universities' debate that ensued focused on the place and future of literature and culture in higher education. Science, in the person of T. H. Huxley, was invited to comment on that debate. In formulating his response, Huxley made the concept of imitation central to his justification of a good literary education. As I argued in the Introduction, the concept of imitation figured significantly in the 'Prolegomena' to Huxley's great essay on 'Evolution and Ethics' (1893–4), where Huxley made imitation the distinctive characteristic of the evolutionary advancement of the human animal, while rendering it unfamiliar precisely by seeing imitation and the human impulse of sympathy, metaphorically, as the reflex instinct of an 'emotional chameleon'. This chapter will argue that Gosse's *Father and Son* also cites imitation approvingly, while going on to make its operations strange and disconcerting – another 'harrowing of self'.

Imitation was a productively unstable concept in late nineteenth-century attempts to explain, using evolutionary frameworks, the desired reproduction of sameness. Such instability produced, however, a supplement in the form of a deconstructive literary inventiveness. This differed from the pedagogic, mimetic account of 'English literature' that Huxley sought to place at the centre of the 1886 controversy. Moreover, this deconstructive literariness troubled the avowed purposes of an intertextual network of late nineteenth-century texts about imitation, cultural dissemination and evolution. These texts were either philological records of cultural evolution, as in the case of the *Oxford English Dictionary*, or narratives of self-culture, as with Gosse's *Father and Son*. Alternatively they narrated macro-stories of universal cultural evolution through micro-observations of imitation in action, as in James Mark Baldwin's popular scientific *Story of the Mind* (1899). However, all the texts are troubled by a 'cunning' degree of play at work in the practice of symbol-based imitation, and in the sign of 'imitation' itself. But in one sense, the very recognition of such degrees of symbolic play was enabled by a sense of cultural relativity and difference that was being shaped by philology, anthropology and evolutionary theory, as among the central interpretive devices of nineteenth-century evolutionary science.

2. MISRECOGNISING SYMBOLS, GRASPING CULTURE: LITERALISM, SYMPATHETIC MAGIC AND TANGLED SKEINS

For Edmund Gosse, his parents' peculiar configuration of Puritan life was embodied in a mode of reading and interpreting that amounted to what the anthropologist Ruth Benedict came to call a 'pattern of culture'.[4] Moreover, though he does not name it as such, Gosse in effect grasps this as a 'culture'. Gosse's sense of the pattern of his parents' interpretive practices derives indirectly from culture's etymological derivatives, and plays upon the concepts of cultivation, the colony and worship:

For her, and for my Father, nothing was symbolic, nothing allegorical or allusive in any part of Scripture . . . Pushing this to its extreme limit, and allowing nothing for the changes of scene or time or race, my parents read injunctions to the Corinthian converts without any suspicion that what was apposite in dealing with half-breed Achaian colonists might not exactly apply to respectable English men and women of the nineteenth century . . . They went . . . to the cultivation of a rigid and iconoclastic literalness. (66)

The younger Gosse constructs his Puritan parents as figures who misrecognise the force of the symbolic, the allegorical and the allusive in Scripture, and he does so in a voice imbued with an ironic, historical relativity of which, he claims, his parents had no conception. Gosse's recognition of a 'respectable', nineteenth-century cultural relativity is performed in the reference to the ethnic hybridity of early Greek colonists ('half-breed Achaians'), and an awareness of the rhetorical distinctiveness of the forms of language that constructed the ancients' objects of worship.[5]

Despite a disavowal of the symbolic, the Gosses of *Father and Son* actually live by a poetics, for they are still supreme cultivators and interpreters of idiosyncratic systems of symbols whose metaphorical nature is systematically misrecognised. Indeed so idiosyncratic are these systems that 'no third person could possibly follow the curious path which they had hewn for themselves through this jungle of symbols' (79):

Hand in hand we investigated the number of the Beast, which number is six hundred three score and six. Hand in hand we inspected the nations, to see whether they had the mark of Babylon in their foreheads. Hand in hand we watched the spirits of devils gathering the kings of the earth in the place which is called in the Hebrew tongue Armageddon. Our unity in these excursions was so delightful, that my Father was lulled in any suspicion he might have formed that I did not quite understand what it was all about. Nor could he have desired a pupil more docile or more ardent than I was in my flaming denunciations of the Papacy. (79–80)

The refrain of 'hand in hand' finds the fanatical father as teacher, guiding the son as initiate through a 'jungle of symbols' grafted onto the modern world: nations are not states, but animate persons possessed of foreheads bearing either signs of purity or the mark of Babylon. Edmund Gosse here appeals to the condition of 'the savage mind' that George W. Stocking finds at work in the anthropology of E. B. Tylor and J. G. Frazer, in that 'the very literal-mindedness and concreteness of the savage mind, the constant confusion of word and thing, of simile and metaphor (the constitutional incapacity, even, for metaphor), paradoxically gave rise to a mental world of make-believe and even madness'.[6] 'Hand in hand' posits the child adopting an identical stance towards the world as his mad teacher, an imitative mirroring of bodies. And yet, imitation cannot simply reproduce the father in the son: the son 'did not quite understand what it was all about'. As the young Gosse is in turn cultivated by reading 'factual' natural history, travel narratives and theology, he repeats the material 'glibly, like a machine'. Yet the child is able, without being fully conscious of his acquisitions, to manipulate the poetics of the literal in which he is cultivated to produce striking, defamiliarising analogies: on being shown a print of a human skeleton, the child is challenged to identify it: 'Isn't it a man with the meat off?' he replies (44). Gosse represents the cultivation of this faculty, in his discovery of the true contours of poetry, a true aesthetic and 'cultured' sensibility that enables him, in the narrative's famous closing words, 'a human being's privilege to fashion his inner life for himself' (211). Yet, this *Bildung* of aesthetic cultivation in *Father and Son* is simultaneously underwritten by the voice of the late nineteenth-century comparative anthropologist, who has collected missionary and military anecdotes from the colonies, and who, in the words of J. G. Frazer, understands the 'moral evolution' that originates in 'a low level of social and intellectual culture'.[7]

The first chapter of Edmund Gosse's *Father and Son* ends with a striking metaphor of restricted cultivation:

> This, then, was the scene in which the soul of the little child was planted, not as in the ordinary open flower-border or carefully tended social parterre, but as on a ledge, split in the granite of some mountain. The ledge was hung between night and the snows on the one hand, and the dizzy depths of the world upon the other; was furnished with soil just enough for a gentian to struggle skywards and open its stiff azure stars; and offered no lodgement, no hope of salvation, to any rootlet which would stray beyond its inexorable limits. (38)

The planting of the constricted, deadened soul in an arid, rocky region, the mingling of the languages of vegetation and salvation; these would of course become familiar to readers of T. S. Eliot's *The Waste Land* (1922). Eliot read Gosse's relation to literary culture critically, for Gosse came to occupy a central and quite innovative position in late nineteenth-century literary culture: he made Scandinavian literature, particularly the works of Ibsen, familiar to English audiences; he was the first modern biographer of John Donne, shaping public taste for the Metaphysicals in a move which predated Eliot's more famous promotional act on behalf of avant-garde criticism.[8]

But to read Gosse on cultivation is to appreciate more precisely the extent to which the generation prior to Eliot's had also been attracted to J. G. Frazer's anthropology of early vegetation cults, and their status as 'survivals' in a crumbling Christian tradition. Grant Allen worked Frazer into his fictional, journalistic and scholarly work on evolution and its relation to 'culture'.[9] Gosse was also indebted to Frazer, so much so that he chose to disclose his otherwise concealed authorial identity in a letter to the Cambridge anthropologist, a letter tentatively offering a 'gift' that is at pains to acknowledge the aura of intellectual authority attached to Frazer's position in the field:

If you come across an anonymous book called *Father and Son*, which is just published by Heinemann, let me tell you that it is I who have written it and that it contains some observations about moral (or savage) ideas in children which such as I should not dare to lay before you, but such as I should be pleased if you thought of value. And with this squinting and trepidatious hint, I leave you to more important studies.[10]

Such observations of savage subjectivity occur during Gosse's account of his imaginative enthralment to the sea after his widowed father's re-location to Devon (84). Confirming Pater's sense of Wordsworth as the anthropological poet of 'survivals' in 'the general history of human culture', Gosse compares his own reaction to the sea with Wordsworth's representation of his 'unconscious intercourse with nature' in the *Prelude*. Wordsworth's account of 'drinking in a pure organic pleasure'[11] reminds Gosse of 'what I have called my "natural magic" practices . . . I recollect that I thought I might secure some power of walking on the sea, if I drank of it – a perfectly irrational movement of mind, like those of savages' (85). This magical fantasy weaves its imagery from allusions to the New Testament. Gosse claims that his childish fantasy was inspired by 'the majestic scene upon the Lake of Gennesaret' (86), or the 'miraculous catch of the fish' narrated in Luke 5.1; but also, the desire to walk on water recalls the images of Christ walking on water in John 6. Gosse's 'natural magic' practices refer to earlier episodes in which the child fantasises about bringing natural history illustrations to life, and imitating and inflecting his father's prayers to God towards the idolatrous worship of a chair (52, 57).

It is appropriate that a passage so intertextually resonant should be linked by Gosse to Frazer's anthropology, for Frazer's anthropology, while it followed in the tradition of Tylor, was also an early associationist theory of what is now recognised as structural linguistics. Frazer's *The Golden Bough* was a high intellectual attempt to theorise the rules of association that produced magic as a system of thought capable of possessing the mind of the savage and 'ignorant and dull-witted people everywhere'. 'It is', Frazer asserts, 'for the philosophic student to trace the train of thought which underlies the magician's practice; to draw out the few simple threads of which the tangled skein is composed'. The assumption that the drinking of water would lead to the power to walk on water was, for Frazer, 'an association of ideas by contiguity', which he categorised as 'contagious magic', and this was governed by the law of contiguity or contact (*Golden Bough*, 12).

On the other hand, the assumption that the destruction of an enemy could be achieved through the making and destroying of an image of that enemy was an example of 'imitative' or 'homoeopathic' magic governed by the law of similarity. Frazer's axes of contiguity and similarity are but short conceptual steps away from Roman Jakobson's later structural linguistic account of the tropes of metonymy (defined by relations of contiguity) and metaphor (defined by relations of similarity and substitution) respectively. And this is no idle connection, because according to Frazer, magic, religion and science are meta-symbolic activities, for

we must remember that at bottom the generalisations of science or, in common parlance, the laws of nature are merely hypotheses devised to explain that ever shifting phantasmagoria of thought which we dignify with the high sounding names of the world and the universe. In the last analysis, magic, religion and science are nothing but theories of thought. (712)

While Frazer's anthropological work was delivered from the high intellectual sphere – the box occupied by the aristocracy of intellectual evolutionists, to use Leslie Stephen's term – it is also an example of the way in which evolutionary methods can never quite elevate their conclusions decisively to the refined air of the dignified; lowly origins, or at best the 'shifting phantasmagoria of thought' and definitions, always haunt and contaminate their conclusions.

   A sense of this can be glimpsed in Frazer's preference for the term 'homoeopathic' magic over 'imitative' or 'mimetic' magic. Frazer argues that the concept of 'imitation' is misleading because it carries connotations of the conscious agency of one who imitates (11). But this implicit sense of 'imitation' fails to grasp the imagined operations of magic, which works independently of, and often against, conscious human agency. As Jacques Derrida has remarked, 'the things in play in mimesis are very cunning', and the play in the concept of imitation can embrace unconscious processes as well.[12] But in this context, Frazer asks his readers to set 'imitative' magic aside, and to see magic operating 'homoeopathically' in an imaginary sphere that he grasps through analogy, by appropriating the concept of 'ether' from the domain of natural science; that is, the 'invisible ether' that is 'postulated by modern science for a precisely similar purpose, namely, to explain how things can physically affect each other through a space which appears to be empty'. It is in the 'ether' of 'secret sympathy' that both 'contagious' and 'homoeopathic' magic operate. Frazer's all-embracing concept of 'sympathetic magic' radically re-inscribes the dominant nineteenth-century language of sympathy, premised as it had been on altruistic impulses of fellow-feeling; Frazer's filaments of sympathetic transmission could embrace the hostile, the fugitive and the transgressive.

Moreover, in Frazer's ethereal domain of sympathy, hard and fast distinctions between 'contagious' and 'homoeopathic' or 'imitative' forms of magic break down, as in practice they are blended in the recorded individual acts of magic that the anthropological collector has gathered from missionaries and native informants all over the world. For instance, Frazer refers to a Malay charm that involves collecting hair, nails, eyebrows and spittle of the intended victim; these are embedded in a likeness of the victim made from beeswax, and then burned for seven nights over a lamp. As Frazer observes, 'the charm combines the principles of homoeopathic and contagious magic; since the image which is made in the likeness of the enemy contains things which once were in contact with him' (*Golden Bough*, 13). Having begun with the intention of intellectually untangling the conceptual skein of magic, Frazer tacitly acknowledges that the skein is of necessity tangled, and explicable with reference to a system of thought – science – that seems to be most opposed to it. The appeal to 'ether' reveals, paradoxically, the presence of 'magical' solutions in scientific explanation.

Frazer's sense of a tangled skein in the conceptual ordering of magic, religion and science enables him to see the same principle in the history of thought in terms of the overlap, inter-weaving and grafting between its evolving systems: at the end of *The Golden Bough* he represents the history of thought in symbolic terms, 'by likening it to a web woven of three different threads – the black thread of magic, the red thread of religion, and the white thread of science'. Frazer goes on:

Could we then survey the web of thought from the beginning, we should probably perceive it to be at first a chequer of black and white, a patchwork of true and false notions, hardly tinged as yet by the red thread of religion. But carry your eye farther along the fabric and you will remark that, while the black and white chequer still runs through it, there rests on the middle portion of the web, where religion has entered most deeply into its texture, a dark crimson stain, which shades off insensibly into a lighter tint as the white thread of science is woven more and more into the tissue. To a web thus chequered and stained, thus shot with threads of diverse hues, but gradually changing colour the farther it is unrolled, the state of modern thought, with all its divergent aims and conflicting tendencies, may be compared. (713)

Frazer's symbolic parable brings the history of thought into the heart of a present that is unclear about the pattern of the cultural future that is being woven. In Frazer's parable the emphasis is on the woven threads themselves that cross over, mingle and shade into one another, holding in suspense the certainty of epochal transformation. In a significant chapter of *The Golden Bough* entitled 'Our Debt to the Savage', Frazer uses the same imagery of 'threads' to describe the way in which apparently all powerful human gods of savage society were really bound by 'threads of custom, "light as air but strong as links of iron", that crossing and recrossing each other in an endless maze bound him fast within a network of observances from which death or deposition alone could release him'. Moreover, Frazer explicitly refuses to dissociate this insight from modernity, for 'when all is said and done our resemblances to the savage are still far more numerous than our differences from him' (263–4).

This complicates the rhetoric of linear progress from superstitious religion to enlightened science that characterises the beginning of Gosse's *Father and Son*. Indeed, despite this rhetoric, Gosse's text plays out these complications, subtly. Gosse's account of his childhood strikingly analyses the way in which the 'death' of his belief in his father's deity occurred simultaneously with his discovery of a 'second self' (50). Gosse describes this second self as 'rudimentary', a piece with his 'natural magic' experiments and product of his 'undeveloped little brain', as though he would progress, ontogenetically, from savagery to civilisation through self-culture as smooth trajectory. However, as we have seen in the case of Herbert Spencer's speculations (chapter 5), the supernatural explanations of mental phenomena such as dreams and hauntings formulated by the 'savage mind' could also be defamiliarising devices for exploring those conflicts and aporias that modern subjectivity has 'forgotten' whilst remaining divided and haunted by their continued presence. Thus, Philip Henry Gosse's subjectivity can be dismantled on more than one occasion; first in the eyes of his son, when the father's status as omniscient god is shattered; and, secondly, in a curious episode towards the end of the narrative, in which the Puritan father meets his match, a Mrs Paget, another member of the Brethren who questions Philip Henry Gosse's spiritual guidance of his son:

My Father found himself brought face to face at last, not with a disciple, but with a trained expert in his own peculiar scheme of religion. At every point she was armed with arguments the source of which he knew and the validity of which he recognised. He trembled before Mrs Paget as a man in a dream may tremble before a parody of his own central self . . . (176)

There is a sense here in which Philip Henry Gosse is symbolically 'victimised' by a curious force, a latter-day blend of imitative and contagious magic: Philip Henry Gosse is confronted by Mrs Paget performing an imitation of his own central self, yet one that is an awful parody of all he represents, of the kind that one may encounter in the fearful, phantas-magoric territory of self-division represented by the dream. In addition, he is withered by a kind of contagious magic, in the sense that his adversary wields theological arguments that have been the possession of his intel-lectual being. In one sense, this can be read as a symbolically appropriate form of 'death', given that Edmund Gosse presents his father as a literal-minded savage in the midst of the modern world. But there is something more complex at stake in Gosse's account; Mrs Paget comes before Philip Henry Gosse not as a 'disciple', but instead as a 'trained expert' in Philip Henry Gosse's cult. Frazer notably described the role of the savage magi-cian as a 'profession' and magicians 'the oldest artificial or professional class in the evolution of society', one that was constantly modified by an intellectual division of labour (*Golden Bough*, 104). Thus, the language of 'training' and 'expertise' brings Edmund Gosse's narrative back into contact with nineteenth-century concerns about intellectual specialisation, profes-sionalisation and cultivation; indeed, with that phase of modernity that Coleridge confronted when he theorised the role of a cultivating class, or 'the clerisy', in the early nineteenth century while erecting a literary and theological front against the claims of materialist science. It is perhaps fit-ting that Mr Paget, a disgraced Baptist minister who had 'committed the Sin against the Holy Ghost', resembled portraits of 'S. T. Coleridge . . . with all the intellect taken out' (*Father and Son*, 173).

The difficulties of definition and the haunting implication that Frazer encounters in connection with the concept of 'imitation', which he nego-tiates through the desired conceptual clarity of homoeopathy, but which transports him back to the overlap between imitation and contagion, is thus a drama that is played out in certain scenes in *Father and Son*. The properties of imitation and contagion that Frazer assigned to magic were simultaneously sources of hope and anxiety in disciplinary contributions to theories of cultural evolution that vied for authority in the cultural field; in part, these emerge from a debate between literature and science over 'culture'; but, in a supplementary sense, they generate 'literature', as a kind of reflection on the cultural ether, or premodern 'magic', that structures the cultivation of the person, and connects indeterminately the spaces between positions in the field of culture.

3. SCIENCE ON LITERATURE: IMITATION AND THE FUTURE OF CULTURE

Chapter 8 of Gosse's *Father and Son* explicitly reflects on the concept of imitation. Seeking to recover formative influences from his childhood,

Edmund Gosse complains that 'the rage for what is called 'originality' is pushed to such a length in these days' (122). Gosse recalls watching and learning from his father's work as a naturalist, extolling the benefits of the act of 'healthy . . . direct imitation', exemplified in the way in which his younger self copied his father's work.

Gosse's sentiment in 1907 strikingly echoes a position on imitation adopted by T. H. Huxley in an earlier acrimonious public debate about the future of 'culture' prompted by Gosse's literary critical work, and conducted in the higher regions of the cultural field. At the beginning of his career in 1885, Edmund Gosse published a book arising from the newly founded Clark Lectures in literature, delivered at the University of Cambridge, entitled *From Shakespeare to Pope: An Inquiry into the Causes and Phenomena of the Rise of Classical Poetry in England*. Both the lecture series and book represented a triumph of social and academic recognition for Gosse, whose Nonconformist background had hardly guaranteed entry to the literary and academic circles that came to receive him. Gosse had not attended the Anglican-dominated ancient English universities; though a civil servant, he 'came up' through work at the British Museum reading room, and had no degree. But in the Preface to *From Shakespeare to Pope*, Gosse laid claim to intellectual authority: his literary history was rigorous, scholarly and meticulously researched.[13]

His claim was undone by a devastating critique of the book that appeared in the *Quarterly Review* for October 1886. The author was John Churton Collins, a university extension lecturer, who demonstrated that many of Gosse's facts were wrong, that he had invented evidence for his claims, and that he apparently had not read some of the works on which he passed judgement.[14] But in entitling the article 'English Literature and the Universities', Collins cast his net wider, seeing the example of Gosse's dilettantism as damaging to progress on a broader front affecting his emergent discipline. Should the ancient universities be endowed with the professorial staff for effecting the 'dissemination of literary culture'?[15] The philological study of Anglo-Saxon and Middle English language was endowed with chairs at Oxford. Philology grew out of established traditions of teaching Greek and Latin, yet it projected itself as professional and scientific: its opponents, however, interpreted professionalism as sectarian narrowness.[16] Accordingly, Collins rejected philology, advancing instead a pedagogic vision of English literature rooted in the study of those Greek and Roman classical models of which it was substantially an imitation. For Collins it was the historic mission of the universities to 'preserve learning from extinction' and 'barbarism'. Culture would be preserved by an 'intellectual aristocracy', which would protect its learned core from what he described as the 'contagion' of 'dilettantism' and 'the multitudes'.[17]

This was the debate about culture that Huxley entered, at the invitation of the *Pall Mall Gazette*, on 22 October 1886. Huxley was one of several prominent figures – including Gladstone, Bright, Arnold and Pater – to be approached by the *Gazette's* editor, W. T. Stead, through a questionnaire prepared by Collins.[18] Huxley's perspective was particularly sought because he had already made a distinctive contribution to defining the relations between literature, culture and science in an address entitled 'Science and Culture', which marked the opening of Sir Josiah Mason's Science College in Birmingham, an institution which made no provision for 'mere literary instruction and education' (see chapter 4). He was thus described by the *Gazette's* editorial as 'hardly less distinguished for culture than for science'. While promoting science, Huxley acknowledged the importance of the literatures of modern languages such as French and German, but especially, given its colonial history and power, English: 'Every Englishman has, in his native tongue, an almost perfect instrument of literary expression; and in his own literature, models of every kind of literary excellence.'[19]

Thus, in his contribution to the debate about 'English Literature and the Universities' in 1886 Huxley responded to the terms prescribed by Collins. At the same time, and for the benefit of the place of scientific education in the cultural field, he re-negotiated the conceptual order that supported Matthew Arnold's literary model of culture. In his *Pall Mall Gazette* piece, Huxley advocates a pedagogic model of literary education based on imitation. In this model, imitation works in two senses. First, students are expected to imitate, or copy, examples of good rhetorical and stylistic practice, which echoes Collins's sense of English literature's imitative relation to the classics. Secondly, the examples of good expression that Huxley alludes to are all drawn from the eighteenth century: the writings of Swift, Goldsmith and Defoe are cited, all of which have in common, Huxley claims, 'clearness' and 'simplicity', or the stylistic virtues of mimetic discourse. It is significant to recall that, in defining the principles of classic literature in the Preface to the 1853 edition of his poetry, Arnold's starting point was the principle of mimesis or imitation. But whereas for Arnold it was the Hellenic Greeks who were the masters of imitations which foregrounded action and elided expression, Huxley constructs a canonical mimesis derived substantially from the Anglo-Scottish eighteenth-century Enlightenment.[20] Huxley's definitive contribution here was his 1879 biography of David Hume for the Macmillan 'English Men of Letters' series, a work in which Hume's radically empirical philosophy became the vehicle for re-defining 'criticism' – another Arnoldian term – as the scientistic police force in the world of thought, 'exterminating' contagious forms of metaphysical or superstitious rhetoric:

> It is the business of criticism not only to keep watch over the vagaries of philosophy, but to do the duty of police in the whole world of thought. Wherever it espies sophistry or superstition they are to be bidden to stand; nay, they are to be followed to their very dens and there apprehended and exterminated, as Othello smothered Desdemona, 'else she'll betray more men.'[21]

The 'English Literature and the Universities' debate was about defending culture from contagion. Huxley's concern with the 'vagaries of philosophy' is another perspective on Frazer's tangled cultural skein, though here 'science' adopts an aggressively corrective stance towards 'superstition' and religion. Moreover, the desire to exterminate contagiously cunning, duplicitous forms of thought to prevent their being further copied and disseminated is gendered; indeed, the gendering of contagious cunning as waywardly feminine will be encountered again in a work of popular evolutionary science: Baldwin's *Story of the Mind*.

In advocating imitation as a form of pedagogy in his *Pall Mall Gazette* piece, Huxley simultaneously refuses to endorse a model of literature teaching dominated by philology, which he dismisses as 'a fraud practised upon letters'. Huxley's rejection of philology is in one sense surprising, for he regularly appealed to its evolutionary methods in his critical writings on cultural and religious topics. For instance, in his anthropological essay on 'The Evolution of Theology' (which appeared in the collection *Controverted Questions*), Huxley reads the Witch of Endor narrative in the Old Testament book of Samuel as a 'fossilised' relic of primitive ghost worship, and it is philological argument that enables him to draw connections between Hebrew terms and their equivalents in Polynesian languages that accommodate comparable practices of worship.[22] Philology thus tended to exercise a defamiliarising effect, rearranging relations between similarities and differences and disturbing the presumption of essences. Huxley seemed to wish to keep a defence of mimetic literary style separate from this critical method, uncontaminated by any contagions that it might carry. In another sense, Huxley's determination to keep philology separate from 'letters' is not surprising; after all, he was rhetorically defending the integrity of the very command of 'letters' through which he crafted his position in the field of debate. Huxley went on to acknowledge that his advocacy of imitation and an eighteenth-century canon would meet with detractors, for 'it has been the fashion to decry the eighteenth century, as young fops laugh at their fathers'. Huxley's view of eighteenth-century literature avows confidence in mimetic representation as a vehicle of cultural transmission and an object of imitation in shaping human consciousness. But he also acknowledges that there is a ludic tendency to diverge from the productions of previous generations in acts that he likens to 'young fops laugh[ing] at their fathers'.

Despite extolling 'healthy, direct imitation', Edmund Gosse narrates a remarkably similar structure of avowal and disavowal regarding the properties of imitation in *Father and Son*. Thus, Huxley's and Gosse's writings glimpse a force of variation, grafting and insertion which disrupts the assumption of high-fidelity copying or faithful imitation, and which recognises the degree of contagious cunning which Derrida sees at play in mimesis. What emerges is 'literature' in a deconstructive mode, though in this context it is a species born of the evolutionary frameworks that generated the discipline of philology. Consequently, there is another conception of 'literature' to set alongside the one that Huxley advocated in the *Pall Mall Gazette*, which deconstructs the assumptions about imitation and teleological cultural evolution. Given this, perhaps Gosse's most conspicuous contribution to an understanding of cultural evolution in his otherwise vilified *From Shakespeare to Pope* was his throwaway comment that literary history consists of 'blind and unconscious' movement.[23]

4. 'IMITATION' IN WORD AND DEED: PHILOLOGY, PARODY AND THE 'LITERARY' UNCONSCIOUS IN EVOLUTIONARY NARRATIVES

Philology is an aid to self-culture, but it also complicates it in *Father and Son*: discovering forbidden fictions, the young Edmund turns to an etymological dictionary, 'Bailey's "English Dictionary"' (an eighteenth-century text), in order to learn unfamiliar words in a novel that he is reading (51). He discovers that dictionaries can complicate, as well as clarify, meaning. Upon overhearing the sour judgement passed by his governess on the character of the forceful Miss Wilkes – 'a minx' – the child consults a dictionary for enlightenment, only to be confronted with two usages, one from the domain of natural history, the other relating to human character, a signifier without a singular referent: '"Minx: the female of minnock; a pert wanton." I was', remarks the narrator ruefully, 'as much in the dark as ever' (119).

If Gosse presents a little allegory on the opacity of the dictionary, there was unsurprising faith in this tool as an authoritative philological archive in late nineteenth-century thinking about the evolution, preservation and reproduction of culture; it was pre-eminently embodied in the *New English*

Dictionary, or *Oxford English Dictionary* (*OED*), from 1895. The *OED* illustrated historically varied usage through both 'letters', or the canonical works of English prose and poetry, and other published materials. A case in point was the very term *imitation*, in which a key mechanism enabling the reproduction and dissemination of culture was itself defined and preserved in the dictionary:

IMITATION c. *Psychol.* The adoption, whether conscious or not, during a learning process, of the behaviour or attitudes of some specific person or model. 1807 WORDSWORTH *Poems* II. 153 The little actor cons another part . . . As if his whole vocation Were endless imitation. 1895. J. M. BALDWIN, *Mental Development* xii.. 351 First . . . biological or organic imitation . . . Second: we pass to psychological, conscious or cortical imitation. . . . 1903 E. C. PARSONS tr. *Tarde's Laws of Imitation* p. xiv. By imitation I mean every impression of inter-psychical photography . . . willed or not willed, passive or active.[24]

We have seen that J. G. Frazer's anthropology invoked 'imitation' warily, setting the word aside in favour of 'homoeopathy' because of an awareness of the contrary connotations that shadowed the term when he sought to apply it to magic; the *OED* entry draws together some of the inflections of meaning that generated tensions latent in the concept of imitation. Wordsworth's scene of imitation (from the ode 'Intimations of Immortality') captures the act of copying by heart from other sources. J. M. Baldwin's definition, taken from his *Mental Development in the Child and the Race* (1894), distinguishes between, whilst seeing a route from and to, organic-biological and human-psychological processes of imitation. E. C. Parsons's usage, from the introduction to her translation from the French of Gabriel Tarde's *Laws of Imitation* (1890), emphasises the impression that passes between two minds: the assumed fidelity of the imitation to its source is signified in its being described as 'photography' that is impressed 'inter-psychically'. Crucially, however, Parsons's usage also distinguishes between conscious and unconscious imitation ('willed or not willed').

It is significant that the entry gathers together usages of *imitation* that had been elaborated in late nineteenth-century work on cultural evolution, and which carried an increasingly international resonance – one example appeared in English translation from a French source, another originated in the United States. The American academic psychologist J. M. Baldwin's experimental psychological observations, set out in *Mental Development in the Child and the Race*, prepared the way for his seminal paper 'A New Factor in Evolution' (1896), which conceived of culture in modified Lamarckian terms as a collective adaptive engine (going beyond Lamarck's original individualistic sense of an organism's 'will'), and therefore as an agent of rapid species adaptation.[25] The French intellectual Gabriel Tarde – prominent for his debates with Durkheim in the 1890s – was also active in the emerging field of criminology during that decade, where he used the concept of imitation to contest the power of Lombroso's racial-determinist paradigm, arguing that 'the field of imitation has been constantly growing and freeing itself from heredity'.[26]

The entry on 'imitation' can be read as exemplifying the *OED*'s story of English linguistic development, set forth in the editor James H. Murray's framing 'General Explanation', and rendered in a diagram representing vocabulary domains comprising the 'core' areas of common, literary and colloquial; these are presented as gate keepers to the more 'peripheral' domains of the scientific, foreign, technical, slang and dialectal. It presents a very different sense of the genealogy of words from the anti-materialist framework set out by Coleridge in, for example, his reading of different historical usages of the term *idea* in *On the Constitution of the Church and State* (see chapter 1), particularly in the attention it devotes to the peripheral (scientific) variants of meaning that Coleridge satirised and eschewed. Murray's 'Explanation' in effect repeats Pater's contention in his essay on 'Style' in the observation that 'scientific . . . words enter the common language mainly through literature'.[27] According to this implied narrative, the sense of *imitation* illustrated from the works of Baldwin and Tarde published in the 1890s is 'psychological' or scientific; but this scientific sense is 'prepared' for entry into the common language by Wordsworth's use of the term in his 'Intimations' ode of 1807.[28] The philological dictionary accordingly sought to order a set of relations between science as the originator of specialist, supplementary meanings, and literature as legitimator of common use.

But this is an implied narrative which elides more complex tensions and struggles between different inflections of the same word, their multiple significations and contexts of iterability. Re-located in its poetic context, Wordsworth's deployment of *imitation* in the 'Intimations' ode does not authorise the safe passage of the term into affirmative late nineteenth-century natural and social scientific usages: instead, 'endless imitation' of 'dialogues of business, love or strife' reproduces the materially direction-less 'earthly freight' which fatally obscure the 'Intimations of Immortality' revealed in the recollections of early childhood. Wordsworth's sense of imitation presents a vision of mimicry without vital power; divinely inspired consciousness and inwardness are haunted by Wordsworth's anxiety about a 'counter-spirit' at work in linguistic and behavioural mimicry (stanzas VII, VIII).²⁹

It was appropriate that Parsons's English translation of Tarde's work on imitation should legitimate its inclusion in the *OED*. For it was precisely this semiotic variation, nuance and struggle that Tarde's sociology of imitation theorised in ways that made the 'unconscious' an important terrain. In conceptualising the 'field of imitation', Tarde formulated a theory of the subject in cultural space structured by signs organised in '*diametrical oppositions*'. Cultural sign-space, Tarde argued,

is so constituted as to admit an infinity of couples whose members are opposed to each other in direction, and our consciousness is so constituted as to admit of an infinity of affirmations opposed to negations, or an infinity of desires opposed to repugnances, each having precisely the same object.³⁰

Tarde argued that imitation had to be seen in the context of linguistic rivalry in which signs and accents of 'affirmation', 'negation', 'desire' and 'repugnance' contest the same referent:

Linguistic progress is effected first by imitation and then by the rivalry between the languages and dialects which quarrel over the same country, and one of which is crowded back by the other, or between the terms or idioms which correspond to the same idea. This struggle is a conflict between opposite theses implicit in word or idiom.³¹

Tarde thus goes beyond Saussure's structural linguistics by advancing a position on the contestation of the sign that bears comparison with the linguistics of the later Bakhtin circle in Russia. Reflecting on different categories of 'belief' – religious, moral, juristic and political – Tarde claims that these are inseparable from 'linguistic beliefs', for 'what an irresistible although unconscious power of persuasion our mother tongue . . . exerts over us'.³² Tarde thus contributes to the late nineteenth-century pursuit of the unconscious, in which Freud's psychoanalytic 'discovery' was only one episode. In doing so, Tarde's sense of the unconscious is less the Freudian account of depth-psychological sublimated motive, and more a Derridean sense of the unconscious as a structural necessity that eludes total epistemological mastery of a field.³³

Tarde's sense of a linguistic unconscious as a structural necessity in the field of cultural imitation is glimpsed in the 'General Explanation' to the *OED*. The editors of the *OED* found themselves assembling a much more complex evolutionary account of the language, as the published 'Explanation' of their practice indicates. In seeking to account for the 'core' of English vocabulary, the 'Explanation' grafts into its rationale an evolutionary biological discourse that simultaneously defines and complicates the dictionary's philological enterprise by finding at the margins of the language's 'core' a blurring of delineations:

> That vast aggregate of words and phrases . . . may be compared to one of those natural groups of the zoologist or botanist, wherein typical species forming the characteristic nucleus of the order, are linked on every side to other species, in which the typical character is less and less distinctly apparent, till it fades away in an outer fringe of aberrant forms, which merge imperceptibly in various surrounding orders, and whose own position is ambiguous and uncertain.[34]

This is another version of Frazer's tangled historical skein of magic, religion and science, this time applied to philologically researched language itself.

The 'aberrant forms', 'ambiguity' and 'uncertainty' that Murray encounters in his attempt to impose a classificatory grid on language is highlighted in microcosm by J. M. Baldwin in *Mental Development in the Child and Race*. For Baldwin acknowledges that the concept of 'imitation' is strained by the multiple uses, animal and human, instinctual and volitional, to which his study puts the term ('the mocking-bird's song is a good imitation' . . . 'the child's movement is a good imitation'); yet this 'strain' and ambiguity are elided in another domain of language, which Baldwin classifies as 'popular language'.[35] This sense of ambiguity, aberrant form and uncertainty haunts the symbolic inscription of scenes of imitation, and compromises the narratives of cultural progress that they promise in Baldwin's *The Story of the Mind* (1899) and Gosse's *Father and Son*.

Baldwin's numerous writings on psychology and cultural evolution argued that a Darwinian selectionist evolutionary paradigm would become ascendant in the intellectual field. His *Darwin and the Humanities* (1910) was a work that followed self-consciously in the wake of the Darwin–Wallace Celebration at the Linnaean Society (the work was published first in America, and then in a London edition). Baldwin sought to re-configure the map of knowledge in Darwinian terms, by urging recognition of a 'genetic order' of disciplines: biology was the pre-eminent, universal discipline, and just beneath that would be found psychology, then ethics and sociology (the ordering of chapters in Baldwin's book); anthropology, philology, political science and literary criticism would also be subject to Darwin's 'great and illuminating conception'. In support of this genetic order, Baldwin did not conceive of two evolutionary processes, divided between 'organic' and 'mental' evolution; instead, his view of evolution had universal application in the form of a 'psycho-physical' process.[36] For Baldwin, organic and psychical developments were mutually reinforcing and inter-connected, with beneficial developments being 'naturally' selected. Baldwin was keen to differentiate his theory from Lamarck's emphasis on variation produced by the individual will of an organism, and its capacity to pass on acquired characteristics to its offspring. Baldwin sees in 'the world of ideas, a curious form of struggle for existence, a competition of ideas to survive', and, unlike Samuel Butler, Lamarck's ideas were not ones that he wished to see preserved.[37] Accordingly, Baldwin stresses the role of 'social heredity' in populations of living organisms, and 'imitation' is central to its transmission. In his observation of 'animal companies', he notes that 'imitation is active to enable the young to learn the actions, calls and general behaviour'.[38]

This was no less applicable to humans. Baldwin narrates a scene of imitation both in *Mental Development in the Child and Race*, and later again in his popular work *The Story of the Mind*, in which he describes a young child in the act of copying an original. Baldwin's theory of 'social heredity' depended in turn on a theory of the subject as a 'socius', that is as 'a normally educated person'.[39] Accordingly, imitation becomes a mechanism in the service of the normalisation of a population, or the replication of the 'same' through contagious action, for 'Beliefs are contagious, ideas run from mind to mind, imitation produces sameness, as Baldwin states in a formulation which implies the 'photographic' quality of inter-psychic imitation.[40] This sense of the contagious basis of sameness frames Baldwin's ideal scene of imitation, in which the male child 'looks at the copy before him; sets all his muscles of hand and arm into massive contraction . . . holds his breath and in every way concentrates his energies upon the copying of the model'.[41] Although Baldwin stresses the trial-and-error nature of the act of imitating – that the child will, necessarily, have to experiment and initially produce low-fidelity imitations – the goal must still be accurate copying, getting it 'right'. Baldwin observes that when a father watches his son, 'he gradually sees emerge from the child's inner consciousness its picture of the boy's own father, whom he aspires to be like'.[42]

The young Edmund Gosse had aspired to be like his father in 1857–8. As Ann Thwaite observes in her biography of Philip Henry Gosse, the popular naturalist did indeed observe his young son's drawings from this period, drawings that imitated the father's own skilful natural history illustrations. What 'saddened' Philip Henry about these, Thwaite records, was their 'lack of originality'. However, Thwaite finds an exception to this rule: it is a naïve drawing of a be-whiskered, booted man, holding a book: the caption heading the page of the exercise book reads 'Beasts, The Man'; the young Edmund's commentary below states, 'It is to many hard to believe that a Man is an animal, however he is.' Thwaite observes that 'Philip Henry Gosse never drew a man in his life. This particular illustration, unremarkable for any other reason, must surely be a portrait of the father himself.'[43] In imitating the work of his father, Edmund Gosse produced a variant, and perhaps this is remarkable for the light it casts on Edmund Gosse's complex reflection on imitation in *Father and Son.*

For these complexities invite a disruptive re-reading of Baldwin's scene of imitation, his building block of cultural evolutionary progress. Despite Gosse's commentary extolling the benefits of 'healthy . . . direct imitation', his scene can be juxtaposed to Baldwin's in the way that it raises questions about the extent to which sameness can be reproduced: the sovereignty of intention and consciousness is challenged by the parodic and the ludic, or play. As we have seen, Gosse looks back to the time of his childhood when his father was composing *Actinologia Britannica* (1860), the work on the marine life of Britain's coasts, and a point at which Gosse's younger self was imitating his father's work, 'preparing little monographs on seaside creatures'. Looking at the preserved remains of his copies, consisting of words and watercolour pictures, Gosse is struck by 'the perseverance and the patience, the evidence of close and persistent labour'. Yet, comparing the copies he produced with his father's originals, Gosse is perplexed by what he sees and, perhaps more significantly, recalls the extent to which these productions perplexed his father, for the imitations were:

ludicrous pastiches . . . they were, moreover, parodies, rather than imitations of his writings, for I invented new species, with sapphire spots and crimson tentacles and amber bands, which were close enough to his real species to be disconcerting . . . If I had not been so innocent and solemn, he might have fancied I was mocking him. (123–4)

We have already seen Philip Henry Gosse represented as a man trembling 'before a parody of his own central self' (176) in the face of Mrs Paget's capacity to imitate his theological expertise. Here Philip Henry is confronted with his son's imitations of his representations of nature that are similar enough to their object to claim fidelity, and yet which are sufficiently divergent from and subversive of the original representations they purportedly imitate to be 'disconcerting'. It is 'disconcerting' for the father – that is to say his masterful self-possession is disturbed, put out of concert – precisely because the imitations are unconscious parodies, for Edmund's solemn and innocent demeanour indicates that there is no intention to mock, or to laugh at the father.

Significantly, 'disconcert' is produced as a consequence of Gosse's shift from imitation to parody, which is represented as an inventive move ('I invented new species'), for 'invention' has implications that disrupt the reproductive logic of imitation. As Derrida argues in 'Psyche: Invention of the Other', invention is an enigmatic concept which is radically distinct from copying ('a copy can never be an invention'), and yet which depends on an established symbolic fabric to make it intelligible.[44] Commonly authorised categories of invention are, as Derrida points out, stories – the fictional or fabulous – and machines, which Derrida defines as devices which generate 'new operational possibilit[ies].'[45] As Derrida's performance progresses, he grafts together the characteristics associated with these conventionally different categories of invention in order to draw analogies between them.[46] This grafting draws attention to the mechanical, unconscious inventiveness of narrative and textual systems, which, in their openness to the other, produce 'new operational possibilities', the contours of which cannot consciously be grasped in advance. For Derrida, the unconscious 'machinery' of written texts generates an inventiveness and openness which 'through a merging of chance and necessity, produce[s] the new of an event' which can move beyond 'the economy of the same'.[47]

A Derridean reading of Philip Henry Gosse's moment of 'disconcert' from *Father and Son* enables a re-reading of the exemplary stories in Baldwin's *Story of the Mind*. In other words, this graft produces a mode of reading which can open up a generically non-literary, popular scientific text about cultural evolution to the play of the literary: a play which disrupts the economy of sameness that one of Baldwin's exemplary stories seeks to uphold. In this episode, Baldwin reflects on children learning through their observation of parental behaviour, which the children then imitate through play; Baldwin repeats the rhetoric, copies it from his previous work; 'if a man study these games patiently in his own children . . . he gradually sees emerge from within the inner consciousness a picture of the boy's own father, whom he aspires to be like, and whose actions he seeks to generalize and apply'.[48]

Baldwin goes on to narrate, in detail, an episode that he has witnessed in which his daughters act out a little maternal scene with a doll. He poses a rhetorical question to an ideal, feminine subjectivity: 'what could be a more direct lesson – a lived out exercise – in sympathy, in altruistic self-denial, in the healthy elevation of her sense of self to the dignity of kindly offices?'[49] The answer to this question is, however, put in doubt when in the middle of the episode of playful domestic imitation that Baldwin narrates, one of Baldwin's daughters invents a supplementary father figure (so marginalising the one standing by, watching the play). She fashions the supplementary patriarch from an ornamental column standing in the corner of the living room. Although Baldwin's text inscribes the daughter in the language of the passive, obedient feminine, it also records her ventriloquial imitation of a deep masculine voice which supposedly emanates from the column: if Baldwin speaks for her 'type' and its replication, the child has pre-emptively spoken for his. Baldwin's mastery within what Tarde would describe as the field of imitation is here rendered uncertain as he encounters a voice which is not conscious of its parodic effect, yet can be read as parodic. This accords with Bakhtin's account of parody, which he conceptualises in terms of dialogic tensions and conflicts between voices, a (persuasive) authoritative 'word of the father' being relativised by other, competing voices that vie for the subject's attention.[50] Baldwin's indirect response to his daughter's invention is to warn the reader that 'play has its dangers also – very serious ones. The game gives practice in cunning no less than forbearance.'[51] Baldwin's text here unconsciously anticipates Derrida's observation that 'the things in play in mimesis are very cunning'. The 'contagion' of sameness that Baldwin claims to find in thoughts passing 'photographically' between minds is undone by the cunning of 'contamination' that Derrida finds at play in his account of the condition of impurity which haunts classificatory drives.[52]

Baldwin's text produces 'new operational possibilities' through 'ethereal' intertextual contact with *Father and Son*, the writings of Tarde, and Derrida's much later texts. For it is possible to read Baldwin's account of his daughters at play through Jacques Lacan's psychoanalytic account of the symbolic order, the Law of the Father, and the phallus as transcendental signifier; and to claim, despite the text's avowed intentions, that it reveals something of the politics of the reproduction of contingent gender differences otherwise projected as natural and universal. This reading must be set in the context of what Derrida insisted were 'public tradition[s]' of discourse, the lines of which can be followed back to the nineteenth century:[53] Lacan's discourse is a variation upon Freud's writings on the unconscious, which were themselves derived from traditions of evolutionary anthropology.[54] It is above all important to stress that Baldwin's moment of disconcert is not the discovery of 'the' unconscious as a domain of mind or thing; rather, we find in Baldwin's textual system, and the grafts through which it can be read, a manifestation of the unconscious as a structural necessity; it generates an inventiveness producing the 'new of an event'. The 'new event' casts a critical light on gender politics through the unconscious parody of masculine mastery that Baldwin's text glimpses and represses. It also casts a critical light on Huxley's gendering of science's drive to exterminate what it constructs as 'feminine' superstition and sophistry.

Gabriel Tarde's late nineteenth-century sociology struggled to conceive and theorise the way in which new events might steer the field of culture in new, unforeseen directions. Tarde was sceptical of the claim, made by Baldwin for example, that a Darwinian evolutionary paradigm could account, universally, for every event. In an effort to conceptualise the new, Tarde called for a philosophy of 'insertion' which could grasp the nature of radical changes of direction in a culture:

> When a new invention, an invisible microbe at first, later on a fatal disease, brings with it a germ which will eventually destroy the old invention to which it attaches itself, how can the latter be said to evolve? Did the Roman Empire evolve when Christianity inoculated it with the virus of radical negations of its fundamental principles? No, this was counter-evolution, revolution perhaps . . . it is a great mistake to consider the sum formed by these elements as a *single* evolution.[55]

Tarde pulls together a striking range of analogies to imagine and explain a cultural change that would be dramatic, and would resist the algorithmic universality proposed by some forms of Darwinian argument: thus he recalls the decline of a great empire, the original invention of vigorous Roman colonists, in the face of a powerful cult (Christianity). And he imagines the agency that brought about the decline as a virus or contagion that might undermine an old order, and invent a new one. What Tarde appears to theorise here is the simultaneously contagious and inventive power of the literary 'insertion', and the supplements that were produced in the dialogic space *between* Gosse's *Father and Son* and the evolutionary textbooks of J. M. Baldwin. Such contagions, insertions and supplements produce openings to ensure, as Raymond Williams might put it, our continuing and absolutely necessary cultural survival.

Conclusion:
culture's field, culture's vital robe

In nineteenth-century England 'culture' signified, variously, occupation and tilling of the land; the 'harrowing of selves'; and, increasingly, a space which writers and critics came to see as 'a court of appeal' for issuing judgements and evaluations of human artistic and intellectual practices, and their educative capacity. The court of appeal was one venerated location within the totality of culture's sphere of operations, a sphere that came increasingly to be imagined as a field, thereby neatly looping back to the horticultural origins of the term. Conceiving the operations of culture's field always involved symbolic imaginings: from Wordsworth's wandering pedlar to J. H. Green's Coleridgean fenced field, cleared of noxious speculative growths, to Herbert Spencer's ghostly 'secondary environment' to J. G. Frazer's 'ether' mysteriously connecting the different strands of the 'tangled skein' of magic, science and religion and, finally, to T. H. Huxley's garden-colony, as both a site of judgement and a volatile 'hothouse' of symbolic activity. In imagining the power and reach of 'culture', scientific discourse, especially from the evolutionary life sciences, sought to engage audiences with the wonders of its new and challenging revelations, and to fashion symbolic substitutes for a crumbling Christian religion. In doing this, the life sciences contributed what Gabriel Tarde described as 'insertions' into various imaginings of culture's work. Those insertions gave rise to powerful supplementary meanings; in short, they have contributed to the emergence of a practice of counter-insertion that we recognise to be 'literary'.

In concluding, I want to return to J. A. Symonds's sense of culture as a 'magic robe' woven between the arts and the sciences, imagined in his essay 'Culture: its Meanings and Uses'. In 1890, Symonds published his *Essays Speculative and Suggestive*; a third edition was published in 1907, the same year as Gosse's *Father and Son*. Gosse had been one of Symonds's literary executors when he died in 1893, and the other, Horatio Brown, steered the third edition through the press. The collection contained an essay 'On the Application of Evolutionary Principles to Art and Literature' in which

Symonds took his readers into 'the wide fields of ordinary culture' which provided countless historical instances of artistic development, as well as articulations of the critical insights that had sought to codify them.[1] For Symonds, an artistic convention was always subject to rules of growth and development, followed by exhaustion and decadence once it had 'performed its curve, fulfilled its cycle, displayed its several aspects' (49). The 'species' of art which broke beyond the logic of this developmental curve was hybridity:

> The arts of Europe, as they now exist . . . are all of them hybrids. The problem for the Evolutionist increases in complexity by reason of crossings, blendings and complicated heredity; by reason of our common European culture being adapted to diverse national conditions; by reason of the rapid interchange of widely separated and specific products. . . . the Novel is one of the most 'hybridisable genera' known to us in literature . . . Personal capacity . . . assert[s itself] . . . with more apparent freedom in these circumstances. The type does not expire because the type has become capable of infinite modification. It is indeed no longer a type . . . but a mongrel of many types. What art loses in force and impressiveness, in monumental dignity and power to embody the strong spirit of creative nations, it now gains in elasticity and disengagement from the soil on which it springs. (51)

Butler's *Erewhon* was a generic hybrid. So was Gosse's *Father and Son*, which continues to impress as something of a model for what Symonds sets out here. As a 'mongrel' form that incorporates many 'types' (documentary, critical essay, autobiography, the novel), it was a vehicle for asserting 'personal capacity', or the singularity of inventive self-harrowing. Hybridity is seen by Symonds as an engine of individuation, elasticity and inventiveness, the very power that liberates 'cultural practice' from its rootedness in a 'soil' bordered by particular national boundaries. Like Clifford Geertz's 'note in a bottle' and Darwin's ocean-crossing seeds, a hybrid may originate in one 'soil', travel as one 'thing' from that location to another, and be read and re-inscribed quite differently. Butler's 'making' of *Erewhon* in New Zealand from Darwin's theories is a good example.

To make this very point, meanings in Symonds's passage cross between the scientific and literary domains of the 'magic robe' of culture, or culture's mediating field: a movement significant in the nineteenth century, but also in the present. The racial sense of 'hybridity' derived from the life sciences is invoked in Symonds's appeal to the racial and zoological unions that result in 'mongrels'. Symonds's usage is explained by the typology of nineteenth-century theories of racial hybridity that Robert J. C. Young has outlined in *Colonial Desire*, for it neatly illustrates Young's contention that 'hybridity . . . shows the connections between the racial categories of the past and contemporary cultural discourse'.[2] In fact, Symonds could be said to have coined a hybrid example of 'hybridity', suspended as it were on the border between technically racial and distinctively artistic usages. In advancing his point, Young looks at the continuing and modified presence of concepts of hybridity in the linguistic theory of M. M. Bakhtin, and the postcolonial theory of Homi Bhabha (20–26).

Indeed, Young could have taken this point further. Bhabha's theory of hybridity (and Bakhtin's, given its emphasis on parodic double-voicedness) can be linked to the practice of mimicry, and provides another genealogical link between critical discourses of the present, and discourses from the nineteenth century. Bhabha's classic essay 'Of Mimicry and Man: the Ambivalence of Colonial Discourse' quotes discourses from nineteenth-century colonial officials, in which the destabilising properties of 'mimic representations' are recognised. In addition, Bhabha cites Jacques Lacan on mimicry, quoting from the essay 'The Line and Light' (in *Of the Gaze*) in which Lacan compares mimicry to camouflage: 'It is not a question of harmonizing with the background, but against a mottled background, of becoming mottled.'[3] The unacknowledged link that Lacan makes here is, I would argue, with the life sciences of the nineteenth century, and with research into 'mimicry' as a biological principle, identified initially by the evolutionary observations of H. W. Bates and A. R. Wallace, though building on and diverging from, as I have argued, established principles of Enlightenment zoology and anthropology.[4] For it appears to be the mimicking capacities of mottled moths to which Lacan alludes, in which, moreover, a mingled discourse of 'culture' and evolution is implicated: mimicry is not about harmonisation with the background (seamless fitting, effortless unification), but about becoming mottled, as 'nature' or some combination of agencies fashions mottled effects. Again, a text such as Gosse's *Father and Son* was a resonant meeting point for the border-crossings between significations of imitation and mimicry that were passed between the life sciences and discourses of criticism respectively – another instance of the text's energetic hybridity, which continues to generate new signifying possibilities in the present.

A complex relationship between the past and the present is always latent in the densely woven workings of the cultural field, which is why Symonds's image of culture as a 'robe' woven between literature and science is particularly resonant. Consequently, analysis of the kind that I have offered in this book ought not to rest on one particular category (such as race in Young's work), but should rather explore the wider patterns of exchange, discursive movement, and contestation that have shaped the literary and scientific interfaces of the present. To take another example, cybernetic discourses, or

discourses of mechanisation and remote control, were also shared between
literary and scientific domains of discourse in the nineteenth century. They
were usually cited negatively in the tradition of 'culture and society' writings
that Raymond Williams identified. However, evolutionary treatments of
machine discourse (Huxley's work on automata, for example) both prob-
lematised and energised it, making it newly available to writers such as
Samuel Butler. Butler pushed what we might now recognise as cybernetic
discourse in new estranging directions:

[Man] is such a hive and swarm of parasites that it is doubtful whether his body is
not more theirs than his, and whether he is anything but another kind of ant-heap
after all. May not man himself become a sort of parasite upon the machines? An
affectionate machine-tickling aphid? (*Erewhon*, 245)

In a world of microbes and parasites, the human body becomes another
colony where assumptions about boundaries, territorial possession and
rights are open to question. Moreover, in an age of mechanical contrivance
in which the boundaries between bodily and machinate organs would begin
to blur, populations of human bodies might in turn become, through a defamiliarising adjustment of the imaginary microscope's focus, parasites upon
a set of host machines. In a colonial context, of course, there are terrible
dangers latent in this kind of image, as Patrick Brantlinger's sobering work
on 'extinction discourse' demonstrates.[5] Consequently, it becomes important to seek critically for what Raymond Williams called the 'resources
of hope' in the intertextualities of culture. For in this image, Butler produced an insertion that would come to be re-written in a different era of
scientific thinking, the neo-Darwinian alliance between natural selection
and the genetics of Crick and Watson. Butler's writing, it seems to me,
is unconsciously mimicked in Richard Dawkins's celebrated passage from
The Selfish Gene about the relationship between genes and the human body:

The replicators that survived were the ones that built *survival machines* for themselves to live in . . . What weird engines of self-preservation would the millennia
bring forth? Four thousand million years on, what was to be the fate of the ancient
replicators? They did not die out, for they are past masters of the survival arts. But
do not look for them floating loose in the seas; they gave up that cavalier freedom
long ago. Now they swarm in huge colonies, safe inside gigantic lumbering robots,
sealed off from the outside world, communicating with it by tortuous indirect
routes, manipulating it by remote control.[6]

The device of defamiliarisation is utilised by Butler and Dawkins; Dawkins
stresses that his book has been written to communicate his own sense of
'astonishment' to others (v). As I have suggested, taking my lead from the

writings of Huxley, Darwin and others, defamiliarisation is not exclusively an approach to a set of familiar literary texts and images that jolts us into unfamiliar perceptions, as codified by Russian formalism after 1917: it is also a discourse that descends from nineteenth-century science as it strove to display 'life' from the astonishing angles that evolutionary science revealed.[7]

The 'colony' is invoked in both Butler and Dawkins as a defamiliarisation of 'life' and its patterns of interaction and agency. While it is implicit in Butler, in Dawkins it is used explicitly as an image of the human body, much as George Henry Lewes used the image when imagining the cooperative interactions of the various component parts of a composite organism in his 'Studies in Animal Life'. It is fitting that the 'colony', as one of the linguistic derivatives of 'culture', should loop back in diverse and complex ways into the politics of culture: for Lewes in the 1860s, the organism-as-colony amounted to 'animal socialism of the purest kind'. Dawkins's image is no less complex, and, despite the title of his book and frequent simplifications of his position, it is socially resonant: the body as 'colony' palliates and even frustrates the selfishness of genes, for while the survival machines are bent on nothing other than their replication, this end is achieved by 'tortuous' indirection, and 'remote control'. It is in the space of tortuous indirection that the symbolic work of culture takes place, and the sympathetic filaments are constructed to bind together, however precariously and uncertainly, Huxley's 'emotional chameleons' and 'artificial personalities'.

My argument is then that traditions of discourse in literature and science, in all their complexity and historic resonance, matter deeply. It is important to remember that Darwin's writings about slave-making ants contribute to the biologist E. O. Wilson's wonderfully defamiliarising image of a 'Dean of Termites' addressing fellow termites about termite culture (comprising, among others, a celebration of 'the centrality of colony life amidst a richness of war and trade among the colonies . . . [and] the aesthetic pleasure of eating from nestmates' anuses after the shedding of the skin').[8] In practice, Wilson's work feeds into another tradition relating science to literature, represented in the late nineteenth century by James Mark Baldwin, as described in my final chapter. Baldwin's theory of the universal applicability of Darwin is with us again; Richard Dawkins, Daniel C. Dennett and E. O. Wilson are to be counted among its exponents, and a neo-Darwinist movement of literary criticism is positioning itself to take a hold on the field of culture. E. O. Wilson has compared their intellectual cartographic task, dauntingly, to the work of 'Columbian' colonisers.[9] If one strives to find resources of hope from colonial discourse, then this is not a promising opening. Of course, literary studies have harboured their own imperial ambitions; in the 1960s, in response to the 'two cultures' thesis of C. P. Snow, F. R. Leavis argued that a true appreciation of the idea of culture, and the 'life' that was needed to sustain it, could be held under the governance of a 'vital English school' (see Introduction). In one sense, Leavis bequeathed something of great value: a nuanced approach to traditions of discourse. What he failed to appreciate was the impact that historic traditions of discourse in the life sciences had exerted upon the very term that marked 'life' and 'culture' as sources of value: 'vitality'. A 'vital' approach to science, literature and culture will be sensitive and alert to the widespread contestations of the sign that produce cultural 'vitality', by offering thick descriptions of the inter-textualities, the signifying practices, and the processes of dissemination and supplementarity that underwrite that vitality.

Notes

INTRODUCTION: LITERATURE, SCIENCE AND
THE HOTHOUSE OF CULTURE

1. Matthew Arnold, *Culture and Anarchy: An Essay in Social and Political Criticism*, 1869, in *Complete Prose Works*, ed. R. H. Super, 11 vols. (Ann Arbor: University of Michigan Press, 1965), v, 93. All future references will be to this edition, and given in the main text.
2. See Buchanan's essay 'The Student and His Vocation' in his collection *David Gray and Other Essays, Chiefly on Poetry* (London: Sampson, Low, Son, and Marston, 1868), 199.
3. George Combe, *The Constitution of Man Considered in Relation to External Objects*, 1828, 8th edn (Edinburgh: MacLachlan, Stewart, and Co., 1847), ch. 11.
4. 'Hence, as more individuals are produced than can possibly survive, there must in every case be a struggle for existence, either one individual with another of the same species, or with individuals of distinct species, or with the physical conditions of life. It is the doctrine of Malthus applied with manifold force to the whole animal and vegetable kingdoms.' Charles Darwin, *The Origin of Species*, 1859, ed. J. W. Burrow, Penguin English Library (Harmondsworth: Penguin, 1982), 117. This is based on the first edition, though Burrow makes an exception by prefacing the work with Darwin's 'Historical Sketch', which did not appear until the sixth edition. Future references will be to this edition (unless stated otherwise), and given in the main text.
5. Jon P. Klancher, *The Making of English Reading Audiences, 1790–1832* (Madison and London: University of Wisconsin Press, 1987), 33.
6. See James Secord, *Victorian Sensation: The Extraordinary Publication, Reception and Secret Authorship of the 'Vestiges of the Natural History of Creation'* (Chicago and London: University of Chicago Press, 2000)
7. See Pierre Bourdieu, *Language and Symbolic Power*, ed. John B. Thompson, trans. Gino Raymond and Matthew Adamson (Oxford: Polity, 1992), 72–6.
8. For a recent account of culture's 'Malthusian turn', see Catherine Gallagher, *The Body Economic: Life, Death and Sensation in Political Economy and the Victorian Novel* (Princeton University Press, 2006); Arnold's work is discussed, though not in the context set out here.

9. Important previous work on this subject includes Donald Ulin, 'A Clerisy of Worms: Darwin's Inverted World', *Victorian Studies*, 35:3 (spring 1992), 295–308. For Ulin, Darwin modifies 'culture' by breaking down some of the dualisms that the dominant nineteenth-century understanding of the concept helped to maintain, such as the distinction between the ideal and the material. Darwin's theory of sexual selection develops a materialist sense of the aesthetic, thus introducing work and struggle into the concept of culture. Darwin is important to Ulin because his writing enables the emergence of a concept of culture connoting both plurality and specificity before the Victorians were able to speak of it as such. This connects Ulin's arguments to another important work, Christopher Herbert, *Culture and Anomie: Ethnographic Imagination in the Nineteenth Century* (Chicago and London: University of Chicago Press, 1991), though as the title indicates, Herbert's concern is principally ethnographic writing, which is a focus for re-constructing the diverse ensemble of texts and discourses which came together to form the '"general intellectual method" of the modern analysis of cultures' (23). Herbert argues that the idea of 'an alien society as a seamless web of institutions with its own inherent "law and order" . . . formed one of the most lethal instruments of dissidence from Victorian thinking' (44). Whereas Herbert proposed to leave the 'development of the idealised sense of the word "culture" . . . almost entirely to one side' (23), my account will stress the often contestatory overlap between this tradition and writings of scientific investigation and speculation, particularly when the question of materialism is at issue. I do, where appropriate, draw on the term 'culture concept', which has been used more widely in discussions of 'culture' in the history of anthropology as a discipline, taking a lead from Clifford Geertz and George W. Stocking: see for example Richard Handler, 'Raymond Williams, George Stocking and Fin-de-Siècle U.S. Anthropology', *Cultural Anthropology* 13:4 (1988), 447–63. Catherine Gallagher's *The Body Economic* discusses the formation of different strands of the culture concept in ch. 6.

10. *Charles Darwin's Notebooks, 1836–1844*, ed. Paul H. Barrett, Peter J. Gautrey, Sandra Herbert, David Kohn and Sydney Smith (Cambridge: British Museum [Natural History] and Cambridge University Press, 1987), 1.

11. As Darwin perused the *Edinburgh New Philosophical Journal* – the third number to be published in 1827 – he would have been aware of an essay tantalisingly entitled 'Of the Changes Which Life has Experienced on the Globe', which had probably been written by the natural historian and comparative anatomist Robert E. Grant, Darwin's mentor at the University of Edinburgh during his abortive period of studying medicine. In 1826–7 Grant had also published in the *Edinburgh New Philosophical Journal* a series of important and influential essays on sea sponges which were underpinned by a theory of transmutation. Robert E. Grant, 'Of the Changes Which Life Has Experienced on the Globe', *Edinburgh New Philosophical Journal* (hereafter *ENPJ*), 3 (1827), 298–301; and see for instance 'Remarks on the Structure of Some Calcareous Sponges', *ENPJ*, 1 (1826), 166–71.

12. An 'Account of Mr Crawfurd's Mission to Ava', *ENPJ*, 3 (1827), 359–70, 359. Future references will be given in the main text.

13. *Darwin's Notebooks*, Notebook B [119], 199. The figure in brackets refers to the entry's place in the sequence of the notebook; the second figure refers to the pagination of the edition. The notebooks are arranged alphabetically, and those concerned principally with the transmutation question are A, B, C, D and E; M and N are concerned with 'Metaphysical Enquiries', as is the notebook known as 'Old and Useless Notes'. References will be given according to the pattern above.

14. See for example the chapter on 'Ruta Baga Culture' in William Cobbett, *Journal of a Year's Residence in the United States of America*, 1818 (Stroud: Alan Sutton, 1983).

15. See David Cannadine, *Ornamentalism: How the British Saw Their Empire* (Harmondsworth: Allen Lane, the Penguin Press, 2001)

16. Crawfurd's narrative presupposes a knowledge of the conflicts which beset the Malay Peninsula and islands of the adjacent Archipelago throughout the first decades of the nineteenth century, as the Dutch and the British fought over the colonial control of territories, imperial conflicts made more complex by the Napoleonic wars, which themselves had been as much about territorial influence in the East as in Europe (Napoleon's Egyptian campaign and the British response, for example). Crawfurd had been present at the British conquest of Java in 1811, and went on to occupy the principal political and civil offices governing the island before 1817 when the Dutch resumed their governance. The mission to Ava represented another episode in the British East India Company's attempt to maintain hegemony and strategic advantage in a maritime region that, connecting China and India, was vital to imperial trade. It came in the wake of British military intervention (the first British–Burmese war, 1824–6), a reluctant peace after the Treaty of Yandabu (from which Britain made significant territorial gains), and an accelerating process of colonisation. The natural historical and commercial and strategic ends of the mission were closely linked: Crawfurd notes the presence of the soondree, a 'valuable timber, the uses of which are well known in our Indian arsenals and timber yards' ('Mission', 367). See the entry for Crawfurd in the *DNB*.

17. J. R. Seeley, *The Expansion of England: Two Courses of Lectures*, 1883 (London: Macmillan, 1895), 89. Seeley's published lectures appeared when British territorial control was at its height and embraced the 'settler' colonies of the Canadian Dominions, New Zealand, Australia and the West Indies; the conquered and governed colonies of Southern Africa; and India. This was at precisely the moment when the integrity of the 'home' imperium – the Union – was being debated through the question of Irish Home Rule, a question which was to dismantle long-established political identifications and affiliations among liberals. In effect, the question of colonial governance had disrupted political affiliations from much earlier, in particular around the Jamaican Morant Bay controversy (1865), and the polarising of English intellectuals around, respectively, cases for the prosecution (J. S. Mill, Darwin, Huxley) and defence (Carlyle, Ruskin,

Dickens, Tennyson) of Governor Eyre. See Catherine Hall, *Civilising Subjects: Metropole and Colony in the English Imagination* (Cambridge: Polity, 2002), 25. Although, as Hall points out, the liberal and scientific intelligentsia came together to prosecute Eyre, John Tyndall supported Eyre, and A. R. Wallace's socialist perspective on colonial governance was to be very different from T. H. Huxley's (see this chapter, and chapter 4).

18. For Darwin's 'squarson' social identity (a combination of squire and parson) and political orientation, see James R. Moore's 'Darwin of Down: the Evolutionist as Squarson-Naturalist', in David Kohn (ed.), *The Darwinian Heritage* (Princeton University Press, 1985), 435–81.

19. The historiography and politics of colonialism has been complicated by a Darwinian, natural historical perspective in other notable ways: see for instance Richard Grove, *Green Imperialism: Colonial Expansion, Tropical Island Edens and the Origins of Environmentalism* (Cambridge University Press, 1995). Grove situates Darwin's theoretical insights at the end of a long tradition of colonial administrative practice that sought to preserve and understand environments, and which became consequently aware of the delicate relationship between a changing environment and indigenous populations of plants and animals.

20. Janet Browne points out that the Admiralty's strategy was to put Britain in a position to exploit the freeing up of trading relations in southern Latin America by charting the unexplored coastline of Buenos Aires. See *Charles Darwin: Voyaging* (London: Jonathan Cape, 1995), 181.

21. For an account of this series, see Angus Fraser, 'John Murray's Colonial and Home Library', *Proceedings of the Bibliographical Society of America* 91:3 (September 1997), 339–408, 350–1.

22. Clifford Geertz, 'Thick Description: Towards an Interpretive Theory of Culture', in *The Interpretation of Cultures: Selected Essays*, 1973 (London: Fontana, 1993), 10.

23. *Darwin's Notebooks*, B [119], 199

24. Charles Darwin, 'Autobiography, May 31st 1876', in Charles Darwin and T. H. Huxley, *Autobiographies*, ed. Gavin de Beer (Oxford University Press, 1983), 71; for Darwin's own record of his reading of Malthus' *Essay on the Principle of Population* (3 October 1838), see *Darwin's Notebooks*, D [134–5], 374–5.

25. *Darwin's Notebooks*, B [3], 171.

26. Cuvier's 'Essay on the Domestication of Mammiferous Animals' was also published in the *Edinburgh New Philosophical Journal*, 4 (April 1828); the author was the brother of Baron Georges Cuvier. Darwin's verbatim note reads: 'But we could only produce domestic individuals and not races, without the occurrence of one of the most general laws of life – the transmission of a fortuitous modification into a durable form, of a fugitive want into a fundamental propensity, of an accidental habit into an instinct' (297); *Darwin's Notebooks*, B [118], 199.

27. Stephen G. Alter, *Darwinism and the Linguistic Image: Language, Race and Natural Theology in the Nineteenth Century* (Baltimore and London: Johns Hopkins University Press, 1999).

28. Raymond Williams, *Culture and Society 1780–1950*, 1958 (Harmondsworth: Penguin, 1963), 16. Future references will be given in the main text.

29. Raymond Williams, *Keywords: A Vocabulary of Culture and Society* (1976), 2nd edn (London: Fontana, 1983), 87.

30. Robert J. C. Young, *Colonial Desire: Hybridity in Theory, Culture and Race* (London: Routledge, 1995), 43.

31. Thomas Carlyle, 'Chartism', in *Critical and Miscellaneous Essays Vol. IV, Works*, Centenary Edition, 30 vols. (London: Chapman and Hall, 1896–99), xxix, 200. Catherine Hall notes the importance of this passage, see *Civilising Subjects*, 30.

32. Seeley, *Expansion of England*, 45.

33. Terry Eagleton, *The Idea of Culture* (Oxford: Blackwell, 2000), 2. Some of the best-known texts comprising Williams's 'culture and society' canon – such as S. T. Coleridge's *On the Constitution of the Church and State* (1830), and Matthew Arnold's *Culture and Anarchy* – have to be seen in the context of arguments about the authority of the Anglican church as an agent of 'cultivation'.

34. Usage of the term 'cult' in English, as outlined in the *OED*, is notable. There are two periods in which the term was most active as a way of talking about some other group's practice of worship, the seventeenth and nineteenth centuries; both were periods of intense religious controversy and fragmentation. A good example of seventeenth-century usage (1679), recorded by the *OED*, is 'let not every circumstantial difference or Variety of Cults be Nick-named a new religion'. In the nineteenth century, the term becomes part of the specialised, professional vocabulary of an ethnography shaped by colonial missionary activity, evinced by the title of George Turner's book of 1880, *Samoa: A Hundred Years After and Long Before: Together with Notes on the Cults and Customs of Twenty-Three Other Islands in the Pacific* (London: Macmillan). Turner's book is in some sense paradigmatic of a set of transforming relationships that spanned the Victorian period: originally published in 1861 under the title *Nineteen Years in Polynesia*, it looked back to missionary observations that commenced in the 1830s. When reissued in 1880, it was prefaced by the authoritative figure of E. B. Tylor, who implicitly links the term 'cult' with 'culture' via scientific ethnography: 'For scientific purposes no one now complains of details, but all is asked for is the minute record even of myths and superstitions, which may anywhere throw light on the culture of the higher nations and on the general history of human thought' (xi). Outside of ethnography, 'sect' became a synonym for 'cult' in more general forms of discussion which sought a relativising perspective on domestic religion and education; see for example T. H. Huxley's 'On the Study of Zoology', 1861, on the average nineteenth-century education: 'He is taught the great laws of morality, the religion of his sect' (which for Huxley represents pretty much the experience of the child exposed to Roman-Christian cults from fifteen centuries before): *Lay Sermons: Essays and Reviews*, 1870 (London: Macmillan, 1891), 100–1.

35. John Addington Symonds, 'Culture: its meanings and uses' in *In the Key of Blue*, 3rd edn, 1893 (London and New York: Elkin Matthews/Macmillan, 1918), 196. Future references will be given in the main text.

36. J. G. Frazer, *The Golden Bough: A Study in Magic and Religion* (London: Macmillan, 1922), 713.

37. F. R. Cowell, *Culture in Private and Public Life* (London: Thames and Hudson, 1959), 4. Further references will be given in the main text.

38. C. P. Snow, *The Two Cultures: And A Second Look* (Cambridge University Press, 1964), 62. Further references will be given in the main text.

39. F. R. Leavis, *Two Cultures? The Significance of C. P. Snow* (London: Chatto and Windus, 1962), 20. Further references will be given in the main text.

40. See the work of David M. Knight on the place of vitalism in the science of the romantic period, for example his essay on Humphrey Davy 'The Scientist as Sage', *Studies in Romanticism* 6 (1967), 65–88, 75–6. For the significance of Coleridge's anti-materialism see Knight's 'Chemistry, Physiology and Materialism in the Romantic Period', *Durham University Journal* 64 (1972), 139–45.

41. V. N. Voloshinov, 'Marxism and the Philosophy of Language', trans. L. Matejka and I. R. Titunik, 1973, in Pam Morris (ed.) *The Bakhtin Reader: Selected Writings of Bakhtin, Medvedev, Voloshinov* (London: Arnold, 1994), 55.

42. Voloshinov, 'Marxism and the Philosophy of Language', 35.

43. For an account of Huxley's 'making' of himself as a 'man of science' as opposed to a 'scientist', see Paul White's study *Thomas Huxley: Making the Man of Science* (Cambridge University Press, 2003).

44. But see James G. Paradis, *T. H. Huxley: Man's Place in Nature* (Lincoln and London: University of Nebraska, 1978), where parallels between Huxley and Arnold are noted, 162.

45. For Huxley's politics at the end of his life, see Adrian Desmond, *Huxley: from Devil's Disciple to Evolution's High Priest* (Harmondsworth: Penguin, 1994), 641.

46. For an account of Huxley's 'garden-colony' metaphor in the context of the politics of colonialism, see also Patrick Brantlinger, 'Huxley and the Imperial Archive', in Alan P. Barr (ed.), *Thomas Henry Huxley's Place in Science and Letters* (Athens: The University of Georgia Press, 1997), 259–76. Brantlinger has extended this analysis into his *Dark Vanishings: Discourse on the Extinction of Primitive Races, 1800–1930* (Ithica and London: Cornell University Press, 2003), where 'Evolution and Ethics' is seen (11–12) as exemplary support for Zygmunt Bauman's contention that 'modern genocide, like modern culture in general, is a gardener's job': *Modernity and the Holocaust* (Ithica and New York: Cornell University Press, 1989), 92. For Brantlinger, Huxley's allegory in 'Evolution and Ethics' has a very precise and systematically violent referent: the clearances of aboriginal populations in Tasmania through the 1870s. While I do not wish to deny or challenge this, or the seriousness of Brantlinger's important work, my own reading of Huxley, and the tradition of Darwinian evolutionary discourse in which he participates, suggests that complexities in this discourse also had implications of reflectiveness, reversal and resistance for discourses of colonialism, and for their relation to 'modern culture' itself.

47. T. H. Huxley, 'Evolution and Ethics', in *Evolution and Ethics and other Essays, Collected Essays*, vol. IX (London: Macmillan, 1894), 46, 50.

48. Huxley, 'Prolegomena', *Evolution and Ethics*, 44. Future references will be given in the main text.

49. Huxley is drawing on a meaning of 'art' that was used in polemics about the economic efficacy of colonialism in the 1830s and 1840s: see for instance Edward Gibbon Wakefield's influential, *A View of the Art of Colonization: With Particular Reference to the British Empire in Letters between a Statesman and a Colonist* (London: John W. Parker, 1849).

50. Darwin, *Origin*, 119. For an account of the 'industrial' origins of the wedge metaphor, see David Kohn's detailed work on Darwin's image of the 'face of nature'. As Ralph Colp and Kohn argue, the 'wedge' is first mentioned in a text from Darwin's Edinburgh days in 1826. An account of a trip to Portobello beach refers to Salisbury Craigs as 'another striking specimen of Scotch taste. – ≪Not of picturesque beauty, but of money. At one time this belted [?] hill was perchance, an ornament to Edinburgh≫ – Now it merely stands as a monument. [to] what Gunpowder & ye Wedge can perform' (DAR.5.49–50), Darwin Papers, Cambridge University Library. As Kohn points out, Darwin is 'above all angry at and simultaneously awed by the destructive power of human industry to turn picturesque beauty into an ugly "monument" to what gunpowder and the wedge can perform': 'The Aesthetic Construction of Darwin's Theory', in Alfred I. Tauber (ed.), *The Elusive Synthesis: Aesthetics and Science*, Boston Studies in the Philosophy of Science, vol. 182 (Dordrecht/Boston/London: Kluwer, 1996), 34–6.

51. See Paradis, *Man's Place in Nature*, ch. 11; for Huxley's original vitalism, see his early publication (1854) 'On the Educational Value of the Natural History Sciences' in *Science and Education, Collected Essays*, vol. 111 (1894), 64.

52. See Robert J. Richards's important work *The Romantic Conception of Life: Science and Philosophy in the Age of Goethe* (Chicago and London: University of Chicago Press, 2002), which argues that 'certain fundamental features of nineteenth-century biology – especially archetype theory and its articulation in morphological and evolutionary thought – came to life in the soil of the German Romantic movement' (512). Richards suggests that 'the proposal that organism, not mechanism, must serve as the grounding concept to explain the activities of nature' originated in Schelling, so in one sense he powerfully re-instates the opposition (310). This shapes Richards's re-reading of Darwin's *Beagle* narrative (Epilogue, ch. 14) as an essentially romantic narrative, and it leads Richards to question conventional accounts of Darwin as a mechanist. It remains important, however, to find a place for the language of mechanism in Darwin's romantically inspired prose, as I suggest in chapter 3.

53. Robert Chambers, *Vestiges of the Natural History of Creation* (1844) Morley's Universal Library (London: George Routledge and Sons, 1887), 260.

54. 'The Natural History of German Life', *Westminster Review*, lxvi (July 1856), 51–79.

55. Dugald Stewart, *Elements of the Philosophy of the Human Mind*, vol.III, in *Collected Works*, ed. Sir William Hamilton, 11 volumes, (Edinburgh: Thomas Constable, 1854), vol. IV,117.

56. Chambers, *Vestiges*, 250.

57. Herbert Spencer, *Principles of Sociology*, 1876, 3 vols., 3rd edn (London and Edinburgh: William and Norgate, 1885), I, 13.
58. Ibid., II, 322–3.
59. Pierre Bourdieu, 'Intellectual Field and Creative Project' (1966), translated from the French by Sian France, *Social Science Information* 8:2 (1969), 89–119, 89.
60. See Paul Barrett's transcription of Darwin's so-called 'Old and Useless Notes' in *Darwin's Notebooks*, 597–629.
61. Catherine Gallagher and Stephen Greenblatt, *Practicing New Historicism* (Chicago and London: University of Chicago Press, 2000), 22.
62. See Secord, *Victorian Sensation*, Prologue. For a comprehensive account of what may be called 'reading' and 'history of the book' studies on the history of science, see Jonathan R. Topham, 'Scientific Publishing and the Reading of science in Nineteenth-Century Britain: A Historiographical Survey and Guide to Sources', in *Studies in the History and Philosophy of Science* 31:4 (2000), 559–612.
63. See Gillian Beer, *Darwin's Plots: Evolutionary Narrative in Darwin, George Eliot and Nineteenth-Century Fiction*, 2nd edn 1983 (Cambridge University Press, 2000), and *Open Fields: Science in Cultural Encounter* (Oxford: Clarendon Press, 1996).

1 'SYMBOLICAL OF MORE IMPORTANT THINGS': WRITING SCIENCE, RELIGION AND COLONIALISM IN COLERIDGE'S 'CULTURE'

1. Richards, *The Romantic Conception of Life*, 544; *Darwin's Notebooks*, 'Old and Useless Notes' [33], 610.
2. Adrian Desmond, *The Politics of Evolution: Medicine, Morphology and Reform in Radical London* (Chicago and London: University of Chicago Press, 1989). Janis McLarren Caldwell is probably correct when she argues that 'Desmond's appealing metanarrative – of the tragic silencing of radicals and the unfortunate domestication of their ideas – does not do justice to the multifaceted appeal of transcendental anatomy'; *Literature and Medicine in Britain* (Cambridge University Press, 2004), 14. However, Desmond's study is still very important for the way in which it recognises the literary and intellectual power of Coleridge's presence in the King's–University College dispute over medicine. Coleridge's work helped to polarise the controversy and shape positions opposed to the materialisms of John Lawrence and Robert Grant. This had important consequences for the future tone of interventions in the intellectual field on the topic of materialism, whatever the nuances, accommodations and inflections that could be achieved in practice.
3. See Isobel Armstrong, 'Arnoldian Repressions: Two Forgotten Discourses of Culture', *News from Nowhere*, 5 (1988), 36–63; see also her *Victorian Poetry: Poetry, Poetics and Politics* (London: Routledge, 1993), chapter 1. W. J. Fox's discourse of 1832 (from the *Monthly Repository*) is cited by Armstrong as one of her 'forgotten discourses of culture': W. J. Fox, *The Monthly Repository*, ns

VI (January 1832), 1–4, quoted in Armstrong, 'Arnoldian Repressions', 38, and *Victorian Poetry*, 25–6.

4. John Stuart Mill, 'Bentham', in *Mill on Bentham and Coleridge*, introduced by F. R. Leavis, 1950 (Cambridge University Press, 1980), 39.

5. Mill, 'Coleridge', 132.

6. Williams, *Culture and Society*, 67.

7. Michel Foucault, *The Order of Things: An Archaeology of the Human Sciences*, 1966, translated by Alan Sheridan (London: Routledge, 1989), 256–7.

8. Mill, 'Coleridge', 99.

9. Homi K. Bhabha, *The Location of Culture* (London: Routledge, 1994), 175.

10. *Collected Letters of Samuel Taylor Coleridge*, ed. Earl Leslie Griggs, 6 vols. (Oxford: Clarendon Press, 1959), IV, 574.

11. S. T. Coleridge, *Aids to Reflection in the Formation of a Manly Character on the Several Grounds of Prudence, Morality and Religion: Illustrated by select Passages from our Elder Divines, especially from Archbishop Leighton*, edited by John Beer, in *The Collected Works of Samuel Taylor Coleridge*, edited by Kathleen Coburn and Bart Winer, vol. IX (Princeton, New Jersey and London: Princeton University Press and Routledge, 1993), 408.

12. William Paley, *Natural Theology: or, Evidences of the Existence and Attributes of the Deity, Collected from the Appearances of Nature*, 1802 (Halifax: Milner, 1848), 5; further references will be given in the text.

13. Erasmus Darwin, *Zoonomia; or, the Laws of Organic Life*, 1794, reprint of the London: J. Johnson edition, 2 vols. (New York: AMS Press, 1974), I, 504.

14. Erasmus Darwin, *The Temple of Nature; or, the Origin of Society: a Poem. With Philosophical Notes*, 1803 (facsimile reprint, Menston and London: Scolar, 1973), Canto I, ll. 233–4. All future references to this edition will be given in the main text. Philosophical footnotes will be page referenced.

15. The extended title of Malthus' text adds 'as it affects the future improvement of society with remarks on the speculations of Mr. Godwin, M. Condorcet, and other writers'.

16. Philip Connell, 'Wordsworth, Malthus and the 1805 *Prelude*', *Essays in Criticism*, 50:3 (July 2000), 242–67, 242. For other accounts of Wordsworth's response to Malthus, see Duncan Wu, *Wordsworth's Reading: 1770–1799* (Cambridge University Press, 1993), p. 94; Thomas Pfau, *Wordsworth's Profession: Form, Class and the Logic of Early Romantic Cultural Production* (Stanford University Press, 1997), 341–82; and David Amigoni, 'Wordsworthian and Darwinian Excursions: Ecology, Colonialism and Cultural Materialist Criticism', in *Key Words: A Journal of Cultural Materialist Criticism*, 2 (1999), 63–80.

17. Paley, *Natural Theology*, 278, 307. For an assessment of Paley's moderate, reformist whiggism, see Mark Francis, 'Naturalism and William Paley', *History of European Ideas*, 10:2 (1989), 203–20, 204.

18. Thomas Malthus, *An Essay on the Principle of Population*, 1798 (Harmondsworth: Penguin, 1982), 197. Malthus' way of seeing was a component in the emerging 'science' of colonialism, as in John Crawfurd's account of his 'Mission to Ava' (see previous chapter). In accordance with Malthus'

theory of the relationship between the rate of population growth and the limiting factor represented by the means of subsistence, Crawfurd subjected wild overestimates putting the population at thirty-three million to Malthusian exactitude: the informed observer, he argued, would look at the kingdom and see 'that the greater part of it is covered with primeval forest, without vestiges of present or former culture, and he will be convinced of the utter improbability of such exorbitant estimates' ('Mission', 370).

19. Michel Foucault, *The Order of Things*: 'labour – that is economic activity – did not make its appearance in world history until men became too numerous to subsist on the spontaneous fruits of the land' (256–7). It was an anthropological turn taken also by Erasmus Darwin in *The Temple of Nature*:

> So human progenies, if unrestrain'd,
> By climate friended, and by food sustain'd
> O'er seas and soils, prolific hordes! would spread
> Erelong, and deluge their terraqueous bed;
> But war, and pestilence, disease, and dearth,
> Sweep the superfluous myriads from the earth.
> Thus while new forms reviving tribes acquire
> Each passing moment, as the old expire;
> Like insects swarming in the noontide bower,
> Rise into being and exist in an hour;
> The births and deaths contend with equal strife,
> And every pore of Nature teems with Life . . .
>
> (IV, ll. 369–80)

20. Malthus, *Essay*, 203.
21. Ibid., 215.
22. Ibid., 201–2.
23. Mill, 'Bentham', 39.
24. *Collected Letters of Samuel Taylor Coleridge*, III, 143.
25. *The Friend*, 2 vols., ed. Barbara E. Rooke, in *Collected Works*, IV (Princeton, New Jersey and London: Princeton University Press and Routledge and Kegan Paul, 1969), 3, 10 August 1809, 45.
26. Ibid., 71–2.
27. *Letters*, III, 144.
28. See Trevor H. Levere, *Poetry Realised in Nature: S. J. Coleridge and Early Nineteenth-Century Science* (Cambridge University Press, 1981), 54.
29. Klancher, *Making of English Reading Audiences*, 38.
30. S. T. Coleridge, *Aids to Reflection*, ed. John Beer, *Collected Works*, vol. IX. All future references will be to this edition, unless otherwise stated, and given in the main text.
31. Language families indicating patterns of common descent were, following the late eighteenth-century work of the Orientalist Sir William Jones, increasingly being researched by the new discipline of comparative philology. See Hans Aarsleff, *The Study of Language in England, 1780–1860* (Minneapolis: University of Minnesota Press, 1983).

32. 'Horne Tooke entitled his celebrated work [*The Diversions of Purley* (1786)], Winged Words, or Language, not only the *Vehicle* of Thought but the *Wheels*.' Coleridge also tracks this metaphor on mobile, living language to the Book of Ezekiel, 'for the spirit of the living creature was in the wheels also', 7. In Britain, the philosophical study of etymology had come to be associated with radical politics as a result of the work of Horne Tooke, the influence of which Erasmus Darwin acknowledges in his notes (see *Temple of Nature* III, 114–15). See Daniel Rosenberg, ''A New Sort of Logick and Critick': Etymological Interpretation in Horne Tooke's *The Diversions of Purley*', in *Language, Self and Society: A Social History of Language*, ed. Peter Burke and Roy Porter (Cambridge: Polity, 1991), 300–29.

33. In his famous discussion of the mechanics of the watch as irrefutable evidence of design and a designer in nature, Paley sees 'contrivance, design: an end, a purpose; means for the end, adaptation to the purpose.' *Natural Theology*, 9. As John Beer points out, Coleridge recasts the word for a distinctive purpose: 'adaptive' is *OED*'s first example of the word (editor's note 38, *Aids*, 247).

34. For the location of this passage in the first edition, see Coleridge, *Aids to Reflection* (London: Taylor and Henry, 1825), iii–iv.

35. *Aids to Reflection* (1825), iii.

36. Scott F. Gilbert and Marion Faber, 'Looking at Embryos: the visual and conceptual aesthetics of emerging form', in Alfred I. Tauber (ed.), *The Elusive Synthesis: Aesthetics and Science*, Boston Studies in the Philosophy of Science vol. 182 (Dordrecht/Boston/London: Kluwer, 1996), 125–151, 131.

37. S. T. Coleridge, *On the Constitution of the Church and State*, 1830, ed. John Colmer, *Collected Works*, vol. x (Princeton, New Jersey and London: Princeton University Press and Routledge and Kegan Paul, 1976), 21. All future references to this edition will appear in the main text.

38. S. T. Coleridge, *Table Talk*, 12 September 1831, ed. Carl Wooding, *Collected Works*, vol. 14 (Princeton, New Jersey and London: Princeton University Press and Routledge, 1990), 148.

39. Secord, *Victorian Sensation*, 95.

40. [Chambers], *Vestiges of the Natural History of Creation*, 168. This is based on the second edition (1844), when Chambers had dropped his reliance on Lord for a theory of embryology, turning instead to Fletcher's theory, which placed more of an emphasis on comparative anatomy given that his embryology focused on the brain as an emblematic organ (168–9).

41. Secord, *Victorian Sensation*, 234.

42. James C. McKusick, 'Coleridge and the Politics of Pantisocracy', in Tim Fulford and Peter J. Kitson (eds.), *Romanticism and Colonialism: Writing and Empire, 1780–1830* (Cambridge University Press 1998), 121, 122.

43. See Tim Fulford, 'Catholicism and Polytheism: Britain's Colonies and Coleridge's Politics', *Romanticism*, 5:2 (1999), 232–53.

44. John Crawfurd, *History of the Indian Archipelago: Containing an Account of the Manners, Arts, Languages, Religious Institutions, and Commerce of its Inhabitants,*

3 vols. (Edinburgh: Archibald Constable, 1820), III, p. 24. In citing this passage (*Constitution*, 89), Coleridge italicises from '*for wherever . . .*' All future references to Crawfurd's *History* will be given in the main text.

45. Bhabha, *The Location of Culture*, 87. See also Bhabha's seminal paper 'Of Mimicry and Man: the Ambivalence on Colonial Discourse', *October*, 28 (spring 1984), 125–33.

46. Crawfurd's exploration of the grafted, hybridised functionality of a plurality of religions in the Malay Archipelago lent itself to the practical context that Coleridge's argument about church and state addressed in 1830. The question of Catholic Emancipation, along with the Test and Corporation Acts which allowed practitioners of non-conformist religions into public life, represented the British state recognising a plurality of religions in the imperial composition of the union. It presented the Church of England with difficulties by weakening its monopoly on political power, legitimated by its claim to spiritual and doctrinal truth. Fulford is correct to argue that Coleridge came to see a negative relationship between polytheistic 'sensuousness' and Catholic ritual (see 'Catholicism and Polytheism', 1999). However, Coleridge's position in *Constitution* is broadly to tolerate Roman Catholic participation in political life, whilst conceding that 'the Romish Priesthood in Ireland does in fact constitute an *imperium in imperio*' (an empire within an empire, an authority within the jurisdiction of another authority) which history has delivered to the present. At the same time, Coleridge points to the historic prejudices and shortcomings manifest in English colonial policy in Ireland, contrasting its failures with the successful and long-lasting Roman colonisation of Spain, evinced in the continuing dominance of a language modeled on 'the Romana Rustica, or Provincial Latin, of the times of Lucan and Seneca'. As John Colmer points out in his editor's notes to *Constitution*, the issue of colonial policy was important to Coleridge: he prepared notes towards a review of Henry Brougham's *An Inquiry into the Colonial Policy of the European Powers* (1803: BM MS Egerton 2800 ff 106–8, CS, 152). Coleridge sets this position out in the second part of *Constitution*, significantly entitled 'Aids to a Right Appreciation of the Bill Admitting Catholics to Sit in Both Houses of Parliament'. In other words, Coleridge aims to settle this political and constitutional question by means of 'appreciation' and right reading, grounded in an historic reflection upon language.

47. Pierpont Morgan Library MS MA 2033G, transcribed in *Constitution*, Editor's Appendix D, 229.

48. For these contexts, see Desmond, *The Politics of Evolution*: Lawrence's controversial contribution to comparative anatomy and the debate about vitalism is discussed, 117–21.

49. J. H. Green, *An Address Delivered at King's College, London, at the Commencement of the Medical Session, October 1 1832* (London: Fellowes, 1832), Preface. Further page references will be given in the text. Colmer suggests that Coleridge's fragment on priesthood was probably written for Green (*Constitution*, 53, n. 2) given Green's relationship to Coleridge, 260–8.

50. Charles James, Bishop of London, *The Duty of Combining Religious Instruction with Intellectual Culture: A Sermon Preached in the Chapel of King's College, London, 8 October 1831* (London: Fellowes, 1831).
51. *The Correspondence of Charles Darwin*, ed. Sydney Smith and Frederick Burkhardt, 10 vols. to date (Cambridge University Press, 1985–) 1, 23–4.
52. For an account of Grant's career, see Desmond, *The Politics of Evolution*, 422.
53. Adrian Desmond and James Moore, *Darwin*, 1991 (Harmondsworth: Penguin, 1992), 360.

2 'OUR ORIGIN, WHAT MATTERS IT?': WORDSWORTH'S EXCURSIVE PORTMANTEAU OF CULTURE

1. Symonds, 'Culture: its Meanings and Uses', 195.
2. See Sally Bushell, *Re-Reading 'The Excursion': Narrative, Response and the Wordsworthian Dramatic Voice* (Ashgate: Aldershot, 2002). Bushell's superb study of the reception of the poem, and its importance to Ruskin, Eliot, Lewes and others, perhaps rather under-represents its importance to the nineteenth-century scientific community. In her otherwise full account of the complex textual and compositional formation of the poem, Bushell does not pay any significant attention to the notes that Wordsworth appended to the poem (though she mentions that the 'Essay on Epitaphs' was appended to book VI of the poem [81]). In fact, they remained a remarkably stable feature of the framework of the poem, as it moved through different editions (though see n.19 below). Their role in promoting 'active' reading is a distinctive part of my approach to the poem.
3. Stephen Gill, *Wordsworth and the Victorians* (Oxford: Clarendon Press, 1998), 200–1; Tyndall, *Address Delivered Before the British Associatiom Assembled at Belfast, With Additions*. Republished in A. S. Weber (ed.), *Nineteenth-Century Science*, 359–384(384).
4. Cited in John O. Hayden, *Romantic Bards and British Reviewers* (London: Routledge and Kegan Paul, 1971), 41.
5. See John Wyatt, *Wordsworth and the Geologists* (Cambridge University Press, 1995), 93, 112.
6. William Whewell, *William Whewell: An Account of His Writings*, edited by Isaac Todhunter, 1876, 2 vols. (Farnborough, Hants.: Gregg International Publishers, 1970), II, 37.
7. Harriet Martineau, *How to Observe: Morals and Manners* (London: Knight and Co., 1838), 3.
8. William Wordsworth, *The Excursion*, in *Poetical Works*, ed. Thomas Hutchinson and Ernest de Selincourt, rev. new edn, 1936 (Oxford University Press, 1981); all future references to this work will be to this edition, and given in the main text, book and line number (1, ll. 364–6).
9. Martineau, *How to Observe*, 'Advertisement'; Herbert, *Culture and Anomie*, 153.

10. *Darwin's Notebooks*, B.
11. Darwin, *Autobiography*, 83, 49. Additional references will be given in the text
12. Gill, *Wordsworth and the Victorians*, 200–1.
13. *Collected Letters of Coleridge*, IV, 574.
14. Wordsworth, *Poetical Works*, 727.
15. See Samuel Johnson on the discipline of writing observations, *A Journey to the Western Islands of Scotland* in Johnson, *Prose and Poetry*, ed. Mona Wilson (London: Rupert Hart-Davis, 1963), 775; Robert Heron, *Observations made in a Journey Through the Western Counties of Scotland in the Autumn of 1792*, 2 vols. (Perth: R. Morison, 1793). Heron's narrative consciously follows in the generic footstep of Samuel Johnson's *Journey*, though Heron promotes the empirical qualities of his own text over Johnson's, which he describes as 'more a series of reflexions' (I, 41).
16. At the same time, Poovey locates the travel writing of Johnson, and by implication Heron, in a tradition of Scottish Enlightenment anthropology that would have unsettled Coleridge's Christian humanism by association: she points to Lord Kames's attempts to attribute racial and temperamental differences to climate and geography as constituting one branch of this enquiry, and to Lord Monboddo's theory that human beings had a simian ancestry. See *A History of the Modern Fact: The Problems of Knowledge in the Sciences of Wealth and Society* (Chicago and London: University of Chicago Press, 1998), 218, 261.
17. Johnson, *Journey*, 675.
18. Wordsworth, *Poetical Works*, 727.
19. Ibid., Heron, I, 89. Heron offers these observations as a means of furthering the ends of the colonisation of new territories in the Antipodes: 'much may be equally done for the civilisation of the natives of New Holland [Australia], by chapmen travelling, with suitable wares from our new . . . settlements at Botany-Bay' (I, 90). Wordsworth's citation of Heron becomes more detailed in later editions: he moves from précis in 1814 ('I regret that I have not the book to quote the passage') to direct quotation in 1841. See the first edition of *The Excursion* (London: Longman, Hurst, Rees, Orme, and Brown, 1814), 425.
20. It is important to note Alan Liu's arguments about the ideological significance of the pedlar figure in his monumental *Wordsworth, The Sense of History* (California: University of California Press, 1989). In his archaeological work on Wordsworth's 'The Ruined Cottage' – an early (and critically more respected) version of Book I of *The Excursion* – Liu argues that the pedlar is an important mediating figure for symbolically displacing the economic 'debts' of the poem's contexts into the lyric values of 'humanity' (see chapter 7, 'Peddling Poetry'). It is, however, equally important to register the shift in the context of Wordsworth's justification of peddling, through his use of Heron, that occurs when the 'Ruined Cottage' is re-located in *The Excursion*, given that poem's concern with representations of trade and 'Albion's' colonial mission (Books

VIII and IX); see also Amigoni, 'Wordsworthian and Darwinian Excursions', esp. 70–1.

21. William Whewell, *History of the Inductive Sciences*, 3 vols. (London: Parker, 1837), III, 484, 399; further references will be given in the text.

22. Simon Shaffer, 'Whewell's Politics of Language', in Menachem Fisch and Simon Schaffer (eds.), *William Whewell: A Composite Portrait* (Oxford: Clarendon Press, 1991), 202.

23. Adam Sedgwick, *Discourse on the Studies of the University of Cambridge*, 1833 (London and Tokyo: Thoemmes Press, 1994), 18–19. Further references will be given in the text.

24. William Camden's *Remaines Concerning Britain* (1637), and John Weever's *Antient Funeral Monuments* (1767).

25. Wordsworth, *Poetical Works*, 729.

26. Ibid.

27. Wordsworth, *Poetical Works*, 732.

28. See 'Essay upon Epitaphs', *The Friend*, in S. T. Coleridge, *Collected Works* IV; see also *Notes and Queries*, CCI (1956), 214–15.

29. William Wordsworth, *Prose Works*, edited by W. J. B. Owen and Jane Worthington Smyser, 3 vols. (Oxford: Clarendon Press, 1974), II, 84–5.

30. Wordsworth, 'Epitaphs', *Poetical Works*, 729.

31. Matthew Arnold, 'Wordsworth', 1879, in *Complete Prose Works*, vol. IX (University of Michigan Press: Ann Arbor, 1973), 50.

32. For a description of this system and its impact on romantic theories of education, see Pfau, *Wordsworth's Profession*, 151–2.

33. Wordsworth, *Poetical Works*, 733.

34. See Wakefield, *The Art of Colonization*.

35. Seeley, *Expansion of England*, 44.

36. For Wordsworth's anti-Malthusianism, as expressed in the 'Postscript' to the 1835 edition of his works, see Amigoni, 'Wordsworthian and Darwinian Excursions', 76–7. Both Philip Connell and Thomas Pfau conclude that Wordsworth, despite a professed anti-Malthusianism, embeds Malthus' thinking in subtle, displaced ways. See Connell, 'Wordsworth, Malthus and the 1805 *Prelude*', and Pfau, *Wordsworth's Profession*.

37. William Gilbert, *The Hurricane: A Theosophical and Western Ecologue to which is Subjoined a Solitary Effusion in a Summer's Evening* (Bristol: R. Edwards, 1796), 68–9.

38. For an account of Gilbert's place in the Coleridge–Wordsworth–Southey circle, see Joseph Cottle, *Reminiscences of S. T. Coleridge and R. Southey*, 1847 (Highgate: Lime Tree Bower Press, 1970).

39. Gilbert alludes to Swedenborg in *Hurricane* IV; the description of the poem's allegorical subject matter is taken from *The Retrospective Review*, in pencil transcription on first leaf, and also inserted in print (neither dated); see copy held in the British Library.

40. Gilbert, *Hurricane*, v.

41. Ibid., 51–2.
42. See Harriet Ritvo, *The Platypus and the Mermaid and Other Figments of the Classifying Imagination* (Cambridge, Mass., and London: Harvard University Press, 1997), 178–9.
43. Gilbert, *Hurricane*, 75.
44. 15–17 April, *Correspondence of Charles Darwin*, I, 221–5. In his *Origin and Progress of Language* (1773–92), Lord Monboddo had argued that the orang-utan was the original man, once in possession of a tail which had gradually worn away through habits of sitting.

3 CHARLES DARWIN'S ENTANGLEMENTS WITH STRAY COLONISTS:
CULTIVATION AND THE SPECIES QUESTION

1. *Darwin's Notebooks*, E [59], 413.
2. Angus Fraser, 'John Murray's Colonial and Home Library', *Proceedings of the Bibliographical Society of America* 91:3 (September 1997), 339–408.
3. Darwin's *Journal of Researches into the Geology and Natural History of the Various Countries Visited by H. M. S. Beagle, under the Command of Captain FitzRoy, R. N. from 1832 to 1836*, was first published in 1839 by Henry Colburn, London, as the third volume of Captain Robert FitzRoy's official account of the *Beagle* voyage. When I refer to the first edition of Darwin's work, I cite (in the main text) from an easily accessible edition: Charles Darwin, *Voyage of the Beagle: Charles Darwin's 'Journal of Researches'*, edited by Janet Browne and Michael Neve, Penguin Classics (Harmondworth: Penguin, 1989). On one occasion, I cite from the original Colburn edition, in the endnotes (the reason being that Browne and Neve have expurgated the relevant passage of text). When I refer to the second edition, I cite from another recent, accessible edition: Charles Darwin, *Voyage of the Beagle: Journal of Researches*, edited by David Amigoni, Wordsworth Classics of World Literature (Ware: Wordsworth, 1997). The latter is a reprint of the 1860 edition, which preserves the text of the 1845 second edition with some minor corrections, listed by Darwin. First edition references will be given as (*Journal* 1839), second edition as (*Journal* 1845). Where there is no difference between first and second editions, I cite from *Journal* 1845.
4. Darwin, *Autobiography*, p. 38.
5. J. F. W. Herschel, *A Preliminary Discourse on the Study of Natural Philosophy*, Cabinet Cyclopaedia edition (London: Longman, Rees, Orme, Brown and Green, 1831); 49, the most likely passage that Darwin alludes to in the *Journal of Researches*.
6. Ibid., 7.
7. Foucault, *Order of Things*, 256–7.
8. Herschel, *Preliminary Discourse*, 2.
9. Ibid., 4.
10. See *Correspondence of Charles Darwin*, III: letters to John Murray, 17 March 1845 (158–9), 5 April 1845 (169–70), 17 April 1845 (178–9).

11. 24 April 1845, *Correspondence of Charles Darwin*, III, 180–1.
12. Chambers, *Vestiges*, 160.
13. Secord, *Victorian Sensation*, 433.
14. 26 April 1845, *Correspondence of Charles Darwin*, III, 181–2.
15. 27th August 1845, ibid., 243–4.
16. Secord, *Victorian Sensation*, 427–8.
17. The second edition was published in three volumes, and constituted nos. 22–4 in the 'Colonial and Home' series. Part III was published on 31 August 1845. Murray did not take up Darwin's advice in respect of Hearne's narrative, which Darwin alludes to in his account of North Arctic Indians and their techniques for catching hares (*Journal*, 1845, 46). Nonetheless, travel narratives and works based on colonial observation and reportage, sometimes by missionaries, were vital to the series: for instance, in 1846, Murray published the Revd Joseph Abbott's *Phillip Musgrave; or, Memoirs of a Church of England Missionary in the North American Colonies* (first published 1842); for an account of the extent of the series see Angus Fraser, 'John Murray's Colonial and Home Library', 396–408.
18. Wordsworth, *Poetical Works*, 90. Wordworth is referring to Samuel Hearne, *A Journey from Prince of Wales's Fort in Hudson Bay to the Northern Ocean. Undertaken by Order of the Hudson Bay Company, for the Discovery of Copper Mines, a North West Passage, & C., in the Years 1769, 1770, 1771, & 1772* (London: Strahan and Cadell, 1795), 345–6.
19. Wordsworth's headnote to the poem reads: 'When a Northern Indian, from sickness, is unable to continue his journey with his companions, he is left behind, covered over with deer skins, and supplied with water, food and fuel . . . The females are equally, or still more, exposed to the same fate.' *Poetical Works*, 90.
20. *Darwin's Notebooks*, c [166], 291.
21. Howard E. Gruber and Paul H. Barrett, *Darwin on Man: A Psychological Study of Scientific Creativity, together with Darwin's Early and Unpublished Notebooks, Transcribed and Annotated* (New York: Dutton, 1974), 291–2.
22. Letter to John Murray, 17 March 1845, *The Correspondence of Charles Darwin*, III, 158.
23. *Collected Papers of Charles Darwin*, ed. Paul H. Barrett, 2 vols. (Chicago and London: University of Chicago Press, 1977), I, 44–5.
24. Percy Bysshe Shelley, 'Mont Blanc: lines written in the vale of Chamouni', in *Poetical Works*, ed. Thomas Hutchinson (London: Henry Frowde, Oxford University Press, 1905), 528–31, ll.75–7. The citation of Shelley in the second edition replaces the brief romantic aesthetic commentary that Darwin provides in the first edition: 'Yet in passing over these scenes, without one bright object near, an ill-defined but strong sense of pleasure is vividly excited.' Darwin has, it seems, passed from pleasurable sensations to reflections of doubt. See first edition (London: Henry Colburn, 1839), 198.
25. Gruber and Barrett, *Darwin on Man*, 101–2.
26. *Darwin's Notebooks*, B [25], 197.

27. See Barrett, ed., *Darwin, Collected Papers*, I, 48.
28. Charles Darwin, 'The Essay of 1844', in *The Foundations of the Origin of Species: Two Essays Written in 1842 and 1844*, ed. Francis Darwin, 1909 (New York: Krause Reprint, 1969), 90.
29. See Allan Bewell, *Wordsworth and the Enlightenment: Nature, Man and Society in the Experimental Poetry* (New Haven and London: Yale University Press, 1989).
30. James Moore, 'Wallace's Malthusian Moment: The Common Context Revisited', in Bernard Lightman (ed.), *Victorian Science in Context* (Chicago and London: University of Chicago Press, 1997), 290–311, 301–2.
31. Peter Raby points out that Wallace transcribed the passage from the concluding chapter of the *Journal of Researches* into his copy of Lindley's *Elements of Botany*; see *Alfred Russel Wallace: A Life* (London: Pimlico, 2002), 19.
32. Letters to H. W. Bates, 1847; Alfred Russel Wallace, *My Life: A Record of Events and Opinions*, 1906, new edition (London: Chapman and Hall, 1908), 143–4.
33. See for instance chapter IX of the 1839 edition. As Darwin reflects on the extinction of giant quadrupeds on the Patagonian plains, he attempts to explain it by reaching for an analogy of the perishable nature of fruit trees that have died despite grafting and fertilisation by rich manure. He speculates that 'a fixed and determined length of life has in such cases been given to thousands and thousands of buds.' For Darwin's powers of theory construction at this point, the connections among buds in a tree or polyps in a zoophyte were analogically expressive of the 'common laws' that bound living organisms together (see *Journal* 1839, 165). By the time of the 1845 edition, Darwin adds significantly to the 'common laws' set out in the conclusion to the chapter (VIII in this edition) by including Malthusian speculations about 'some check [that] is constantly preventing the too rapid increase of every organized being left in a state of nature', and dispelling a sense of mystery from the disappearance of species by drawing naturalistic analogies between individual illness leading to death, and rarity in species leading to extinction (*Journal* 1845, 168). Darwin had already written this in the essay of 1844, and was to self-consciously repeat the analogy ('I may repeat what I published in 1845') in the first edition of the *Origin* (323; see also 150).
34. *Darwin's Notebooks*, B [119], 199.
35. Darwin, 'Essay of 1844', 184–90; see also *Origin*, 351.
36. Darwin, *Origin*, 390.
37. Ibid., 215.
38. Secord, *Victorian Sensation*, 433.
39 See H. W. Bates, 'Contribution to an Insect Fauna of the Amazon Valley: *Lepidoptera: Heliconidae*', *Transactions of the Linnaean Society*, 23 (1862), 495–566. Darwin reviewed this work, and the work of Wallace, in 'Mimetic Butterflies', *Natural History Review* (1863); see Barrett (ed.), *Darwin, Collected Papers*, II.
40. Darwin, *Origin*, 234.

41. *Athenaeum*, 1673 (Nov. 1859), 662.
42. Ibid., 659–60.

4 'IN ONE ANOTHER'S BEING MINGLE': BIOLOGY AND THE DISSEMINATION OF 'CULTURE' AFTER 1859

1. Young, *Colonial Desire*, 55.
2. Adrian Desmond gives an account of the event in *Huxley*, 345.
3. T. H. Huxley, *Lay Sermons: Addresses and Reviews*, 1870 (London: Macmillan, 1891), 1.
4. Ibid., 4–6.
5. Huxley, Ibid., 14.
6. J. Baxter Langley, 'Postscript: the History of Sunday Evenings for the People', in Sir John Bowring, 'Siam and the Siamese' *Sunday Evenings for the People* (London: St Martin's Hall, 1867), 17 February, 11.
7. Polygenesis was the approved position held by adherents of James Hunt's racist (given its pro-Confederacy alignment in the American Civil War) Anthropological Society. Crawfurd's position was, however, a complex one given that he espoused it from the rival (and more liberal) Ethnological Society, which, on the whole, subscribed to monogenesis. Wallace, on the basis of the more nuanced position that he came to formulate, argued for an alliance between the organisations. For an account see Desmond, *Huxley*, 343–4.
8. John Crawfurd, 'The Plurality of the Races of Man: A Discourse', *Sunday Evenings for the People* (London: Trübner, 1867), 5.
9. Ibid., 3.
10. See Catherine Hall, *Civilising Subjects*; for Darwin's involvement in the controversy, see Desmond and Moore, *Darwin*, 540–1.
11. See Patrick Joyce, *Democratic Subjects: The Self and the Social in Nineteenth-Century England* (Cambridge University Press, 1994), 161–76. I am grateful to Martin Hewitt for generously sharing with me his archival research on Langley in Manchester.
12. See Langley's dedication to Professor Partridge, his tutor in anatomy (and President of the Royal College of Surgeons) at King's College, in *Via Medica: A Treatise on the Laws and Customs of the Medical Profession* (London: R. Hardwicke, 1867).
13. J. Baxter Langley, *A Literary Sandwich: Being a Collection of Miscellaneous Writings* (London: John Darton, 1855), v.
14. J. Baxter Langley, 'Address Delivered in St Martin's Hall at the Sunday Evenings for the People', 13 January 1867, appended to Crawfurd, 'The Plurality of the Races of Man', 11.
15. Ibid., 8.
16. Ibid., 4.
17. See E. B. Tylor, *Primitive Culture: Researches into the Development of Mythology, Religion, Language, Art and Custom*, 2 vols., 1871 (London: John Murray, 1913), II, 449–53.

18. Langley, 'Address', 11.
19. Ibid., 12; see also Arnold, *Culture and Anarchy*, 113.
20. Langley, 'Address', 12.
21. Young, *Colonial Desire*, 60.
22. Tylor, *Primitive Culture*, 1, 1.
23. George W. Stocking, 'Matthew Arnold, E. B. Tylor and the Uses of Invention' in *Race, Culture and Evolution*, 1968 (Chicago and London: University of Chicago Press, 1982), 72. Stocking's argument is valuable for the way in which it questions a commonplace which, once established in the history of anthropology as a discipline, became hard to dislodge from those narratives which it informed: that Tylor coined the relativist, pluralist anthropological meaning of cultures as distinctive ways of life, a moment of definition that was assumed by American anthropologists of the 1950s, and which filtered implicitly into Williams's *Culture and Society*; see *Culture and Society*, 229, where Williams implicitly accepts twentieth-century anthropology's claim to have elaborated the culture concept as 'a whole way of life', though he routes its transmission to anthropology via 'the literary tradition'. By the time of *Keywords*, however, Williams was more critical of North American anthropology's claim on this inflection of the term (91).
24. George W. Stocking, *The Ethnographer's Magic and Other Essays in the History of Anthropology* (Madison: University of Wisconsin Press, 1992), 115; cited in Handler, 'Raymond Williams, George Stocking', 455.
25. T. H. Huxley, 'Science and Culture', in *Science and Culture and Other Essays* (London: Macmillan, 1880), 15.
26. T. H. Huxley, 'The Coming of Age of *The Origin of Species*', *Science and Culture*, 311.
27. For accounts of the formation and function of *Nature*, see Bernard Lightman, '*Knowledge* confronts *Nature*: Richard Proctor and Popular Science Periodicals', Peter C. Kjaergaard, '"Within the Bounds of Science": Redirecting Controversies to *Nature*', and Ruth Barton, 'Scientific Authority and Scientific Controversy in *Nature*: North Britain against the X Club', in Louise Henson *et al.* (eds.), *Culture and Science in the Nineteenth-Century Media* (Aldershot: Ashgate, 2004).
28. Huxley, 'Coming of Age of *The Origin*', 310.
29. Barton, 'Scientific Authority and Scientific Controversy in *Nature*', 233.
30. *Westminster Review*, 17 (1860), 541.
31. 'Prospectus of the "Westminster and Foreign Quarterly Review", under the direction of new editors', *Westminster Review*, n.s., 1 (1852), iii–vi, in James R. Moore (ed.), *Religion in Victorian Britain: Sources* (Manchester University Press, 1988), 432–3.
32. Desmond and Moore, *Darwin* 393.
33. T. H. Huxley, 'Time and Life: Mr Darwin's *Origin of Species*', *Macmillan Magazine*, 1 (Dec. 1859), 142–48, 146.
34. Ibid., 146–7.
35. Ibid., 148.

36. 'Colloquy of the Round Table', *Macmillan's Magazine* 1 (Dec. 1859), 148–9.
37. Walter Pater, 'Style', in *Essays on Literature and Art*, ed. Jennifer Uglow, Everyman (London: Dent, 1973).
38. Laurel Brake, *Walter Pater*, Writers and Their Work (London: Northcote House, 1994), 18.
39. Walter Pater, 'Coleridge's Writings', *Essays on Art and Literature*, 1. Future references will be given in the main text.
40. 'Studies in Animal Life', *Cornhill Magazine*, 1 (1860), 61–74, 198–207, 283–95, 438–47, 598–607, and 682–90; 61. Future references will be given in the text.
41. See Alter, *Darwinism and the Linguistic Image*.
42. For the direct application of the concept of natural selection to linguistic change, see Friedrich Max Müller's *Lectures on Science of Language: Second Series* (London: Longman Green, 1864), 309–10.
43. Williams, *Culture and Society*, 256–7.
44. See Victor Shklovsky, 'Art as Technique', 1917, translated Lee T. Lemon and Marion J. Reis, in David Lodge (ed.), *Modern Criticism and Theory: A Reader* (London: Longman, 1988), 15–30, 21.
45. Letter to Wallace (13 March 1869); quoted in Martin Fichman, *An Elusive Victorian: The Evolution of Alfred Russel Wallace* (Chicago and London: University of Chicago Press, 2004), 36.
46. Alfred Russel Wallace, *The Malay Archipelago: The Land of the Orang-Utan and the Bird of Paradise: A Narrative of Travel with Studies of Man and Nature*, 1869 (London: Macmillan, 1894), Appendix, 462; all future references will be given in the main text.
47. Alfred Russel Wallace, *A Narrative of Travels on the Amazon and Rio Negro, with an Account of the Native Tribes and Observations of the Climate, Geology and Natural History of the Amazon Valley* (London, 1853), 28.
48. T. H. Huxley, *Man's Place in Nature and Other Anthropological Essays*, 1894 (London: Macmillan, 1895), 1.
49. *The Strange Adventures of Andrew Battell of Leigh, in Angola and the Adjoining Regions. Reprinted from 'Purchas his Pilgrimes'*, 1847, Second Series edition, with notes and a concise history of Congo and Angola by E. G. Ravenstein (London: Hakluyt Society, 1901).
50. Huxley, *Man's Place in Nature*, pp. 5–6; see also *Strange Adventures of Andrew Battell*, pp. 54–5.
51. As an example of disfigurement, Huxley cites a mistranslation of Battell's key contention about the Pongo's lack of both speech and understanding: the translation which Buffon uses distorts this meaning, presenting the beast as lacking in speech *although* it possesses more understanding than other animals ('qu'il ne peut parler *quoiqu'il ait plus d'entendement que les autres animaux*'); *Man's Place in Nature*, 20.
52. Susan D. Bernstein, 'Ape Anxiety: Sensation Fiction, Evolution and the Genre Question', *Journal of Victorian Culture*, 6.2 (autumn 2001), 250–71.
53. Wallace argued that 'Our system is also one of monopoly by a few of all the means of existence: the land, without access to which no life is possible; or

capital, or the results of stored-up labour, which is now in the possession of a limited number of capitalists . . . the remedy is freedom of access to land and capital for all': *Social Environment and Moral Progress* (London: Cassell, 1913), 155. As Martin Fichman notes in his important recent study of Wallace, the latter was not an activist land reformer when he wrote these concluding paragraphs to the *Malay Archipelago*. But the chapter came to the attention of prominent liberal thinkers such as John Stuart Mill and John Morley. Mill persuaded Wallace to join the Land Tenure Reform Association in 1870, ten years prior to the formation of the more radical Land Nationalisation Society; see *An Elusive Victorian*, 45.

54. *Chambers's Journal*, 8 (third series), 26 September, 1857, 201–4; see Raby, *Alfred Russel Wallace*, 107–8, n. 16, 304.
55. Wallace, *My Life*, 179–80.
56. Fichman, *An Elusive Victorian*, 37.
57. See Wallace's chapter 'Moral Progress Through a New Form of Selection', in *Social Environment and Moral Progress*, esp. pp. 148–9. See also Martin Fichman's account of Wallace on gender politics in 'Biology and Politics: Defining the Boundaries', in Lightman (ed.), *Victorian Science in Context*, 94–118, 109–14.
58. Matthew Arnold, *Essays in Criticism*, 1865, *Complete Prose Works*, III, 140, 144, 149.
59. Carlo Ginzburg, 'Making Things Strange: The Prehistory of a Literary Device', *Representations*, 56 (Fall 1996), 8–28, 13–14.
60. Fichman, *An Elusive Victorian*, 194.
61. Leslie Stephen, 'What is Materialism? A Discourse', South Place Religious Society, pamphlet 9, 2.
62. Ibid., 1.
63. Tyndall alluded to some of the controversies in the 'Preface' added to the expanded version of the address: John Tyndall, *Address Delivered Before the British Association Assembled at Belfast, with Additions* (London: Longmans, Green and Co., 1874), v–viii, vii.
64. Tyndall, *Belfast Address, with Additions* (full text, excepting the 'Preface'), in A. S. Weber (ed.), *Nineteenth-Century Science: A Selection of Original Texts* (Ontario: Broadview, 2000), 359–85, 375. Future references will be to this edition.
65. T. H. Huxley, 'On the Hypothesis that Animals are Automata and its History', *Science and Culture*, 239.
66. Herbert Spencer, *First Principles*, 6th edn, The Thinker's Library (London: Watts and Co., 1937); see chapters 1–3.
67. Tyndall, *Belfast Address*, 378, 360.
68. Andrew Wilson, *Leisure Time Studies: Chiefly Biological. A Series of Essays and Lectures* (London: Chatto and Windus, 1879), 27.
69. John Robertson, 'Culture and Action: A Discourse', collected in South Place Religious Society 1–16, pamphlet 15 (London: E. W. Allen, no date), 77, British Library bound volume (pagination continuous beginning from pamphlet 10).

70. Ibid., p. 70.
71. Grant Allen, 'The Origins of Cultivation', *Fortnightly Review*, ns, 55 (1894), 578–92, 584.
72. Spencer, *Principles of Sociology*, 1, 134. Spencer seeks to imagine these breakdowns in primitive epistemology through modern frameworks and vocabularies: 'an invisible, intangible entity such as mind . . . is a high abstraction, unthinkable by him [the savage], and unexpressible by his vocabulary' (1, 132). Spencer's cultural anthropology of the savage mind consequently works through processes of defamiliarisation: 'the hypothesis of a sentient, thinking entity, dwelling within a corporeal framework, is now so deeply woven into our beliefs and into our language that we can scarcely imagine it to be one that the primitive man did not entertain, and could not entertain' (1, 132).
73. Karl Pearson, 'Enthusiasm of the Market Place and of the Study: A Discourse', South Place Religious Society, 1885 (pamphlet 5), 6, 4.
74. Ibid., 2.
75. George Levine traces some of the intellectual tensions that emerged over this insight in his account of the argument between Pearson and Benjamin Kidd over religion and altruism; see *Darwin Loves You: Natural Selection and the Re-enchantment of the World* (Princeton University Press, 2006), chapter 3.
76. Pearson, 'Enthusiasm of the Market Place', 1.
77. Ibid., 7.
78. Leslie Stephen, *Hobbes*, English Men of Letters (London: Macmillan, 1904), 68.
79. George Jacob Holyoake, 'Hostile and Generous Toleration: A New Theory of Toleration', South Place Religious Society, pamphlet 7 (28 February 1886). Dramatically, Holyoake reminded his audience of the events of 1841, shortly before his imprisonment for the 'blasphemy' published in *The Oracle of Reason*, when he himself sat in the congregation of South Place chapel, listening to W. J. Fox's indictment of an intolerant and unjust legal system. See also Holyoake's autobiographical recollection of Fox's powers of oratory: *Sixty Years of An Agitator's Life*, 1892, 2 vols. (London: T. Fisher Unwin, 1906), II, p. 227. Holyoake's lecture self-consciously imitated liturgical rituals, including an opening prayer, which called upon 'a listening ear' in that 'illimitable and coherent mystery which we call the Universe' to 'above all teach the people that they dwell in a self-acting Universe, and that its conjectured author can derive no honour save in beholding a self-helping, independent and gladsome world'. Despite its appeal to the ear of a 'conjectured author', the prayer drew upon the radical language of the self-helping and self-transmuting organism from the 1830s and 1840s; see Desmond, *Politics of Evolution*, 74, 111.
80. Henry Festing Jones, *Samuel Butler: A Memoir*, 2 vols., 1919, 2nd impression (London: Macmillan, 1920), II, 28.
81. Ibid., I, 417.
82. See for instance his essays 'Are We Englishmen?', *Fortnightly Review*, ns 28 (October 1880), 472–87, and 'The Origin of the Sublime', *Mind*, 3:2 (July 1878), 324–39.

83. *Cornhill*, ns 11 (January 1888), 37. Arnold had written disparagingly of Spencer's language in *God and the Bible* (1875); Spencer replied in an appendix to the 1875 edition of *First Principles*.

84. 'Carving a Cocoa-Nut', *Cornhill*, 36 (October 1877); for an account of this article see David Amigoni, 'Carving Coconuts, the Philosophy of Drawing Rooms and the Politics of Dates: Grant Allen, Popular Scientific Journalism, Evolution, and Culture in the *Cornhill Magazine*', in Louise Henson *et al.*, (eds.), *Culture and Science in the Nineteenth-Century Media*, 251–61.

85. In chapter II, Lord Henry Wotton observes that 'A new Hedonism – that is what our century wants.' Oscar Wilde, *The Picture of Dorian Gray*, World's Classics (Oxford University Press, 1998), 22.

86. Grant Allen, 'The New Hedonism', *Fortnightly Review*, ns (1894), 376–392, 376; further references in main text.

87. Raymond Williams, 'Culture is Ordinary', 1958, in *Resources of Hope* (London: Verso, 1989), 6.

88. See Allen's 'Of Dates', *Cornhill Magazine*, ns, 10 (1888), 520–32, ostensibly an excursion in the natural history of the date palm tree which playfully registers Allen's opposition to the British occupation of Egypt from 1882, and its financial and fiscal basis. See David Amigoni, 'Carving Coconuts, the Philosophy of Drawing Rooms, and the Politics of Dates: Grant Allen, Popular Scientific Journalism, Evolution and Culture in the *Cornhill Magazine*', 259–60.

89. J. Arbuthnot Wilson [Grant Allen], 'The Great Tropical Fallacy', *Belgravia: An Illustrated London Magazine* 35 (June 1878), 413–25, 420–3.

90. Grant Allen, *Physiological Aesthetics* (London: Henry S. King, 1877), 56.

91. Ibid., 17.

92. Ibid., 3, 2.

93. Ibid., 2.

94. Stephen, 'What is Materialism?', 15.

95. Oscar Wilde, 'The Decay of Lying', *Complete Works*, 1966 (London: Harper Collins, 1994), 1073.

96. Stephen, 'What is Materialism?', 14.

97. Tyndall, *Belfast Address*, 384.

98. Leslie Stephen, *History of English Thought in the Eighteenth Century*, 1876, 2 vols. (London: Harbinger Books/Rupert Hart-Davis, 1962), I, 11–12.

99. Stephen, 'What is Materialism?', 8–9.

100. Wordsworth, *Poetical Works*, 'Miscellaneous Sonnets I', XXXIII, 206.

101. For a rich account of the relationship between scientific thought, Pater, and the revival of paganism in the late nineteenth century see Gowan Dawson, *Darwin, Literature and Victorian Respectability* (Cambridge University Press, 2007), ch. 3. I am grateful to Dr Dawson for permitting me to see this work prior to publication.

102. Pater, 'Coleridge's Writings', 3.

103. Pater, 'Wordsworth', *Essays on Art and Literature*, 107–8.

5 SAMUEL BUTLER'S SYMBOLIC OFFENSIVES: COLONIES AND
MECHANICAL DEVICES IN THE MARGINS
OF EVOLUTIONARY WRITING

1. Samuel Butler, 'The Deadlock in Darwinism', *Essays on Life, Art and Science* (London: Fifield, 1908), 251.
2. Samuel Butler, *Life and Habit*, 1877, Streatfeild edn 1910 (reprinted London: Jonathan Cape, 1924), 26
3. Samuel Butler to Francis Darwin, 25 November 1877, in Henry Festing Jones, *Samuel Butler: A Memoir*, 2 vols., 1919, 2nd impression (London: Macmillan, 1920), 1, 257–60, 259. All future references will be given as (*Memoir*) in the main text.
4. Butler, *Life and Habit*, 255.
5. Tyndall, *Belfast Address*, 366.
6. Butler, *Life and Habit*, ch. 1, 28.
7. Samuel Butler, *A First Year in Canterbury Settlement, with Other Early Essays*, ed. R. A. Streatfeild (London: A. C. Fifield, 1914), 34. Future references to this volume will be given in the main text.
8. Samuel Butler, *Erewhon; or Over the Range*, 1872, revised (10th) edn (London: Jonathan Cape, 1924), 234. All subsequent references will be given in the main text.
9. Beer, *Darwin's Plots*, 254.
10. Samuel Butler, *Evolution Old and New: or, The Theories of Buffon, Dr. Erasmus Darwin, and Lamarck, as Compared with That of Charles Darwin*, 1879, 3rd edn (London: Jonathan Cape, 1921), 9.
11. Ernst Krause, *Erasmus Darwin. Translated from the German by W. S. Dallas, with a Preliminary Notice by Charles Darwin* (London: John Murray, 1879), 216.
12. Secord, *Victorian Sensation*, Epilogue, ch. 12.
13. Charles John Abraham, 'A Letter to Dr Hawtrey, Describing Life in New Zealand', British Library [printed source], *Letters, 1850–1911*, 1–4, 2.
14. Samuel Butler, *The Way of All Flesh*, ed. Michael Mason, Oxford World's Classics (Oxford University Press 1993), 214–15; all subsequent page references refer to this edition and appear in the main text.
15. Samuel Butler, *Unconscious Memory* (London: A. C. Fifield, 1910), 11.
16. Butler approached the topic cautiously: 'please do not mention the name, though I think that at the distance of space and time I might mention it to yourself': *Memoir*, 1, 124.
17. The editor was James Edward Fitz-Gerald, also first superintendent of the Province; Butler was a friend, and once stood in as editor for a number of months during Fitz-Gerald's absence. See *Memoir*, I, 99.
18. Butler would have been aware of Abraham as another literary, educated man in the colony. In his letter of 1850 to Eton's Dr Hawtrey, Abraham complained that 'the Bishop and myself are the only persons in the Colony almost that possess libraries' (1). Abraham's published writings – earnest evangelical sermons and

a very dull Christian history of mankind, cribbed from the work of approved authors (no Gibbon or Hume), and based on his lectures at Eton – provide little evidence of the wit and inventiveness of 'Barrel-Organs.' His sermon on 'The Divine Principles of Christian Mission to the Heathen', delivered to the University of Cambridge in May 1869, projects an anti-scientism that is characteristic of the sentiments expressed in 'Barrel-Organs', though Abraham's target in the sermon on missionary activity was positivism rather than Darwinian evolution (12–13). Moreover, Abraham's conception of the unity of Christian history (see 'Divine Principles', 16, and *The Unity of History: or, Outlines of Lectures on Ancient and Modern History, Considered on Church Principles,* Eton: E. P. Williams, 1846) looks superficially like the claim in 'Barrel-Organs' that all speculative questions have, ultimately, to be resolved into questions of faith. However, Abraham's rather crude constructions of Christian teleology are very different to the sense of conceptual repetition and circularity that is the central argument of 'Barrel-Organs'.

19. Butler, 'Thought and Language', in *Essays on Life, Art and Science*, 191, 213. All future references to this essay will refer to this volume and be given in the main text.

20. Samuel Butler, *Hudibras*, ed. John Wilders (Oxford: Clarendon Press, 1967); Butler quotes from First Part, Canto I, ll. 149–50. For the poet's satire on scientific learning, see Second Part, Canto III.

21. For Huxley's alliance with the Colonial Office over the collection of ethnographic data using staff and resources of the colonial service after 1870–1, see Desmond, *Huxley*, 397.

22. E. B. Tylor, *Anthropology: An Introduction to the Study of Man and Civilization* (1881), 2 vols., The Thinker's Library (London: Watts and Co., 1930), I, 86, 91, 5.

23. Butler, *Evolution Old and New*, 44–5.

24. Ibid., 305–6.

25. Ibid., 49.

6 EDMUND GOSSE'S CULTURAL EVOLUTION: SYMPATHETIC MAGIC, IMITATION AND CONTAGIOUS LITERATURE

1. Edmund Gosse, *Father and Son: A Study of Two Temperaments*, ed, A. O. J. Cockshut (Keele: Ryburn, Keele University Press, 1994), 29. All further references will be to this edition, and given in the main text.

2. Peter Keating, *The Haunted Study: A Social History of the English Novel*, 1989 (London: Fontana, 1991), 308–11.

3. Vivian and Robert Folkenflik have argued for the importance of symbolist conventions and moments of epiphany in Gosse's text; see 'Words and Language in *Father and Son*', *Biography: An Interdisciplinary Quarterly*, 2 (1979), 157–74.

4. Ruth Benedict, *Patterns of Culture*, 1934 (Boston: Houghton Mifflin, 1989), 55; for her comments on the culture of New England Puritans, and the relativity of perspectives, see 277.

5. Yet, as Ann Thwaite's biography of Philip Henry Gosse indicates, Philip Henry Gosse's formation was a good deal more complex than this, being shaped out of occupations in various colonies during the 1830s and 1840s: he worked in Newfoundland, Canada and Jamaica as shipping clerk, farmer and naturalist respectively. Building on the fairly limited education acquired in his hometown of Poole, Philip Henry Gosse became an avid self-educator, and was the model 'colonial and home' reader identified by the publishing house of Murray. As Thwaite indicates, Paul's letter to the Corinthians, with its emphasis on extinction and new birth – 'old things are passed away: behold, all things are become new' – became both a source of stability and a tool for reassessment, in the face of radically defamiliarising experiences, not least the horrors of slavery in Alabama, where Philip Henry Gosse worked briefly as a teacher after his departure from Canada. Ann Thwaite, *Glimpses of the Wonderful: The Life of Philip Henry Gosse* (London: Faber and Faber, 2002), 51.

6. George W. Stocking, *After Tylor: British Social Anthropology 1888–1951* (London: Athlone, 1996), 141.

7. Frazer, *The Golden Bough: A Study in Magic and Religion* (London: MacMillan, 1922). For examples of Frazer's use of nineteenth-century military reports from Bengal of human sacrifice offered to ensure good crops, see 434–5; for moral evolution, see 92; for his use of 'culture' in the sense authorised by Tylor, see 84 and 539. Further reference will be given in the text.

8. What Eliot drew attention to at the end of Gosse's career was precisely the latter's influential position in the intellectual field as critic, 'man of letters', patron and reputation-maker when he remarked that 'the place that Sir Edmund Gosse filled in the literary and social life of London is one that no one can ever fill again, because it is, so to speak, an office that has been abolished.' Eliot was reviewing Charteris's *Life and Letters of Edmund Gosse* in *Criterion*, July 1931; see Thwaite, *Edmund Gosse*, 506. This judgement marked the end of a surprisingly persistent critical dialogue with the, in Eliot's eyes, spurious authority that Gosse had come to embody. For instance, in the introduction to Eliot's collection of essays *The Sacred Wood* (1920), Eliot cites Gosse's complaint, articulated in a *Sunday Times* review, about the quality of the 'men of poetry' that were coming to prominence. However, Eliot implies that Gosse was a symptom of the problem rather than its authoritative diagnostician. Williams suggests that Eliot's work was 'casually' informed by anthropological and sociological inflections of 'culture' (*Culture and Society*, 229). However, Eliot's essay 'Experiment in Criticism', *The Bookman*, 70 (1929), suggests a more sustained commitment; as Marc Manganaro observes, Eliot appealed to the authority of biology and anthropology as a means for literary critics to order 'the much larger arsenal of cultural "facts"' that critics and poets were obliged to deal with in reaching an understanding of culture as 'tradition'. See *Myth, Rhetoric and the Voice of Authority: A Critique of Frazer, Eliot and Frye* (New Haven: Yale University Press, 1992), 74–5.

9. Allen's earlier popular South Sea castaway narrative of cannibalism and savagery, *The Great Taboo* (1890), significantly wove *The Golden Bough* into its

plot some thirty years before T. S. Eliot wove Frazer's work into *The Waste Land.*

10. Ann Thwaite, *Edmund Gosse: A Literary Landscape* (Oxford University Press, 1984), 438.
11. From Wordsworth, *The Prelude* (1850); *Poetical Works*, Book 1, 614–15.
12. '"This strange thing called literature": an interview with Jacques Derrida', in Derek Attridge (ed), *Jacques Derrida: Acts of Literature* (New York and London: Routledge, 1992), 57.
13. Edmund Gosse, *From Shakespeare to Pope: An Inquiry into the Causes and Phenomena of the Rise of Classical Poetry in England* (Cambridge University Press, 1885), vi.
14. For instance, Gosse implies that Sidney's *Arcadia* is a work of poetry rather than prose (*From Shakespeare to Pope*), pp. 25–6. For John Churton Collins on this point see 'English Literature and the Universities', *The Quarterly Review* (October 1886), 289–329, 296.
15. Ibid., 325–6, 328.
16. On the other hand, the appreciation of English literature as such was viewed suspiciously as amateur and intellectually second rate, as Gerald Graff argues in *Professing Literature: An Institutional History* (Chicago and London: University of Chicago Press, 1987). Graff is writing specifically about the development of higher education literature teaching in United States, but his anatomy of the conflict between scientistic philological researchers and generalist critic-teachers expresses the divisions which drove the 'English Literature and the Universities' debate in Britain. So much so that Churton Collins's book of 1891, *The Study of English Literature: A Plea for its Recognition and Reorganization at the Universities*, which addressed the situation in Britain, was debated extensively at MLA gatherings during the 1890s. See Graff, *Professing Literature*, chapter 5, and 72.
17. Churton Collins, 'English Literature and the Universities', 290, 294.
18. This amounted to a well-organised campaign; Collins launched his damaging salvo against Gosse from the *Quarterly*, and then, with Stead's assistance, sustained the debate in the newsapaper columns of the *Pall Mall Gazette*. See Anthony Kearney, 'Literary Journalism and the English Debate in the 1880s', *Durham University Journal*, 54:1 (January 1993), 39–44, 40–1.
19. Huxley, 'Science and Culture', 19. Arnold responded to Huxley in 1882 with his own address to the University of Cambridge entitled 'Literature and Science', which re-stated the case for a literary, humanistic understanding of culture rooted in the classics.
20. 'We all naturally take pleasure, says Aristotle, in any imitation or representation whatever; this is the basis of our love of poetry.' 'Preface of 1853', in *The Poems of Matthew Arnold*, ed. Kenneth Allott, Annotated English Poets (London: Longman, 1965), 591. For the point about action over expression, see ibid., 595.
21. T. H. Huxley, *Hume*, English Men of Letters (London: Macmillan, 1879), 58.

22. T. H. Huxley, 'The Evolution of Theology: An Anthropological Study', in *Essays on Controverted Questions* (London: Macmillan, 1892), 131–208, 163.

23. Gosse, *From Shakespeare to Pope*, p. 21.

24. *Compact Oxford English Dictionary*, 2nd edn (Oxford: Clarendon Press, 1991). All references are to this edition.

25. J. M. Baldwin, 'A New Factor in Evolution', *American Naturalist*, 30 (1896), 441–51, 536–53.

26. Gabriel Tarde, *The Laws of Imitation*, trans. Elise C. Parsons, 1903, in Terry N. Clark (ed.), *Gabriel Tarde: On Communication and Social Influence* (Chicago and London: University of Chicago Press, 1969), p. 190.

27. *OED*, xi.

28. Murray's governing framework was in place when the dictionary first appeared. However, the *OED* was initially published in serial parts: the parts covering IJK (which would have included the entry on *imitation*) were in preparation and appearing between 1899–1901. The entry from Baldwin (1895) could have been included, though not the entry from Parsons/Tarde (1903), which would most likely have been collected in preparation for the *Supplement* (1928–33), when many additional 'scientific' usages were included.

29. Wordsworth, *Poetical Works*, 461.

30. Tarde, *Laws of Imitation*, 166–7.

31. Ibid., 182.

32. Ibid., 178.

33. 'Contrary to the terms of an old debate full of the metaphysical investments that it has always assumed, the "unconscious" is no more a "thing" than it is any other thing, is no more a thing than it is a virtual or masked consciousness.' See Derrida's discussion of Freud and Nietzsche in 'Différance', *Margins of Philosophy*, trans. Alan Bass (Brighton: Harvester, 1982), 21. For a discussion of the place of the 'unconscious' as a strategy in Derrida's thought, see Christopher Norris, 'Deconstruction, Ontology and the Philosophy of Science', in his *New Idols of the Cave: On the Limits of Anti-Realism* (Manchester University Press, 1997), 84–5.

34. *OED*, xi.

35. J. M. Baldwin, *Mental Development in the Child and the Race: Methods and Processes*, 1894, 3rd edn (London and New York: Macmillan, 1906), pp. 252–3.

36. J. M. Baldwin, *Darwin and the Humanities*, 2nd edn, The Ethical Library (London: Swann Sonnenschein, 1910), 8.

37. Ibid., 53.

38. Ibid., 29.

39. Ibid., 50.

40. Ibid., 54.

41. J. M. Baldwin, *Story of the Mind*, Library of Useful Stories (London: Newnes, 1899), 94.

42. Baldwin, *Mental Development in the Child and the Race*, 343; see also; *Story of the Mind*, 111.

43. Thwaite, *Glimpses of the Wonderful*, 245.

44. Jacques Derrida, 'Psyche: the Invention of the Other', in Attridge (ed.), *Acts of Literature*, 310.
45. Ibid., 322.
46. Ibid., 333.
47. Ibid., 340.
48. Baldwin, *Story of the Mind*, 111.
49. Ibid., 115.
50. M. M. Bakhtin, 'Discourse in the Novel', in *The Dialogic Imagination*, trans. Caryl Emerson and Michael Holquist (Austin: University of Texas Press, 1981), 342ff.
51. Baldwin, *Story of the Mind*, 116.
52. Jacques Derrida, 'The Law of Genre', in Attridge (ed.), *Acts of Literature*, 225.
53. Derrida, 'Psyche', 333.
54. See for instance Freud's 'Totem and Taboo' (1912–13), in *The Penguin Freud Library*, vol. 13, *The Origins of Religion* (Harmondsworth: Penguin, 1985).
55. Tarde, *Laws of Imitation*, 184.

CONCLUSION: CULTURE'S FIELD, CULTURE'S VITAL ROBE

1. J. A. Symonds, 'On the Application of Evolutionary Principles to Art and Literature', *Essays Suggestive and Speculative*, 1890, 3rd edn (London: John Murray, 1907), 48. Future references will be to this edition.
2. Young, *Colonial Desire*, 18 (Symonds invokes the 'amalgamation thesis'), 27.
3. Homi Bhabha, 'Of Mimicry and Man: the Ambivalence of Colonial Discourse', *October*, 28 (spring 1984), 125–133, 125.
4. See Dylan Evans's essay 'From Lacan to Darwin', which demonstrates the various ways in which Lacan was interested in animal ethology before turning decisively to a poststructuralist linguistic model; in Jonathan Gottschall and David Sloan Wilson (eds.), *The Literary Animal: Evolution and the Nature of Narrative* (Evanston, Illinois: Northwestern University Press, 2005).
5. See Brantlinger, *Dark Vanishings*.
6. Richard Dawkins, *The Selfish Gene*, 1976, 2nd edn (Oxford University Press, 1989), 19–20.
7. See Jeff Wallace, 'Difficulty and Defamiliarisation – Language and Process in *The Origin of Species*' in David Amigoni and Jeff Wallace (eds.), *Charles Darwin's 'Origin of Species': New Interdisciplinary Essays* (Manchester University Press, 1995), 1–46.
8. Quoted in Ian McEwan, 'Literature, Science and Human Nature', in Gottschall and Wilson (eds.), *The Literary Animal*, 11–12
9. E. O. Wilson, 'Foreword from the Scientific Side', ibid., viii.

Bibliography

NINETEENTH-CENTURY NEWSPAPERS AND PERIODICALS

Athenaeum
Belgravia: An Illustrated London Magazine
Chambers Journal
Cornhill Magazine
Edinburgh New Philosophical Journal
Edinburgh Review
Fortnightly Review
Macmillan's Magazine
Mind
Pall Mall Gazette
Quarterly Review
The Times
Westminster Review

OTHER PRIMARY AND SECONDARY MATERIALS

Aarsleff, Hans, *The Study of Language in England, 1780–1860* (Minneapolis: University of Minnesota Press, 1983)

Abraham, Charles John, 'A Letter to Dr Hawtrey, Describing Life in New Zealand', British Library [printed source], *Letters, 1850–1911*, 1–4
  The Unity of History: or, Outlines of Lectures on Ancient and Modern History, Considered on Church Principles (Eton: E. P. Williams, 1846)

[Allen, Grant], 'The Great Tropical Fallacy', *Belgravia: An Illustrated London Magazine*, 35 (June 1878), 413–25
  'The New Hedonism', *Fortnightly Review*, ns, 55 (1894), 376–92
  'The Origins of Cultivation', *Fortnightly Review*, ns, 55 (1894), 578–92
  'The Origin of the Sublime', *Mind*, 3.2 (July 1878), 324–39
  Physiological Aesthetics (London: Henry S. King, 1877)

Alter, Stephen G., *Darwinism and the Linguistic Image: Language, Race and Natural Theology in the Nineteenth Century* (Baltimore and London: Johns Hopkins University Press, 1999)

Amigoni, David, 'Carving Coconuts, the Philosophy of Drawing rooms and the Politics of Dates: Grant Allen, Popular Scientific Journalism, Evolution, and Culture in the *Cornhill Magazine*', in Louise Henson *et al.* (eds), *Culture and Science in the Nineteenth-Century Media* (Aldershot: Ashgate, 2004), 251–61

'Wordsworthian and Darwinian Excursions: Ecology, Colonialism and Cultural Materialist Criticism', *Key Words: A Journal of Cultural Materialist Criticism*, 2 (1999), 63–80

Amigoni, David, and Wallace, Jeff (eds.), *Charles Darwin's 'Origin of Species': New Interdisciplinary Essays* (Manchester University Press, 1995)

Armstrong, Isobel, 'Arnoldian Repressions: Two Forgotten Discourses of Culture', *News from Nowhere*, 5 (1988), 36–63

Victorian Poetry: Poetry, Poetics and Politics (London: Routledge, 1993)

Arnold, Matthew, *Complete Prose Works*, ed. R. H. Super, 11 vols. (Ann Arbor: University of Michigan Press, 1960–1977)

The Poems, ed. Kenneth Allott, Annotated English Poets (London: Longman, 1965)

Attridge, Derek (ed.), *Jacques Derrida: Acts of Literature* (New York and London: Routledge, 1992)

Bakhtin, M. M., *The Dialogic Imagination*, trans. Caryl Emerson and Michael Holquist (Austin: University of Texas Press, 1981)

Baldwin, J. M., *Darwin and the Humanities*, 2nd edn, The Ethical Library (London: Swann Sonnenschein, 1910)

Mental Development in the Child and the Race: Methods and Processes, 1894, 3rd edn (London and New York: Macmillan, 1906)

'A New Factor in Evolution', *American Naturalist*, 30 (1896), 441–51, 536–53

Story of the Mind, Library of Useful Stories (London: Newnes, 1899)

Barr, Alan P. (ed.), *Thomas Henry Huxley's Place in Science and Letters* (Athens: The University of Georgia Press, 1997)

Bates, H. W., 'Contribution to an Insect Fauna of the Amazon Valley: *Lepidoptera*: *Heliconidae*', *Transactions of the Linnaean Society*, 23 (1862), 495–566

[Battell, Andrew], *The Strange Adventures of Andrew Battell of Leigh, in Angola and the Adjoining Regions. Reprinted from 'Purchas his Pilgrimes'*, 1847, Second Series edition, with notes and a concise history of Congo and Angola by E. G. Ravenstein (London: Hakluyt Society, 1901)

Bauman, Zygmunt, *Modernity and the Holocaust* (Ithica and New York: Cornell University Press, 1989)

Beer, Gillian, *Darwin's Plots: Evolutionary Narrative in Darwin, George Eliot and Nineteenth-Century Fiction*, 1983, 2nd edition (Cambridge University Press, 2000)

Open Fields: Science in Cultural Encounter (Oxford: Clarendon Press, 1996)

Benedict, Ruth, *Patterns of Culture*, 1934 (Boston: Houghton Mifflin, 1989)

Bernstein, Susan D., 'Ape Anxiety: Sensation Fiction, Evolution and the Genre Question', *Journal of Victorian Culture*, 6.2 (autumn 2001), 250–71

Bewell, Allan, *Wordsworth and the Enlightenment: Nature, Man and Society in the Experimental Poetry* (New Haven and London: Yale University Press, 1989)

Bhabha, Homi K., *The Location of Culture* (London: Routledge, 1994)
  'Of Mimicry and Man: The Ambivalence of Colonial Discourse', *October*, 28 (spring 1984), 125–33
Bourdieu, Pierre, *Language and Symbolic Power*, ed. John B. Thompson, trans. Gino Raymond and Matthew Adamson (Oxford: Polity, 1992)
  'Intellectual Field and Creative Project' (1966), trans. Sian France, *Social Science Information*, 8:2 (1969), 89–119
Brake, Laurel, *Walter Pater* (London: Northcote House, 1994)
Brantlinger, Patrick, *Dark Vanishings: Discourse on the Extinction of Primitive Races, 1800–1930* (Ithaca and London: Cornell University Press, 2003)
  'Huxley and the Imperial Archive', in Alan P. Barr (ed.), *Thomas Henry Huxley's Place in Science and Letters* (Athens: The University of Georgia Press, 1997), 259–76
Browne, Janet, *Charles Darwin: Voyaging* (London: Jonathan Cape, 1995)
Buchanan, Robert, *David Gray and Other Essays, Chiefly on Poetry* (London: Sampson, Low, Son, and Marston, 1868)
Bushell, Sally, *Re-Reading 'The Excursion': Narrative, Response and the Wordsworthian Dramatic Voice* (Ashgate: Aldershot, 2002)
Butler, Samuel [b. 1612] *Hudibras*, ed John Wilders (Oxford: Clarendon Press, 1967)
Butler, Samuel, *Erewhon; or Over the Range*, 1872, revised (10th) edn (London: Jonathan Cape, 1924)
  Essays on Life, Art and Science (London: Fifield, 1908)
  Evolution Old and New: or, the theories of Buffon, Dr. Erasmus Darwin, and Lamarck, as Compared with that of Charles Darwin, 1879, 3rd edn (London: Jonathan Cape, 1921)
  A First Year in Canterbury Settlement, with Other Early Essays, ed. R. A. Streatfeild (London: A. C. Fifield, 1914)
  Life and Habit, 1877, Streatfeild edn 1910 (reprinted London: Jonathan Cape, 1924)
  Unconscious Memory (London: A. C. Fifield, 1910)
  The Way of All Flesh, ed. Michael Mason, Oxford World's Classics (Oxford University Press 1993)
Caldwell, Janis McLarren, *Literature and Medicine in Britain* (Cambridge University Press, 2004)
Cannadine, David, *Ornamentalism: How the British Saw Their Empire* (Harmondsworth: Allen Lane, the Penguin Press, 2001)
Carlyle, Thomas, *Works*, Centenary Edition, 30 vols. (London: Chapman and Hall, 1896–99)
Chambers, Robert, *Vestiges of the Natural History of Creation*, 1844, Morley's Universal Library (London: George Routledge and Sons, 1887)
Clark, Terry N., ed., *Gabriel Tarde: On Communication and Social Influence* (Chicago and London: University of Chicago Press, 1969)
Cobbett, William, *Journal of a Year's Residence in the United States of America*, 1818 (Stroud: Alan Sutton, 1983)
Coleridge, Samuel Taylor, *Aids to Reflection in the Formation of a Manly Character on the Several Grounds of Prudence, Morality and Religion: Illustrated by Select*

Passages from our Elder Divines, Especially from Archbishop Leighton (London: Taylor and Henry, 1825)

Collected Letters, ed. Earl Leslie Griggs, 6 vols. (Oxford: Clarendon Press, 1959)

The Collected Works, general eds. Kathleen Coburn and Bart Winer, 16 vols. (Princeton, New Jersey and London: Princeton University Press and Routledge Kegan Paul)

Collins, John Churton, 'English Literature and the Universities', *The Quarterly Review* (October 1886), 289–329

Combe, George, *The Constitution of Man Considered in Relation to External Objects*, 1828, 8th edn (Edinburgh: MacLachlan, Stewart, and Co., 1847)

Connell, Philip, 'Wordsworth, Malthus and the 1805 *Prelude*', *Essays in Criticism*, 50:3 (July 2000), 242–67

Cottle, Joseph, *Reminiscences of S. T. Coleridge and R. Southey*, 1847 (Highgate: Lime Tree Bower Press, 1970)

Cowell, F. R., *Culture in Private and Public Life* (London: Thames and Hudson, 1959)

Crawfurd, John, 'An Account of Mr Crawfurd's Mission to Ava', *Edinburgh New Philosophical Journal*, 3 (1827), 359–70

History of the Indian Archipelago: Containing an Account of the Manners, Arts, Languages, Religious Institutions, and Commerce of its Inhabitants, 3 vols. (Edinburgh: Archibald Constable, 1820)

'The Plurality of the Races of Man: A Discourse', Sunday Evenings for the People (London: Trübner, 1867)

Darwin, Charles, 'Autobiography, May 31st 1876', in Charles Darwin and T. H. Huxley, *Autobiographies*, ed. Gavin de Beer (Oxford University Press, 1983)

Collected Papers, ed. Paul H. Barrett, 2 vols (Chicago and London: University of Chicago Press, 1977)

Correspondence, ed. Sydney Smith and Frederick Burkhardt, 10 vols. to date (Cambridge University Press, 1985–)

The Foundations of the Origin of Species: Two Essays Written in 1842 and 1844, ed. Francis Darwin, 1909 (New York: Krause Reprint, 1969)

Journal of Researches into the Geology and Natural History of the Various Countries Visited by H. M. S. Beagle, under the Command of Captain FitzRoy, R. N. from 1832 to 1836 (London: Henry Colburn, 1839)

[Voyage of the Beagle] Journal of Researches, ed. Janet Browne and Michael Neve, Penguin Classics (Harmondworth: Penguin, 1989)

[Voyage of the Beagle] Journal of Researches, ed. David Amigoni, Wordsworth Classics of World Literature (Ware: Wordsworth, 1997)

Notebooks, 1836–1844, ed. Paul H. Barrett, Peter J. Gautrey, Sandra Herbert, David Kohn and Sydney Smith (Cambridge: British Museum [Natural History] and Cambridge University Press, 1987)

The Origin of Species, 1859, Penguin English Library, ed. J. W. Burrow (Harmondsworth: Penguin, 1982)

Darwin, Erasmus, *The Temple of Nature; or, the Origin of Society: a Poem. With Philosophical Notes*, 1803, reprint of the London: J. Johnson edition (Menston and London: Scolar, 1973)
  Zoonomia; or, the Laws of Oganic Life, 1794, reprint of the London: J. Johnson edition, 2 vols. (New York: AMS Press, 1974)
Dawkins, Richard, *The Selfish Gene*, 1976, 2nd edn (Oxford University Press, 1989)
Dawson, Gowan, *Darwin, Literature and Victorian Respectability* (Cambridge University Press, 2007)
Derrida, Jacques, *Margins of Philosophy*, trans. Alan Bass (Brighton: Harvester, 1982)
Desmond, Adrian, *Huxley: from Devil's Disciple to Evolution's High Priest* (Harmondsworth: Penguin, 1994)
  The Politics of Evolution: Medicine, Morphology and Reform in Radical London (Chicago and London: University of Chicago Press, 1989).
Desmond, Adrian and Moore, James, *Darwin*, 1991 (Harmondsworth: Penguin, 1992)
Dictionary of National Biography from the Earliest Times to 1900, ed. Leslie Stephen and Sidney Lee, 1885–1900, second reprinting, 22 vols. (London: Oxford University Press, 1937–8)
Oxford Dictionary of National Biography in Association with the British Academy from the Earliest Times to the Year 2000, ed. H. G. C. Matthews and Brian Harrison, 60 vols. (Oxford University Press, 2000)
Eagleton, Terry, *The Idea of Culture* (Oxford: Blackwell, 2000)
[Eliot, George], 'The Natural History of German Life', *Westminster Review*, lxvi (July 1856), 51–79
Festing Jones, Henry, *Samuel Butler: A Memoir*, 2 vols., 1919, 2nd impression (London: Macmillan, 1920)
Fichman, Martin, *An Elusive Victorian: The Evolution of Alfred Russel Wallace* (Chicago and London: University of Chicago Press, 2004)
Folkenflik, Vivian and Folkenflik, Robert, 'Words and Language in *Father and Son*', *Biography: An Interdisciplinary Quarterly*, 2 (1979), 157–74
Foucault, Michel, *The Order of Things: An Archaeology of the Human Sciences*, 1966, trans. Alan Sheridan (London: Routledge, 1989)
Francis, Mark, 'Naturalism and William Paley', *History of European Ideas*, 10:2 (1989), 203–20
Fraser, Angus, 'John Murray's Colonial and Home Library', *Proceedings of the Bibliographical Society of America*, 91:3 (September 1997), 339–408
Frazer, J. G., *The Golden Bough: A Study in Magic and Religion* (London: Macmillan, 1922)
Fulford, Tim, 'Catholicism and Polytheism: Britain's Colonies and Coleridge's Politics', *Romanticism*, 5:2 (1999), 232–53
Gallagher, Catherine, *The Body Economic: Life, Death and Sensation in Political Economy and the Victorian Novel* (Princeton University Press, 2006)
Gallagher, Catherine, and Greenblatt, Stephen, *Practicing New Historicism* (Chicago and London: University of Chicago Press, 2000)

Geertz, Clifford, *The Interpretation of Cultures: Selected Essays*, 1973 (London: Fontana, 1993)

Gilbert, Scott F. and Faber, Marion, 'Looking at Embryos: The Visual and Conceptual Aesthetics of Emerging Form', in Alfred I. Tauber (ed.), *The Elusive Synthesis: Aesthetics and Science*, Boston Studies in the Philosophy of Science 182 (Dordrecht/Boston/London: Kluwer, 1996)

Gilbert, William, *The Hurricane: A Theosophical and Western Eclogue to which is Subjoined a Solitary Effusion in a Summer's Evening* (Bristol: R. Edwards, 1796)

Gill, Stephen, *Wordsworth and the Victorians* (Oxford: Clarendon Press, 1998)

Ginzburg, Carlo, 'Making Things Strange: the Prehistory of a Literary Device', *Representations*, 56 (Fall 1996), 8–28

Gosse, Edmund, *Father and Son: A Study of Two Temperaments*, ed. A. O. J. Cockshut (Keele: Ryburn, Keele University Press, 1994)

From Shakespeare to Pope: An Inquiry into the Causes and Phenomena of the Rise of Classical Poetry in England (Cambridge University Press, 1885)

Gottschall, Jonathan and Wilson, David Sloan (eds.) *The Literary Animal: Evolution and the Nature of Narrative* (Evanston, Illinois: Northwestern University Press, 2005)

Graff, Gerald, *Professing Literature: An Institutional History* (Chicago and London: University of Chicago Press, 1987)

Green, J. H., *An Address Delivered at King's College, London, at the Commencement of the Medical Session, October 1 1832* (London: Fellowes, 1832)

Grove, Richard, *Green Imperialism: Colonial Expansion, Tropical Island Edens and the Origins of Environmentalism* (Cambridge University Press, 1995)

Gruber, Howard E. and Barrett, Paul H., *Darwin on Man: A Psychological Study of Scientific Creativity, together with Darwin's Early and Unpublished Notebooks, Transcribed and Annotated* (New York: Dutton, 1974)

Hall, Catherine, *Civilising Subjects: Metropole and Colony in the English Imagination* (Cambridge: Polity, 2002)

Handler, Richard, 'Raymond Williams, George Stocking and Fin-de-Siècle U.S. Anthropology', *Cultural Anthropology* 13:4 (1988), 447–463

Hayden, John O., *Romantic Bards and British Reviewers* (London: Routledge and Kegan Paul, 1971)

Hearne, Samuel, *A Journey from Prince of Wales's Fort in Hudson Bay to the Northern Ocean. Undertaken by Order of the Hudson Bay Company, for the Discovery of Copper Mines, a North West Passage, & C., in the years 1769, 1770, 1771, & 1772* (London: Strahan and Cadell, 1795)

Henson, Louise, *et al.* (eds.), *Culture and Science in the Nineteenth-Century Media* (Aldershot: Ashgate, 2004)

Herbert, Christopher, *Culture and Anomie: Ethnographic Imagination in the Nineteenth Century* (Chicago and London: University of Chicago Press, 1991)

Heron, Robert, *Observations made in a Journey Through the Western Counties of Scotland in the Autumn of 1792*, 2 vols. (Perth: R. Morison, 1793)

Herschel, J. F. W., *A Preliminary Discourse on the Study of Natural Philosophy*, Cabinet Cyclopaedia edition (London: Longman, Rees, Orme, Brown and Green, 1831)

Holyoake, George Jacob, 'Hostile and Generous Toleration: A New Theory of Toleration', South Place Religious Society, 1886 (pamphlet 7)

   Sixty Years of An Agitator's Life, 1892, 2 vols. (London: T. Fisher Unwin, 1906)

Huxley, T. H., *Essays on Controverted Questions* (London: Macmillan, 1892)

   Evolution and Ethics and Other Essays, Collected Essays, vol. IX (London: Macmillan, 1894)

   Hume, English Men of Letters (London: Macmillan, 1879)

   Lay Sermons: Addresses and Reviews, 1870 (London: Macmillan, 1891)

   Man's Place in Nature and Other Anthropological Essays, 1894 (London: Macmillan, 1895)

   Science and Culture and Other Essays (London: Macmillan, 1880)

James, Charles [Bishop of London], *The Duty of Combining Religious Instruction with Intellectual Culture: A Sermon Preached in the Chapel of King's College, London, 8 October 1831* (London: Fellowes, 1831)

Johnson, Samuel, *Prose and Poetry*, ed. Mona Wilson (London: Rupert Hart-Davis, 1963)

Joyce, Patrick, *Democratic Subjects: The Self and the Social in Nineteenth-Century England* (Cambridge University Press, 1994)

Kearney, Anthony, 'Literary Journalism and the English Debate in the 1880s', *Durham University Journal*, 54:1 (January 1993), 39–44

Keating, Peter, *The Haunted Study: A Social History of the English Novel*, 1989 (London: Fontana, 1991)

Klancher, Jon P., *The Making of English Reading Audiences, 1790–1832* (Madison and London: University of Wisconsin Press, 1987)

Knight, David M., 'Chemistry, Physiology and Materialism in the Romantic Period', *Durham University Journal*, 64 (1972), 139–45

   'The Scientist as Sage', *Studies in Romanticism*, 6 (1967), 65–88

Kohn, David (ed.), *The Darwinian Heritage* (Princeton University Press, 1985)

   'The Aesthetic Construction of Darwin's Theory', in Alfred I. Tauber (ed.), *The Elusive Synthesis: Aesthetics and Science*, Boston Studies in the Philosophy of Science 182 (Dordrecht/Boston/London: Kluwer, 1996)

Krause, Ernst, *Erasmus Darwin. Translated from the German by W. S. Dallas, with a Preliminary Notice by Charles Darwin* (London: John Murray, 1879)

Langley, J. Baxter, 'Address Delivered in St Martin's Hall at the Sunday Evenings for the People', 13 January 1867, appended to John Crawfurd, 'The Plurality of the Races of Man'

   A Literary Sandwich: Being a Collection of Miscellaneous Writings (London: John Darton, 1855)

   'Postscript: the History of Sunday Evenings for the People', in Sir John Bowring, *Siam and the Siamese*, Sunday Evenings for the People (London: St Martin's Hall 17 February, 1867)

Via Medica: A Treatise on the Laws and Customs of the Medical Profession (London: R. Hardwicke, 1867)

Leavis, F. R., *Two Cultures? The Significance of C. P. Snow* (London: Chatto and Windus, 1962)

Levere, Trevor H., *Poetry Realised in Nature: S. J. Coleridge and Early Nineteenth-Century Science* (Cambridge University Press, 1981)

Levine, George, *Darwin Loves You: Natural Selection and the Re-enchantment of the World* (Princeton University Press, 2006)

[Lewes, George Henry], 'Studies in Animal Life', *Cornhill Magazine* 1, (1860), 61–74, 198–207, 283–95, 438–47, 598–607, 682–90

Lightman, Bernard (ed.), *Victorian Science in Context* (Chicago and London: University of Chicago Press, 1997)

Liu, Alan, *Wordsworth, the Sense of History* (California: University of California Press, 1989)

McKusick, James C., 'Coleridge and the Politics of Pantisocracy', in Tim Fulford and Peter J. Kitson (eds), *Romanticism and Colonialism: Writing and Empire, 1780–1830* (Cambridge University Press, 1998)

Malthus, Thomas, *An Essay on the Principle of Population*, 1798 (Harmondsworth: Penguin, 1982)

Manganaro, Marc, *Myth, Rhetoric and the Voice of Authority: A Critique of Frazer, Eliot and Frye* (New Haven: Yale University Press, 1992)

Martineau, Harriet, *How to Observe: Morals and Manners* (London: Knight and Co., 1838)

Mill, John Stuart, 'Bentham', 'Coleridge', 1840, in *Mill on Bentham and Coleridge*, introduced by F. R. Leavis, 1950 (Cambridge University Press, 1980)

Moore, James R., 'Darwin of Down: the Evolutionist as Squarson-Naturalist', in David Kohn (ed.), *The Darwinian Heritage* (Princeton University Press, 1985), 435–81

'Wallace's Malthusian Moment: the Common Context Revisited', in Bernard Lightman (ed.), *Victorian Science in Context* (Chicago and London: University of Chicago Press, 1997), 290–311

Morris, Pam (ed.), *The Bakhtin Reader: Selected Writings of Bakhtin, Medvedev, Voloshinov* (London: Arnold, 1994)

Müller, Friedrich Max, *Lectures on the Science of Language: Second Series* (London: Longman Green, 1864)

Norris, Christopher, *New Idols of the Cave: On the Limits of Anti-Realism* (Manchester University Press, 1997)

Paley, William, *Natural Theology: or, Evidences of the Existence and Attributes of the Deity, Collected from the Appearances of Nature*, 1802 (Halifax: Milner, 1848)

Paradis, James G., *T. H. Huxley: Man's Place in Nature* (Lincoln and London: University of Nebraska, 1978)

Pater, Walter, *Essays on Literature and Art*, ed. Jennifer Uglow, Everyman's Library (London: Dent, 1973)

Pearson, Karl, 'Enthusiasm of the Market Place and of the Study: A Discourse', South Place Religious Society, 1885 (pamphlet 5)

Pfau, Thomas, *Wordsworth's Profession: Form, Class and the Logic of Early Romantic Cultural Production* (Stanford University Press, 1997)

Poovey, Mary, *A History of the Modern Fact: The Problems of Knowledge in the Sciences of Wealth and Society* (Chicago and London: University of Chicago Press, 1998)

Raby, Peter, *Alfred Russel Wallace: A Life* (London: Pimlico, 2002)

Richards, Robert J., *The Romantic Conception of Life: Science and Philosophy in the Age of Goethe* (Chicago and London: University of Chicago Press, 2002)

Ritvo, Harriet, *The Platypus and the Mermaid and Other Figments of the Classifying Imagination* (Cambridge, Mass., and London: Harvard University Press, 1997)

Robertson, John, 'Culture and Action: a Discourse', South Place Religious *Society* (pamphlet 15)

Rosenberg, Daniel, '"A New Sort of Logick and Critick": Etymological Interpretation in Horne Tooke's *The Diversions of Purley*', in Peter Burke and Roy Porter (eds.) *Language, Self and Society: A Social History of Language* (Cambridge: Polity, 1991)

Secord, James, *Victorian Sensation: The Extraordinary Publication, Reception and Secret Authorship of the 'Vestiges of the Natural History of Creation'* (Chicago and London: University of Chicago Press, 2000)

Sedgwick, Adam, *Discourse on the Studies of the University of Cambridge*, 1833 (London and Tokyo: Thoemmes Press, 1994)

Seeley, J. R., *The Expansion of England: Two Courses of Lectures*, 1883 (London: Macmillan, 1895)

Shaffer, Simon, 'Whewell's Politics of Language', in Menachem Fisch and Simon Schaffer (eds.), *William Whewell: A Composite Portrait* (Oxford: Clarendon Press, 1991)

Shelley, Percy Bysshe, *Poetical Works*, ed. Thomas Hutchinson (London: Henry Frowde, Oxford University Press, 1905)

Shklovsky, Victor, 'Art as Technique', 1917, translated Lee T. Lemon and Marion J. Reis, in David Lodge, (ed.), *Modern Criticism and Theory: A Reader* (London: Longman, 1988)

Snow, C. P., *The Two Cultures: And A Second Look* (Cambridge University Press, 1964)

Spencer, Herbert, *First Principles*, 1861, 6th edn, The Thinker's Library (London: Watts and Co., 1937)

Principles of Sociology, 1876, 3 vols., 3rd edn (London and Edinburgh: William and Norgate, 1885)

Stephen, Leslie, *History of English Thought in the Eighteenth Century*, 1876, 2 vols. (London: Harbinger Books/Rupert Hart-Davis, 1962)

Hobbes, English Men of Letters (London: Macmillan, 1904).

'What is Materialism? A Discourse', South Place Religious Society, 1886 (pamphlet 9)

Stewart, Dugald, *Collected Works*, ed. Sir William Hamilton, 11 vols. (Edinburgh: Thomas Constable, 1854)

Stocking, George W., *After Tylor: British Social Anthropology 1888–1951* (London: Athlone, 1996)

'Matthew Arnold, E. B. Tylor and the Uses of Invention', in *Race, Culture and Evolution*, 1968 (Chicago and London: University of Chicago Press, 1982)

Symonds, J. A., *Essays Suggestive and Speculative* 1890, 3rd edn (London: John Murray, 1907)

In the Key of Blue, 1893 3rd edn (London and New York: Elkin Matthews/Macmillan, 1918)

Tauber, Alfred I. (ed.), *The Elusive Synthesis: Aesthetics and Science*, Boston Studies in the Philosophy of Science 182, (Dordrecht/Boston/London: Kluwer, 1996)

Thwaite, Ann, *Edmund Gosse: A Literary Landscape* (Oxford University Press, 1984)

Glimpses of the Wonderful: The Life of Philip Henry Gosse (London: Faber and Faber, 2002)

Turner, George, *Samoa: A Hundred Years After and Long Before: Together with Notes on the Cults and Customs of Twenty-Three Other Islands in the Pacific* (London: Macmillan, 1880)

Tylor, E. B., *Anthropology: An Introduction to the Study of Man and Civilization*, 1881, 2 vols. The Thinker's Library (London: Watts and Co., 1930)

Primitive Culture: Researches into the Development of Mythology, Religion, Language, Art and Custom, 1871, 2 vols. (London: John Murray, 1913)

Tyndall, John, *Address Delivered Before the British Association Assembled at Belfast. With Additions* (London: Longmans, Green and Co., 1874)

Ulin, Donald, 'A Clerisy of Worms: Darwin's Inverted World', *Victorian Studies*, 35:3 (spring 1992), 295–308

Wakefield, Edward Gibbon, *A View of the Art of Colonization: with Particular Reference to the British Empire in Letters between a Statesman and a Colonist* (London: John W. Parker, 1849)

Wallace, Alfred Russel, *The Malay Archipelago: The Land of the Orang-Utan and the Bird of Paradise: A Narrative of Travel with Studies of Man and Nature*, 1869 (London: Macmillan, 1894)

My Life: A Record of Events and Opinions, 1906, new edition (London: Chapman and Hall, 1908)

A Narrative of Travels on the Amazon and Rio Negro, with an Account of the Native Tribes and Observations of the Climate, Geology and Natural History of the Amazon Valley (London, 1853)

Social Environment and Moral Progress (London: Cassell, 1913)

Wallace, Jeff, 'Difficulty and Defamiliarisation – Language and Process in *The Origin of Species*', in David Amigoni and Jeff Wallace (eds.), *Charles Darwin's 'Origin of Species': New Interdisciplinary Essays* (Manchester University Press, 1995), 1–46

Weber, A. S. (ed.), *Nineteenth-Century Science: A Selection of Original Texts* (Ontario: Broadview, 2000)

Whewell, William, *History of the Inductive Sciences*, 3 vols. (London: Parker, 1837)

William Whewell: An Account of His Writings, ed. Isaac Todhunter, 1876, 2 vols. (Farnborough, Hants.: Gregg International Publishers, 1970)

White, Paul, *Thomas Huxley: Making the Man of Science* (Cambridge University Press, 2003)

Wilde, Oscar, 'The Decay of Lying', in *Complete Works*, 1966 (London: Harper Collins, 1994)

The Picture of Dorian Gray, World's Classics (Oxford University Press, 1998)

Williams, Raymond, *Culture and Society 1780–1950*, 1958 (Harmondsworth: Penguin, 1963)

Keywords: a Vocabulary of Culture and Society, 1976, 2nd edn. (London: Fontana, 1983)

Resources of Hope (London: Verso, 1989)

Wilson, Andrew, *Leisure Time Studies: Chiefly Biological. A Series of Essays and Lectures* (London: Chatto and Windus, 1879)

Wordsworth, William, *The Excursion* (London: Longman, Hurst, Rees, Orme, and Brown, 1814)

Poetical Works, ed. Thomas Hutchinson and Ernest de Selincourt, rev. new edition, 1936 (Oxford University Press, 1981)

Prose Works, ed. W. J. B. Owen and Jane Worthington Smyser, 3 vols. (Oxford: Clarendon Press, 1974)

Wu, Duncan, *Wordsworth's Reading: 1770–1799* (Cambridge University Press, 1993)

Wyatt, John, *Wordsworth and the Geologists* (Cambridge University Press, 1995)

Young, Robert J. C., *Colonial Desire: Hybridity in Theory, Culture and Race* (London: Routledge, 1995)

Index

CAMBRIDGE STUDIES IN NINETEENTH-CENTURY
LITERATURE AND CULTURE

General editor
Gillian Beer, *University of Cambridge*

Titles published

Lightning Source UK Ltd.
Milton Keynes UK
UKOW02f1242260815

257552UK00001B/91/P

9 780521 174053